ERR

page
Intelligence Branch of the Bengal Police
(IB) 1105/1914 (57/14) ...

page 120, last sentence should read:
As expected, the Sikh agent reported on
18 December that a constitution with
the following rules had been drawn up:

**page 168, under 'Memoirs/
Reminiscences'**
O'Malley, L.S.S., *Census of India 1911*
(two references) are included in the list
of 'Official Records', p. 167.

Voices of *Komagata Maru*

Imperial Surveillance and
Workers from Punjab in Bengal

Voices of *Komagata Maru*

Imperial Surveillance and
Workers from Punjab in Bengal

SUCHETANA CHATTOPADHYAY

Tulika Books

Published by
Tulika Books
44 (first floor), Shahpur Jat, New Delhi 110 049, India
www.tulikabooks.in

First published in India in 2018

ISBN: 978-81-934015-8-3 (hardback)

Printed at Chaman Offset, Delhi 110 002

This work is dedicated to
Herr Professor Manabendra Bandopadhyay,
author, translator, mentor and uncle.
In his Bangla short story '*Thik jano ak galpo*' (Just like a story),
he invented the character of Manuel Noreño, a Brazilian footballer.
Noreño's imaginary ancestry could be traced back to an escaped
Sikh inmate of *Komagata Maru* who had miraculously boarded
a Portuguese vessel at Vancouver Bay and ended up in Bahia
where he had met a daughter of African slaves.

Contents

List of Illustrations   viii

Acknowledgements   ix

Introduction   1

CHAPTER ONE
They Shall Not Reach Calcutta   13

CHAPTER TWO
Closely Observed Ships   48

CHAPTER THREE
In the Public Sphere and Underground   78

CHAPTER FOUR
The Long Memory   113

CONCLUSION
Dismantling the Cage   140

Bibliography   167

Index   173

Illustrations

Launch on the River Hooghly, *c.* 1979–80   6

Ships at Chandpal Ghat, 1912   28

Ships in Calcutta docks   52

The Bara Sikh Sangat as it appears now   89

Slum at 100 Bakulbagan Road, Bhabanipur   96

Old house at Bakulbagan Road, Bhabanipur   97

Old house at Manoharpukur Road, Bhabanipur   98

66 Corporation Street   102

Babu Singh   105

Genda Singh   130

6, Ganga Prasad Mukherjee Road   146

Banta Singh   147

Dhanna Singh   147

Pakkar Singh   147

Bhagat Singh   148

48 Chakraberia Road (South), where the Naujawan Sabha was located   157

Gurudwara Jagat Sudhar, 1940   158

Sikh taxi-driver and co-pilot with American GIs in Calcutta, 1945   160

Acknowledgements

The Sunday morning was filled with brilliant sunshine. The guide from the First Nation pointed at some stones along the coast. She said that they were the graves of the people belonging to the place she came from; the graves were the last evidence that they had inhabited the island of Victoria long before it was named after the Empress of British India. The stones were being pulled out by cranes and thrown into the sea to make way for million-dollar beach-front property. Staring at the gleaming Pacific, the guide said: 'We once existed in hundreds, now there are only a few.'

The thought of writing this book jump-started with her words.

I am grateful to Davina Bhandar, Rita Kaur Dhamoon, Renisa Mawani and Satwinder Bains for inviting me to Victoria BC in May 2014 to participate in an extraordinary workshop to commemorate the journey of the *Komagata Maru* and the many dimensions of that voyage. There, I met and was enriched by discussions with them as well as with Milan Singh, Alia Somani, Sonia Manak, Roshni, Kaori Mizukami, Ian Fletcher, Yael Fletcher, Ena Dua, Rajender Kaur, Tariq Malik, Nasreen Malik, Chandar Sundaram, Sailaja Krishnamurti, Larry Hannant, Jamie Lawson, Nishant Upadhyay, Radhika Mongia and the other participants. Rita, especially, has helped me in so many ways. It was also a surprise to meet Seema Sohi and learn that in her paper and publications she has almost literally agreed with me on imperial perceptions of racially minoritized outsiders as a 'menace', a position I had outlined in 2006 when writing on the Bolshevik challenge to the British empire. I spent a wonderful evening with Davina and her partner, Mike, her mother and the rest of the family during the last evening of my stay, and I thank them for the warmth, hospitality and conversation. At Jadavpur University, Nilanjana Gupta and Kavita Panjabi provided a space in August 2014 where I could present my research on the ship and its local impact. I am indebted to them and to the late Jasodhara Bagchi for constructive suggestions and encouragement. It was in Patiala in December 2014 that I was again prodded in this direction by Indu Banga and Karamjit Malhotra as organizers of a conference on the *Komagata Maru*'s history and legacy. I am deeply indebted to them for their immense generosity. Professor Banga's comments as well as the insights of other speakers and participants, especially those of Harish K. Puri, J.S. Grewal, Anjali Gera Roy, Amrit Varsha Gandhi, Jaswindar Singh, Arun Bandopadhyay, Malwinderjit Singh Waraich, Chaman Lal and Chhanda Chatterjee, have enriched my thinking. Student volunteers, Vikram and Surjit, were more than kind. I will always remember the driver*ji* who drove from Patiala to Delhi for seven hours by road.

This work would not have materialized without the support I received from my senior colleague and historian of Punjabi Sikh identities, Himadri Banerjee. His invaluable insight and generous sharing of some of the sources, used in the last two chapters, helped me to complete this research. I was also assisted in ways too innumerable to mention by my friends Abdul Kafi, Chirashree Das Gupta, Fabien Tarrit, Preeta Bhattacharya, Phil Hutchinson, Saswata Bhattacharya, Subrata Sinha and Titas Chakraborty. Chirashree's parents were affectionate and kind when I stayed with them in Delhi on my way to Punjab. In Toronto, Kaushalya 'Tinni' Bannerji, Billy and Amina Ally enlivened our long discussions on the themes that have surfaced in this book. Himani Bannerji's insights on race, migration and class and her detailed comments on the manuscript were of indispensable value. Michael Kuttner's advice and proofreading of the preliminary draft of the manuscript were immensely useful. The intellectual and material support of my parents, Ratnabali Chatterjee and Tirthankar Chattopadhyay, was of crucial importance. I could not have finished this work without them. My aunt and uncle, Chandra Ghosh and Norman Hindson, extended their characteristic concern towards me and my work. The same is true of Aniruddha Ray, Amiya Kumar Bagchi, Antoinette Burton, Chitrarekha Gupta, Devleena Ghosh, James Holstun, Madhushree Datta, Malini Bhattacharya, Mrinal Gupta, the late Sarbani Chaudhuri and Sibani Raychaudhury.

I am indebted to all my colleagues of the Department of History, Jadavpur University for their kindness in allowing me to take a year off from teaching and other duties to complete this research. The office staff of the History Department, Purnimadi, Pratimadi, Sajalda and our departmental librarian, Bananidi and her assistant Jayasree, were kind and helpful. The staff of West Bengal State Archives, especially Moumita, Madhurimadi, Rina, Ranidi, Sarmisthadi, Sashi Subba, Subhadeep Das and Prabir, were very kind. I am indebted to the staff of National Library, Calcutta. My students Anal Pal, Atrayee Lahiri, Bachhu Bauri, Bithika, Sahana, Farhin Khanam, Farheen Tabassum, Gobinda Bhadra, Hasnara Khatun, Manojit Hira, Rakib, Sattwik Banerjee and Srimanti Roy provided key research assistance. Sanchita Bose and Ritaj Gupta took the trouble to locate some of the addresses which appear in this book, and accompanied me when I photographed them. The archival photo of a ship at Chandpal Ghat, Calcutta (1912) is from a collection stored at the Royal Commission on the Ancient and Historical Monuments of Scotland (RCAHMS). My friend Indranil Roy photographed and kindly supplied an image of a ship cruising along the Hooghly. Bijoya Goswami provided a rare pamphlet from the collection of her father, the late Sneangshu Acharyya. Elaine Pinkerton graciously allowed access to her late father, Richard Bear's photo of Gurudwara Jagat Sudhar. Ram Rahman shared images of his father, the late Habib Rahman's modernist architectural design of the *Komagata Maru* memorial at Budge Budge from the 1950s. For the kindness and help I received from them in the course of this research, I wish to thank Abir Neogy, Agnibho Gangopadhyay, Amitava Malakar, Ananya Dasgupta, Alexis Wearmouth, Amrita Ghosh, Anil Persaud, Anirudh Deshpande, Anita Dixit, Arnab Bhattacharya, Diya Ray, Donatella Alessandrini, Dorothy Das, Ella 'Bg' Roy, Foqia Khan, George Orton, Ghayur Bangash, Gregory Cameron, Indraneel Dasgupta, Hans Harder, Indrani Datta-Gupta, Ishita Ghosh, Jacqui Freeman, Jayeeta Bagchi, Joyeeta Roy Ghosh, Kaushik Ray, Kakali Mukherjee, Kingshuk Dasgupta, Mahua Datta-Chatterjee, Meenakshi Rudra, Melissa Chatterjee, Nilanjana Paul, Nina Balogh, Nupur Dasgupta, Prakriti Mitra, Rani Ray, Ranjana Dasgupta, Ranjini Basu, Rajyeswar Sinha, Sagarika Datta, Sanjay Datta, Santanu Chakraborty, Sarmistha Datta-Gupta, Saswati Bose, Selvyn Jussy, Sobhi Samour, Sourav Baksi, Surajit Mazumdar, Subho Basu, Sutanuka Bandopadhyay, Swati Biswas, Swati Ganguly, Tilottama Mukherjee and Vijay Prashad. Bhimda, Mamtadi, Gitadi, Lakshmidi, Pushpadi, Shivkumarda and Sondhyadi facilitated this work by helping me in various ways. Many others assisted me while I was writing, and I regret my inability to mention each of those generous individuals by name. Parts of this research were handed over for publication in different anthologies and journals. I wish to thank the editors for their kindness and engaging with my writing. Nilanjana Dey's painstaking reading of the manuscript was of immense help. Finally, I am grateful to my publisher, Indu Chandrasekhar, for her continued interest in my work. All errors are mine.

Introduction

You watched the stylish yachts and ships;
one of them had a long trip ahead of it,
while salty oblivion awaited others.
You've seen the refugees going nowhere,
you've heard the executioners sing joyfully.
You should praise the mutilated world.
– Adam Zagajewski, 'Try to Praise the Mutilated World'

'It is a sad story; it is a shameful story.' In April 1915, while sorting potentially 'seditious' material arriving in wartime Calcutta, the Postal Censor
came across these lines inscribed in a pamphlet written by Anna Ross from
Canada, referring to the journey of the *Komagata Maru*.[1]

A ship sailed in 1914, circumnavigating half the world. Its passage ended
at a geographic point where it was forcibly driven by the rulers of land and
sea. This is an attempt to trace the last stretch of the journey of its passengers
after they touched land, to trace their suppressed voices and to find the
resonance of their actions in Bengal. The *Komagata Maru*'s voyage did not
end with the confrontation and massacre at Budge Budge Railway Station.
The ship's passengers inaugurated a protest mentality that made its way
into the movements of Punjabi Sikh workers in different forms as contexts
shifted and decades passed. This study seeks to uncover the trajectory of the
Komagata Maru's passengers within the immediate locale of Bengal with a
focus on Calcutta and its hinterland, and treat the response of the imperial
apparatuses of state repression through surveillance and policing. The

research examines the trans-regional and inter-continental implications of state action, the positions taken by the region's urban intelligentsia in the colonial public sphere, and the far-reaching impact of the ship's arrival and the protest strains from below on clashes with authority. In this sense, this monograph, by focusing on Bengal, acts as a link in the existing works of scholarship that have traced the spread of radical anti-colonial currents among the Punjabi Sikh diaspora, which connected Punjab with Southeast and East Asia and the Americas.

From the second half of the nineteenth century, migration from Punjab was fuelled by depeasantization in the countryside. Colonial land-revenue policies drove many out of agrarian livelihoods; the displaced peasants travelled as manual workers, petty traders, soldiers and artisans. In search of work within the circuits of global capitalism in Southeast and East Asia, they provided cheap labour in the formally organized as well as informal empires of capital. Their livelihoods as migrant workers were subject to controls placed by the monopolistic bourgeoisie of European extraction. From British-occupied Burma and Malaysia to Dutch-occupied Java to American-controlled Philippines to imperialized China, the interplay of race, class and migration lowered their bargaining power as workers in the labour market.

By the early twentieth century, these migrant workers, designated as members of 'lesser races', were seeking low-paid employment on the Pacific Coast of the Americas. To prevent an inflow of non-white labour and thereby control the size of an exploitable labour force, anti-immigrant policies directed against Asian workers from Japan, China, Korea and India were introduced by authorities of the United States of America (USA) and Canada. The strategy of racial exclusion took the shape of a 'continuous journey regulation' in Canada, a racist order instituted in 1908 to impede migrant workers, especially from India and Japan, and to regulate the number of working population needed for purposes of production. The measure was adopted with full support from colonial authorities in India and after consulting the top echelons of the imperial bureaucracy in London. The Canadian government stipulated that immigrants hoping to enter Canada must travel continuously from the country of their birth, or of which they were citizens. Since many labourers of Sikh origin came to Canada after having lived and worked in East Asia, the middle ground between them and North America, the measure was seen as an effective step to block their entry. As racism mounted, a revolutionary group comprising workers, political émigrés and students from India emerged in San Francisco.

Established in 1913, on the eve of the First World War, the Ghadar Party (Indian Revolt) was rooted among the South Asian diaspora, drawing in Punjabi Sikh migrant workers who inhabited the regions stretching from Southeast Asia to the western shores of the Americas. The group's network included Hindus and Muslims as well as bhadralok (Bengali Hindu upper-caste) revolutionaries. They received support from, and were influenced by, anarchist and socialist currents directed against private property, profit accumulation, colonialism and empire-building. Various pre-war radical currents, including the strand represented by the Industrial Workers of the World (IWW),[2] which was active in white-settler-dominated countries such as Australia and the USA, shaped the anti-imperialist and anti-capitalist outlook of the Ghadar Party. Building solidarity from below, the Ghadar-influenced migrant collectives were pitted against racist harassment, discrimination and exclusion; they generated confidence among workers in search of livelihood in unfamiliar and inhospitable terrains. The group articulated its political and social positions through an Urdu and Punjabi weekly, *Hindustan Ghadar*, and an anthology of lyrical rebel poetry, *Ghadar-di-Gunj*, written by Punjabi Sikh immigrants. The crucial ingredient of 'labour' was combined with those elements of ethno-linguistic identity formation that enabled a rejection of oppressive power relations encompassing day-to-day survival. These components, shaping the outlook and actions of the Ghadar activists and their mass base, turned the movement in radical directions from the beginning. Their militant responses to labour conditions under capitalism and affiliation to anti-colonial currents seeking national liberation for India at a time when the Indian National Congress (INC) still sought political autonomy within the British empire (dominion status) worried the authorities in USA, Canada and India.

In 1914, the journey of the *Komagata Maru* reinforced the organic link between Indian immigrants from Punjab and the Ghadar Movement. In the following year, the Ghadar Party coordinated with other revolutionary groups, but they failed to bring about an uprising from Punjab to Singapore. Consequently, a series of repressive measures adopted by the British, Canadian and US governments led to the suppression of Ghadar activists between 1915 and 1918. At the end of the war, the Ghadar strain came to be distributed across a range of novel political initiatives. The political and social energies contained within the Ghadar Movement merged with other militant formations – from nationalist to communist. A large section of Ghadar activists turned to the Bolshevik Revolution of 1917 for inspiration and an explicitly 'class'-oriented anti-imperialist programme. They were active within India and beyond during the inter-war years. As conscious champions of social transformation from below, they aspired for the hegemony of workers, envisioning the future through multiple organic intellectual exercises and protest actions. Their presence could be registered during the formative era of the communist and labour movements.[3]

In March 1914, Gurdit Singh, a labour contractor with Ghadar sympathies, chartered the *Komagata Maru*, a Japanese vessel, from Hong Kong. The ship left Hong Kong in April. More than 300 passengers were on board when it sailed into Vancouver harbour in May. The vessel remained stranded as a court case was fought on behalf of the migrants by a Shore Committee constituted of Indians already living there. In July, the Supreme Court of British Columbia upheld the law of racial exclusion. The ship was expelled from Canadian waters. On their way back, the destitute and exhausted passengers, stranded on board for almost five months, decided to launch judicial proceedings in India against racial discrimination within the British empire, especially in settler colonies such as Canada. The British imperial authorities did not allow the returning migrants to disembark in the British-controlled port-cities of Asia. They planned to arrest Gurdit Singh and his followers as Ghadarite troublemakers. Meanwhile, the First World War erupted in July. By the time the ship entered the Bay of Bengal, the British colonizers, dependent on military labour from Punjab, were worried that a campaign against imperial race relations would disrupt the war effort. Based on surveillance and policing, they imposed a coercive strategy upon the passengers when the ship reached Budge Budge, to the south of Calcutta, at the end of September 1914. While the migrants were waiting under strict vigilance to board a train to Punjab, an armed confrontation turned into a full-scale massacre. Twenty-one passengers were killed as colonial troops opened fire on the migrants in the railway station at Budge Budge on 29 September. This event has been recorded in history.[4] But what were the consequences, which remain underexplored and unaddressed, of the ship's eventful arrival?

This work examines radical responses to racialized subjecthood imposed on Punjabi, especially Sikh, migrant workers in Calcutta and its suburbs during wartime and in the post-war era. 'Racialized subjecthood' is interpreted in this context as certain mutually constituted exploitative conditions, which regulated the work and life of the migrants. Developed under the aegis of colonialism, these were class-bound subordinations

related to ejection from small agricultural holdings into an unstable world
of migrant wage labour formation, racial stereotyping (drawing on ethno-
linguistic and religious classification of Sikhs as a cheap labour reserve fit
to bear the physical strains of manual work) and an attendant complex
of state repressions to facilitate and impede their movements within the
labour markets of the British empire and beyond. Recognition of ethno-
racial barriers as constitutive of oppressive labour practices underlined the
politicized self-awareness and emergence of radical collectives among the
Punjabi Sikh migrants. Their initiatives were based on encounters with
the concrete conditions of 'subjection' to the institutionalized imperial
strategies of labour control. As they came to identify the points of conflict,
they contested racialized subjecthood. In the process, they confronted the
colonial state, representing and upholding the interests of those above them.

The operation of the colonial repressive state apparatus to deal with
the passengers of the *Komagata Maru* and Punjabi migrants influenced
the intersections of anti-colonial strands in the city of Calcutta and its
surroundings during 1914–15; this clash of positions, a point of combat
from above and below, shaped future militancy and the organized post-
war transmission of the ship's memory as a symbol of resistance among the
Sikh workers in the industrial centres of southwest Bengal. By tracing these
processes, it becomes possible to unravel certain neglected aspects of the last
stretch of the ship's journey, and both its immediate and long-term local
effect. Existing historiography on the ship's voyage has failed to note certain
facets of colonial surveillance and prior arrangements made by the British
authorities even before its arrival, as well as the suppressed voices of detained
passengers after the massacre. The close relationship between inter-imperial
geographies of surveillance, and the interlocked power of the colonial state
and colonial capital, have never been emphasized. The responses of the local
Hindu and Muslim intelligentsia to the ship's controversial voyage have
also remained underexplored. No attempt has been made to understand
and record the entry of the Sikh working class diaspora into the local
revolutionary, left and labour movements. A historical treatment of wartime
Ghadar and post-war Punjab Kirti Dal's (Kirti Kisan Party's) influence on
the actions of Sikh workers in South Bengal has been missing. Finally, the
interplay between acts of recollection and regional formation of radical
collectives in the wake of the ship's voyage remains uncharted. By drawing
on untapped yet voluminous and readily available colonial archival records,
and the fragmentary references found in autobiographical accounts, this

research attempts to fill the gaps and steer the history of the *Komagata Maru*'s journey in new directions.[5]

The first chapter analyses the local context of opposition in Bengal when the *Komagata Maru* reached its shores. Driven by war-induced panic, the colonial authorities feared the ship's passengers would find support for their anti-racist and anti-colonial campaign in Calcutta, a city brimming with ill-concealed hostility towards imperial rule. A German warship, *Emden*, was active in destroying British installations and merchant vessels in Bay of Bengal at this point; it was upsetting trade routes, passenger service and inter-imperial communication. The combined effect of deep unease made the authorities adopt a policy of open coercion when the ship arrived. It was decided in advance, with close involvement of heads of surveillance at every level, that the *Komagata Maru* would not be allowed to sail up the River Hooghly into Calcutta. Instead, the ship would be stopped at Budge Budge, an industrial town located to the south of the metropolis. Gurdit Singh, the organizer of the expedition, and his close followers were arrested under the provision of wartime security acts, and the rest of the migrants speedily dispatched to Punjab by a special train. The escalation of accumulated tensions and the warlike position of the administration triggered a confrontation followed by a full-scale massacre. While an official account was circulated, and individual statements of police officers and soldiers on duty echoed the official narrative, the repressed voices of the arrested passengers in police stations and prison and Gurdit Singh's later recollections offered a counter-version of the event.

Launch on the River Hooghly, *c.* 1979–80 (Photo by Suvankar Chatterjee)

The second chapter examines the ways in which the reception of the *Komagata Maru* set the blueprint of future surveillance and policing. Ships and migrants, especially those carrying Punjabi Sikh labourers and potentially radical 'suspects', were subjected to intensified scrutiny and repression. The watch on the Hooghly assumed local, inter-provincial and inter-imperial dimensions as intelligence material and imperial perspectives came to be exchanged across a wide geographic zone. Various branches of colonial authority along with monopolistic business corporations erected by colonial capital closed ranks to ensure the security of a seaborne empire from a set of migrant travellers. This imperial offensive aimed to curb the defiance of those returning, expressed through words and action as they faced layers of coercive strategy on board and upon landing.

The third chapter treats the ways in which the issue of immigration within the British empire and to North America became the focal point of a controversy in Bengal's colonial public sphere during the passage of the *Komagata Maru* and following the grisly aftermath at Budge Budge. Vocal criticisms were expressed in the local press run by the Indian intelligentsia. The voice of print was saddled with the pressure to display 'loyalty' to a beleaguered empire-at-war. No such constraints inhibited the revolutionary underground in Calcutta and its surroundings. A tiny segment of Sikh workers entered the political sphere for the first time as militant revolutionaries. They joined the local secret society network aiming to overthrow the colonial state. This step was taken after the killing and victimization of the *Komagata Maru* passengers in a climate of mounting repression. Despite colonial stereotyping and official backlash, the Sikh rebels paved the way for activism from below among Punjabi Sikh workers residing in Bengal.

The fourth chapter records the presence of Punjabi Sikh activists and workers in the post-war landscape of labour movements and left politics as the emergency measures imposed by a wartime imperial order receded, and mass protests gained ground. Finally, an attempt is made to read the transformation of protests and campaigns among Punjabi migrant workers from the time of the *Komagata Maru's* arrival in Bengal to the later decades, which was riddled with cycles of sectional and wider activism.

The organizers and activists among Punjabi workers in Bengal left behind records of 'a history from below'. With the exception of Gurdit Singh, the other figures who engaged in regional movements of anti-colonial resistance and whose militant activities could be traced to the multiplication of protest settings, came from the ranks of workers. As taxi drivers, chauffeurs and janitors, they encountered and contributed to various political actions affiliated with political formations in metropolitan Calcutta and in the industrial hinterland spread along the banks of the Hooghly. The records indicate their efforts to connect with the community through a shared experience of 'labour', and to step beyond the diasporic network held together by ethno-religious-linguistic affiliations and regulated by colonial state and capital into spaces of labour struggles alongside workers from other backgrounds. Through the interplay of class and community in their milieu, where communal concerns could and did gain ascendancy, a complex picture of affiliations with nationalist, socialist and communist organizations unfolded. Depending on the character of mobilization, this interplay could generate a ground for self-assertion among migrants as workers. The layers of identity at critical anti-colonial conjunctures and during periods of organized activity revealed a tendency to privilege their material location as workers, as activists fighting for all workers within the circles of community and as warriors in a 'common cause' who resisted the enmeshed authorities of state and private enterprise. Instead of a readymade 'essentialist' solidarity based on inherited identities, they invented processes to work with workers and activists from other identity structures. Through the experience of confronting victimization and exploitative practices, they forced the rulers to take notice of them and to repeatedly label them as archetypes of 'danger' and 'sedition'. At the receiving end of state power, they rejected its manifestations, refracted through ever-present policing and managerial offensives to shape a pliant workforce.[6] 'Class' underpinned the conflict between the power of colonial capital exercised through the colonial state and Punjabi Sikh workers as a migratory labour force. Through episodes of resistance and periodic protests, the workers refused to submit to the entwined work and political regimes imposed from above. If class consciousness is born and asserted through class struggle, then the emphasis on self-rule based on dignity of labour, a latent class position, was present among Punjabi Sikh activists. Inspired by Ghadar and radical labour movements, they went beyond economistic demands for improved working conditions and better wages by articulating visions of an egalitarian society of the future.

This research is also an exercise in the convergence of micro-history[7] with histories of the urban, the local and the everyday in temporal and long-term settings. By exploring the resonance of the *Komagata Maru* incident, and the actions of Punjabi Sikh workers empowered by the Ghadar tendency and the post-war decades of labour activism, this study explores the mutations of a political space connected with the Punjabi diaspora in Calcutta and Bengal which has remained unobserved. Within the framework of the interlinked power complex of imperialism, capitalism and labour migration spanning the globe, it attempts to recover a lost sub-regional terrain of resistance and protest from below.

Leading marginal lives, mostly as workers employed in the service-sector industry, the Punjabi Sikh migrants engaged in programmes aimed at overthrowing and disrupting the existing order in their immediate surroundings as well as in the wider world. The variations in their actions touched upon moments and moods of resistance and fatigue within the wider frame of surge and eclipse of political and labour initiatives. They demonstrated the expansion and contraction of their political agency by organizing, preparing for, participating in and living through endeavours to combat working conditions and state authority, while coping with the pressures of day-to-day survival. The personal aspects of their daily lives converged with specific moments and gestures recorded by the state and by those who knew them – a pressure on the fingers while pulling the trigger, turning the wheel of a taxi-cab, waiting in a prison cell, being photographed in handcuffs before being led away, cheering in public rallies, speaking at closed-door meetings, selling newspapers in a dusty corner of the street, and marching through the hours, months and decades.

A few words on the nature of the primary sources used are relevant in this connection. The archival collection of police records in the West Bengal State Archives in Calcutta, under-explored in existing historiography, forms the fulcrum of this research. The city of Calcutta during the early twentieth century was not just a point of passage within the British empire, but a key centre of colonial power and a crucial laboratory of imperial repressive practices cultivated and applied elsewhere. The urban space and the hinterland served as zones of employment for migrant labour related to the powerful institutional edifices of colonial capital in eastern India with international reach across global markets. The archival collection of colonial official and unofficial sources stored in the city, far from being 'peripheral', yields detailed resources that cannot be ignored if one wishes to arrive at a comprehensive understanding of the *Komagata Maru*'s voyage and its consequences. The histories of the Ghadar Movement or the *Komagata Maru*'s trail, while describing the circumstances in detail and offering rewarding perspectives on Punjabi Sikh migrants, have overlooked this aspect of concentrated colonial power in the city and the region, and failed to adequately investigate why the ship was brought to Bengal and why overwhelming imperial vigilance, locally organized, was imposed on the ships that arrived soon afterwards.

This research has depended chiefly on archival records, drawing substantially on colonial police accounts; the dossiers reveal quotidian tracking of Punjabi Sikhs who had attracted the attentions of the state through their actions, affinities and associations. Though the Sikhs represented a minor religious community in Bengal, they had developed a network through gurudwaras, neighbourhood enclaves, and circuits of casual and migrant labour since the early twentieth century. In the inter-war period, as the size of the community grew, the presence of Punjabi Sikhs in the public sphere was noted through the emergence of associations, print-activism and newspapers published in the Gurumukhi script. The diasporic community comprised of long-term residents and mobile workers. While the former tended to link people together with the transient segment, they maintained connections with Punjab as well as with the wider world, since the trail of migration branched out in various geographic directions between India and the Pacific. Since women were a minority within a predominantly male diaspora in Bengal, their voices have seldom surfaced in the records. Their self-articulations have been near-impossible to trace. This has been somewhat easier in the case of men but within the limits placed by the character of colonial intelligence-gathering, with its usual recourse to distorted representations, exaggerations and omissions. The unknown situations and obscure figures, the concealed strands and short-lived associations, therefore, yield an unfinished set of portraits. Even the addresses associated with them in Calcutta have mostly disappeared, making way for houses of the urban gentry. The sources, however, do offer an insight into a continuous overlapping of class locations and protest methods which emerged among Punjabi Sikh workers.

As migrations compelled by collapsing material sustenance across and within borders grow under global capitalism, regimes of extreme insecurity and exploitation are unleashed on those who must move precariously from one geographic point to another, possessing nothing but their labour power in a planet of jobless 'growth'. They scale ever-taller barbed wire fences represented by border controls, xenophobic state policies and aggressively hostile social responses. In such a climate, this research traces a fragment of their past through a microscopic history of varied resistance and opposition among a segment of migrant workers who surfaced more than a hundred years ago.

Notes and References

[1] *Weekly Reports of Intelligence Branch, Bengal Police 1915.*

[2] The IWW was a radical labour organization influenced by Socialist and Anarchist ideas, with a working-class following in North America.

[3] For a pioneering study of the Ghadar Movement against the backdrop of agrarian poverty and migration from Punjab, see Harish K. Puri, *Ghadar Movement: Ideology, Organization and Strategy*, Amritsar, 1983. Puri offers a comprehensive historical understanding of the Ghadar Movement from 1913 to 1918, and its relationship with the world of migrant labour, revolutionary networks in East Asia and impact on India, especially Punjab, during the First World War. He also treats the journey of the *Komagata Maru* and its significance within the broad rubric of Ghadar-led anti-racist activism. For a revealing account of the Ghadar Movement among South Asian immigrants, expatriates, exiles and students in North America, see Malini Sood, *Expatriate Nationalism and Ethnic Radicalism: The Ghadar Party in North America*, Hamden, 2000. For an account of Ghadar revolutionaries in China from 1913 to 1930, see B.R. Deepak, *India–China Relations: In the first half of the 20th Century*, Delhi, 2001, pp. 61–85. For a recent treatment of the inter-war activities of those formerly or tangentially connected with the Ghadar milieu, see Maia Ramnath, *Haj to Utopia: How the Ghadar Movement Charted Global Radicalism and Attempted to Overthrow the British Empire*, Berkeley, 2011.

For an explanation of the relationship between colonialism and migration from Punjab to America, see Sucheta Mazumdar, 'Colonial Impact and Punjabi Emigration to the United States', in Lucie Cheng and Edna Bonacich, eds, *Labor Immigration under Capitalism: Asian Workers in the United States Before World War II*, Berkeley, 1984, pp. 316–36. Also, the theoretically rich analysis of the wider context of emigration from Asia to North America in Lucie Cheng and Edna Bonacich, 'Introduction', in ibid., pp. 1–56. For a recent history of migrants from the Indian subcontinent, see Vivek Bald, *Bengali Harlem and the Lost Histories of South Asian America*, Cambridge, Mass., 2013. For a comparative perspective in an Asian setting and an enriching analysis of the links between colonial labour surplus, exploitation of migrant workers and the power exercised by empires of capital, see Ken Kawashima, *The Proletarian Gamble: Korean Workers in Interwar Japan*, Durham and London, 2009. For a critical discussion on the colonial agrarian conditions in Punjab, see Mridula Mukherjee, *Colonizing Agriculture: The Myth of Punjab Exceptionalism*, Delhi, 2005. To understand the entwined world of capitalism, colonialism and imperialism, see Amiya Kumar Bagchi, *Perilous Passage: Mankind and the Global Ascendancy of Capital*, Delhi, 2006.

[4] For an account of the *Komagata Maru*'s journey, see Hugh Johnston, *The Voyage of the Komagata Maru: The Sikh Challenge to Canada's Colour Bar*, Vancouver, 1995. Also, Darshan S. Tatla, 'Introduction', in Baba Gurdit Singh, *Voyage of Komagata Maru or India's Slavery Abroad*, edited by Darshan S. Tatla, Chandigarh, 2007, pp. 1–53; Malwinder Jit Singh Waraich and Gurdev Singh Sidhu, eds, *Komagata Maru, A Challenge to Colonialism: Key Documents*, Chandigarh, 2005. For recent

discussions following the centenary of the ship's voyage, see Anjali Gera Roy and Ajaya K. Sahoo, 'Introduction to the Special Issue: The journey of the Komagata Maru: national, transnational, diasporic', *South Asian Diaspora*, 2016. Also, Anjali Gera Roy and Ajaya K. Sahoo, *Diasporas and Transnationalisms: The Journey of the Komagata Maru*, New York, 2017; Anjali Gera Roy, *Imperialism and Sikh Migration: The Komagata Maru Incident*, New York, 2017.

[5] Recently, certain key documents related to the arrival of the *Komagata Maru* and stored in the West Bengal State Archives have been compiled and published. See Ananda Bhattacharyya, *Remembering Komagata Maru: Official Reports and Contemporary Accounts*, Delhi, 2016.

[6] For an understanding of the ways in which working masses have made themselves count in historical records, see Eric Hobsbawm, 'On History from Below', in *On History*, London, 1999, pp. 266–88. On the role of class and community in the formation of labour protests based on the works of E.P. Thompson, see Subho Basu, 'Introduction', in *Does Class Matter? Colonial Capital and Workers' Resistance in Bengal, 1890–1937*, Delhi, 2004, pp. 1–36.

[7] The need for adopting a 'micro-historical' frame in the context of the *Komagata Maru*'s voyage has been emphasized by Radhika Mongia in 'Terms of Analysis: Methodological Lessons from the Komagata Maru', an unpublished paper read at a workshop on 'Charting Imperial Itineraries 1914–2014: Unmooring the Komagata Maru', University of Victoria, 2014.

CHAPTER ONE

They Shall Not Reach Calcutta

While the ship was sailing towards the shores of Bengal, the local colonial authorities resolved that the *Komagata Maru* must not reach Calcutta. Outbreak of the First World War formed the critical context that underlined the schemes of surveillance and repression to deal with the vessel. Certain local considerations were also at work. The wider social and political tensions in the city and its hinterland, reflected in war-induced material hardship, rumours and public meetings, were a source of mounting anxiety to the colonizers. The mood of anti-colonial hostility, not only in Calcutta but also in the rest of Bengal, was cited to shape, justify and legitimize a repressive colonial strategy culminating in massacre. Local tensions and currents of opposition in the city and its surroundings merged with the wider considerations at work in the adoption of a combative strategy by the colonizers in relation to the passengers of the *Komagata Maru*. Interplay between imperial and local currents influenced the state's actions. This, in turn, came to be contested by different passenger-survivors who questioned the official standpoint as being the 'truth'. The condition of the passengers during the last stretch of the *Komagata Maru*'s journey can be understood by comparing the voices of colonial authority with that of those hunted by them; their victimization, as imperialized subjects of labour and population control along racist lines, was to exercise a direct impact on radical activism in the region.

War-induced Scarcity

An apocalyptic mood descended on Calcutta and on the rest of Bengal in the climate of war. The conversion of social life from a colonial-civilian to a colonial-martial mode generated a sense of imminent catastrophe. The wartime conditions in the city and the region could be situated within a wider imperial canvas; the extraordinary drain of resources in the form of money, men and material from South Asia by the British state, which directly contributed to a sharp decline in the living standards of ordinary people; the support extended by mainstream nationalist leaders to the imperial war effort, in the hope of securing India's autonomy within the altered post-war political geography of the British empire; the aim of different revolutionary groups to subvert and overthrow the temporarily beleaguered colonial order; the strategy of the colonial government to hold on to the subcontinent through heightened repression.[1]

In the colonial metropolis, embedded urban inequality was magnified by war. Those in the middle and at the bottom of the social hierarchy were hit by spiralling food prices and house rents in the absence of any government control. The unequal distribution of material benefits, organized through a convergence of race and class, was reinforced by wartime privations, and intensified the gulf separating the colonizers from the colonized. While big capital, represented by European interests in the city, remained unaffected, the living conditions of the bulk of the colonized subjects nosedived. The micro-enclaves of prosperity among the Indian rich also highlighted class and other fissures existing within the colonized subject populations, social divisions that could not be papered over by a shared subordination to the imperial state and colonial capital. The burden of surviving the war devolved on ordinary people and overwhelmed them. The material desperation in the city and the region found its way into wartime newspaper reports. Immediately before and during the war, the city came to be projected as the lost pulse of an emaciated hinterland. As Calcutta was drawn into the war effort, gloomy and dejected forecasts of a regional famine were advanced. With the sharp rise in prices, fear of imminent and widespread hunger soon became a reality. The *Moslem Hitaishi* noted: 'Food-stuffs are getting dearer and dearer in Calcutta. . . . [F]ish and meat are extremely scarce. . . . The poor and middle classes are feeling the pinch. Many of the wage-earning classes have been thrown out of work. . . . [E]ven house-rents are rising.'[2] The non-intervention of the government was also registered: 'The terrible war now raging in Europe will not perhaps let this Government do much to help the people.'[3] The *Dainik Bharat Mitra* (8 August 1914) demanded government intervention in the form of legislation to check high prices in the markets 'which are going up by leaps and bounds'. If food prices continued to rise, the paper observed, 'it is unimaginable what the situation would be after some more time has elapsed'. It predicted 'serious future consequences', including 'unrest in the shape of dacoities (robbery) and thefts if matters are allowed to run their course'.[4] To prevent mass starvation, the paper wanted the 'Government of India to throw off its indifference and adopt precautionary measures beforehand'. The *Basumati* (15 August 1914) was 'surprised at the statement, made by His Excellency Lord Carmichael at the last meeting of the Legislative Council, regarding prices not having gone up in Calcutta'.[5] The paper stressed that prices of foodstuffs had

> gone up so enormously as to require the intervention of the police, and articles such as Horlick's malted milk, Barley powder, arrowroot, soap, biscuits etc., are selling at very high prices. Even potatoes cannot be had for anything under 3 annas 6 pies a seer, though the usual price is 2 annas 3 pies.[6]

The high prices, alleged the paper, 'may not cause any inconvenience to His Excellency the Governor, but they are inflicting no end of hardship on poor folk'. In August 1914, the steep rise in the prices of food – by 25 per cent in some cases – was noted by the police authorities.[7]

As scarcity mounted, the hardships of the poor – including that of the lower middle class – received increased attention from sections of the local middle-class intelligentsia. The non-intervention of the colonial government in the districts of eastern Bengal was noted.[8] Yet no attempt was made to give a coherent political direction to popular wartime grievances. The mainstream nationalist leaders supported the imperial war effort in the hope of future political reforms. In the absence of any ideology of labour to mobilize them, the poor were consigned to hunger, starvation and occasional rioting.[9] Those who carried the crushing weight of war were concentrated in the lowest echelons of society. Cast out of any position of ownership, their indigent and destitute voices could be ignored.

Opposition

The war heightened the awareness of racialized subjecthood among the colonized, re-emphasizing contestations of the white superiority complex.

Racist assaults by European soldiers in Calcutta and the suburbs regularly found their way into the pages of Indian newspapers. They criticized 'misbehaving soldiers': 'recently some soldiers, while returning by a train from a football match at Budge Budge, behaved very improperly towards an Indian female in a train in the next station and even tried to enter into her compartment'.[10] The *Mohammadi* (17 July 1914) observed: 'European soldiers, when they get loose, become brutes as it were. We hope that the authorities will take particular care to prevent them from molesting the public.' The *Moslem Hitaishi* referred to a fracas between soldiers and students at Sealdah Railway Station in 1914.[11]

Wartime Calcutta was perceived by the colonial authorities as a disturbed zone where unmanageable forces of opposition lurked; they feared that the *Komagata Maru* passengers could find support among and blend with such forces. Surveillance reports conveyed a mood of dissent and resistance. At a Young Men's Christian Association (YMCA) meeting in late August, a speaker projected the conflict between the big powers as the outcome of inter-imperialist rivalry and envisioned a decolonized future:

> On the 25th August, a Mr. Watkins of the Y.M.C.A. delivered a lecture at the Theosophical Society Hall in College Square. The subject of the lecture was 'Peace in the Present Crisis'. The speaker explained the present crisis by cuttings from several newspapers and the writings of great men. He referred to the utterings of European powers and their pretended policy of peace while in reality they were trying to strengthen their military power. He also quoted some passages from the Bible including a prophecy of God that sometime the East will become strong. He said that like China and Japan, India will also rise. About 100 people including one European lady and gentleman were present.[12]

An unsuspecting British official was parted from his gun, which was for sale, by a band of revolutionary youths through a mischievous trick in September 1914. Liaqat Hussain, a millenarian-nationalist preacher, stressed in a newspaper letter in August, that empire-loyalists of the city should sacrifice their own and send their kin to fight in the battlefields of the war in Europe. A few days after the arrival of the ship in early October, he was heard thundering in a city park, 'Which *sala* is the King? There should be no talk of any king raised in any *swadeshi* meeting.'[13] The visions of a decolonized future, emerging in the backdrop of mounting challenges to a wartime crisis-ridden empire, were juxtaposed with the prospect of a German invasion.

The Emden Effect

Fantastic German vessels, pouring destruction upon the city by air and water, overwhelmed the popular imagination during the early months of the war. European officials, European voices representing the colonial capital in newspapers and the colonized subjects waited for this possibility with varying degrees of fear, dejection, thrill and excitement. Despite repeated declarations of loyalty to the empire by various associations and individuals, the popular mood in Calcutta was often interpreted as 'informally pro-German', or at least expectant of a resounding British defeat. Stray incidents making their way into police records vividly painted such a scenario. On an August evening, thousands of 'natives' were caught stargazing in the 'maidan' (the open space at the centre of the city) and the streets; they had mistaken a terrestrial body glittering in the sky as a German airship sent to pulverize the imperial order. The European police official recording the incident was struck by the crowd's 'credulity' behind the 'solemn' glances: 'In reality it was Venus seen through a small cloud. The planet is at present exceedingly bright, being at the furthest visible eastern distance from the sun, and after sunset for a short time is the most brilliant object in the sky.'[14]

Away from the music of the spheres, floating rumours related losses of sea-going vessels in the maelstrom of war as signals of the impending collapse of British power. Clerks of Mackinnon-Mackenzie, a Scottish business firm with a large share in the shipping trade, allegedly spun an imaginary tale, and it was repeated by their friends working for the Bengal Chamber of Commerce, that the majority of the company's ships, twenty-two out of forty, requisitioned for the war had been sunk by the German navy. They also spoke of the deaths of 20,000 Indian troops being carried in these vessels. They held 'that the steamship Golconda, one of the remaining ships and one of the finest owned by Messrs. Mackinnon Mackenzie, is lost sight of and that no news of her whereabouts is forthcoming, and she is believed to be missing'.[15] They believed that the Indian troops already dispatched overseas would not fight alongside the Allied forces. The clerks insisted that their European employers, the sahibs, had forbidden them to divulge any news related to the war, and had threatened them with dismissal. Britain's naval losses and the novel experience of aerial bombing in West Europe, initiated by German airships (Zeppelin) during August–September 1914, formed the backdrop of these rumours.[16] Circulation of rumours reached a high point in August, when a Special Branch officer heard that two regiments of Sikh soldiers had rebelled somewhere in Punjab and that the government was trying to suppress this news as rumour.[17]

Although the authorities were at pains to refute their 'slender foundations' at the beginning of the war, the rumours gave way to full-blown panic in September. This was triggered by the sudden arrival of the German cruiser, *Emden*, in the Bay of Bengal. The belief in the unshakeable hold of the largest empire of capital over the eastern seas, cultivated since the eighteenth century, came to be abruptly challenged by an unexpected rival. The enemy ship's appearance ruffled the calm confidence of the British colonizers. The *Emden* quickly became known for its stealth. The ship appeared unnoticed in the mouth of the River Hooghly on 15 September, and destroyed five English vessels coming down from Calcutta.[18] On the night of 22 September, it shelled the tanks of the Burma Oil Company and the storage batteries in the Madras docks.[19] During the early months of the war, the *Emden* destabilized sea routes, commerce and mail connections between the British, French and Dutch colonial empires in East Asia.[20]

Shipping in Calcutta was directly disrupted by the *Emden* effect. Rising unemployment among casual labourers[21] was accompanied by the refusal of many passengers to embark at the port. On a November afternoon, the *SS Egypt* arrived with 117 passengers at the Kidderpore (Khidirpur) docks. Five hundred and fourteen passengers had been on board when the boat left London; the majority, 'suffering, apparently, from what may be termed "Emden Fever" got off at Bombay'. The ship sailed surreptitiously 'from Colombo to Calcutta in two and a half days, hugging the coast, the whole of the way lights extinguished'.[22] The *City of Marseilles* reached Outram Ghat on a late November afternoon from Liverpool. A large crowd had gathered to receive the ship, 'which carried about 196 passengers for Calcutta'. The vessel had stopped at Naples, Port Said, Suez, Aden and Colombo, and met 'friendly war-ships at various points'. Its course had been slightly altered 'in order to avoid an encounter with the Emden.'[23]

European opinion-makers regarded the *Emden* as a source of menace and danger, as an agent of devastation in the realm of profit-seeking and capital accumulation. Losses were anticipated and bemoaned. The *Emden*'s rapid success in destroying British capital assets was seen as 'so monotonously frequent' that 'its possible depredations' were 'taken into account as a normal business risk in times of war'.[24] As the ship retreated further eastwards and its threatening presence from the immediate vicinity of Calcutta was removed, the *Emden* became a source of thrilling entertainment and drama to the

European public in the city. While the ship was being vested with an aura of mythical invincibility, the ordinary people in the metropolis were gripped by an apocalyptic vision. From 16 September, the day after the *Emden* had raided and sank the British steamers, the colonial officials noted that the panic-driven rumours were gaining ground. Word was spreading that the government was planning to transplant its seat of power to the interiors of Bengal by shifting from Calcutta to Dhaka; that German cruisers were about to invade Calcutta; and that the German navy had greater strength in the waters of East Asia. Many contemplated an escape from the city by removing their families from Calcutta.[25] The final flight of the colonizers was visualized at a time when they had already removed their central administrative headquarters to New Delhi. In the face of a concentrated German offensive, British authority was seen as a force of imperialism-in-retreat, ready to abandon the city to its doom. A social disaster of unknown magnitude was imagined, induced by the exit of the existing masters and the erasure of the civic infrastructure by the invading German forces.

The spectre of German invasion remained unrealized. It nestled for a while in the imagination of the colonizers and their subjects. It was observed on behalf of the colonial capital that 'consuming countries are now in the position that they must have jute or gunnies, as the case may be; so business is proceeding in spite of the Emden's successful deception'.[26] With the resumption of the super-profitable jute trade, which initially suffered from the vanishing of the continental market, particularly in Germany and Austria-Hungary,[27] the anxiety of European proprietors subsided. The colonized subjects also realized that the colonizers were not yet ready to leave the city. Their sense of dread and dissent against colonial authority at a time of rising hardship were expressed through other outlets. However, wartime watch on the river by the colonial authorities persisted, as did the rumours surrounding the vessels arriving from the east. Soon, the imaginary battleships navigating through the sky and the sea were replaced by ships of sedition. The *Emden* effect was followed, accompanied and replaced by the 'Ghadar' effect tied with the arrival of the *Komagata Maru*, and the spectre of the return of the repressed.

To Chalk Out Repression

Even before the ship had reached the shores of Bengal, the colonial state apparatus was making arrangements in advance to deal with 'the disappointed emigrants from the Punjab to Canada by Komagata Maru'.[28] As early as May, the Bengal Intelligence Branch had been alerted to the possibilities of a Ghadar-led uprising supported by Indian migrants abroad. A British Superintendent posted in the Dinajpur district of Bengal reported that his brother, who had spent twenty-five years in India, met some Indians in Vancouver, Canada. They had told him that the revolutionary party was certain a 'general rising' was to occur in the course of the next two years and they were biding their time till England got entangled in war. Ever-vigilant of any threat to the empire, he had obtained two copies of *Ghadar*, a seditious leaflet, and sent them by post to his sibling. San Francisco and Vancouver were identified as the revolutionary headquarters, and it was recorded that a 'tremendous amount' of seditious literature was sent to India from these cities.[29] Though aware of the revolutionary challenge, the local authorities in Bengal were not in a position to connect the Ghadar tendency with the controversy surrounding the *Komagata Maru's* journey and Indian labour emigration to North America.

As the ship came closer in September, imperial anxieties surfaced. The police authorities of Punjab and Bengal, in consultation with the central authorities in Simla and Delhi, secretly planned to imprison Gurdit Singh and his close followers the moment they touched land, and to send the rest by a special train to Punjab. They anticipated an adverse response to this action, and decided that if the passengers supportive of Gurdit Singh showed signs of resenting his detention, he would be kept in Calcutta temporarily and sent to Punjab later. They were determined not to allow the ship to reach Calcutta. The *Komagata Maru* had already attracted public attention. If it was permitted to sail into the volatile port-city, the regional headquarters of colonial authority and the nerve centre of anti-colonial dissent in the region, a crowd could gather to welcome the ship and its passengers; this was 'undesirable' and had to be prevented. David Petrie, a high-ranking police officer who was present at Budge Budge and had been sent by Cleveland, Director of Criminal Intelligence, with whom he had discussed a strategy of containment for a fortnight, explained this in confidential accounts while stationed in Calcutta to supervise and implement the official plan. According to Petrie, the Bengal government was

> particularly interested in excluding from Calcutta persons whose entry might easily be productive of mischief. They considered it desirable, too, that the emigrants should not come up the river to Calcutta itself, where crowds would

probably collect and so stir up public excitement, which all our operations were specially designed to prevent.[30]

For a while, the idea of bringing them up to suburban Garden Reach, then quietly removing them by ferry to Howrah Station for transport by train to Punjab, and ultimately detaining them at Fort Ludhiana, was considered. Sir William Duke, a member of the Executive Council of Bengal, was against this plan. He thought 'it was undesirable to bring the Sikhs into Calcutta at all, if it could by any means be avoided'.[31] Duke suggested that the ship should be berthed at Budge Budge, 13 miles south of Calcutta, and the special train should be kept ready at the station.[32] Intra-imperial intelligence aided the efforts of the colonial authorities in India in advance. A confidential letter from W.C. Hopkinson of Immigration Branch, British Columbia, had reached the Director of Criminal Intelligence in early September. It referred to a previous letter from late July offering details on potential troublemakers who were likely to challenge imperial authority, and contained copies of certificates issued to Gurdit Singh and seven others. Hopkinson sent 'extra photos' for their easy identification and warned that a large number of 'East Indians' were returning from Canada to India probably without the intention of turning back. Other passenger lists were also forwarded from Canada. Unregistered 'Hindus' who had left for India on the *Empress of India* from Vancouver and Victoria on 22 August, and on the *Canada Maru* from Victoria on 1 September, were mentioned. Seven passengers travelling on the *Canada Maru* were specifically marked as 'suspicious characters'.[33] While the prior information helped the government to prepare for the arrival of the *Komagata Maru*, the entire exchange convinced the Indian authorities that a political threat, inspired by the experience of racist harassment in Canada and the Ghadar tendency, was looming in the horizon. It was embodied in the form of returning immigrants.

The Bengal government was entrusted with a range of responsibilities. Within the course of a week (14–21 September), in consultation with and guided by the provincial authorities of Punjab and central authorities from Delhi and Simla, a programme of repression was chalked out. A list of fourteen passengers was drawn up; they were to be prevented from returning to Punjab and detained in Bengal under the wartime security measure, Ingress into India Ordinance, 1914. Gurdit Singh's internment was emphasized. The government's priority, as outlined by Cleveland, was to 'neutralize' those arriving with the intention of stirring up 'trouble'; having been forcibly turned away from Vancouver and refused entry at Singapore, the troubled passengers were perceived as dangerous malcontents, capable of rising against colonial authority in India. From his headquarters in Simla, Cleveland wrote to Cumming, Chief Secretary to the Bengal Government, on 17 September:

> In this time of stress we are all avoiding unnecessary writing. . . . I am sending down Petrie of my department (for this job) to explain to you exactly what arrangements are contemplated and to discuss them with you, or with any officer of your government whom you may select, and the best method of dealing with the whole matter so as to suit the convenience of your Government, of the Punjab Government and of the GOI.[34]

More importantly, the passengers could inconvenience and embarrass the government at a time of war, when it was banking on the loyalty of Indians and on the resources of the subcontinent in the form of men and money. By launching a potentially popular public campaign against imperial racism, they could disrupt the war effort. The colonial authorities suppressed telegrams – such as the one sent to Sardar Harchand Singh of Lyallpur – from the passengers to their sympathizers in Punjab and Bengal. *Bengalee*, a Calcutta newspaper which had campaigned against the racist persecution of the passengers by Canadian authorities, was also suppressed. The message, which never arrived, had been signed by Gurdit Singh. It urged Indian nationalist leaders to receive the ship at the Calcutta docks followed by an appeal to begin a movement to force the government to investigate the circumstances leading to its return. The passengers specifically desired the government to appoint a commission to look into their 'grievances'. An official note from Punjab observed:

> The Lieutenant Governor thinks it advisable, in the present crisis, to prevent the arrival of these men from being used as the occasion for a recrudescence of the agitation with regard to Indian emigration in the British colonies, and he therefore proposes to take action under Ordinance No. V of 1914, dated the 5th Sept. 1914, to procure their return to their homes immediately on landing.

Paradoxically, the majority of the ship's passengers were described in confidential correspondence as 'harmless', 'destitute' and disinclined to follow 'the leader of the expedition',[35] the implicit assumption being that they would be easier to control.[36] The return of the natives revealed the imperial strains of assessing their obedience and disobedience; to protect authority, a strategy that claimed to be outwardly protective while hiding a repressive agenda, was required.

Armed with the prior intent of suppression rather than dialogue, the British officials were ready to detain those labelled as ring-leaders of the campaign to embarrass imperial authority: Gurdit Singh; his secretary, Daljit Singh; Gurdit's close aide, Amir Mohammad Khan; Pohlo Ram; Jawahar Mal, a Sindhi passenger who had embarked at Kobe on the return trip; Narain, Jawahar Mal's brother; Kehar Singh; and Harnam Singh. According to Petrie:

> As to the case of No. (1), no remark is needed. No. (2) was his secretary and chief helper; his attitude on board was often very insolent. No. (3) shared GS's cabin, and was mentioned by the Captain as being an active mischief-maker. No. (4) was mentioned by the Hoshiarpur authorities as a person who was likely to stir up trouble on his return to India. Nos. (5) and (6) are Sindhi brothers who came aboard under suspicious circumstances at Kobe; No. (5) was mentioned in a telegram from Japan and was also described by the Captain as an actively dangerous man who had been lecturing and stirring up disaffection on board. No. (7) had written a diary of events at Vancouver which showed a strong under-current of disloyal feeling. No. (8) was a man who had been previously deported from Canada and his experience on the KM with his attitude on board made him from whom trouble could be reasonably expected.[37]

These, according to him, were men 'against whom there existed ample prima facie ground for taking action'. It was decided that they would be quickly put on board a police launch and transferred to Alipore Central Jail in Calcutta once the passengers were taken off the ship under police escort.[38]

The nitty-gritty of the administration of repression was then worked out in practical terms; the costs of boarding the train were to be disbursed in Calcutta by the Bengal government without delay along with all practical arrangements. The Bengal authorities were stretched to the point of desperation at this point. By their own admission, this was due to the triangular pressures of war, sentiments of popular opposition and violent 'sedition'.[39] It was probably in order to avoid any disagreeable response from their Bengal counterpart and the surfacing of intra-bureaucratic tensions that the instruction from Punjab via Simla on 17 September carried a cajoling note: 'Sir Michael O'Dwyer feels sure that he can rely on the Government of Bengal in this matter.'[40]

Extreme Measures

Encased within a wider strategy of repression, imperial surveillance made way for confrontation and massacre. The massacre as the pivotal 'event' at the end of the *Komagata Maru's* passage unfolded in multiple stages, with different levels of coercive pressure applied from above by colonial authorities at each moment of dealing with the ship's passengers.[41] On 27 September, a deceptively calm telegram reached the authorities in Simla from Calcutta: 'KM met today by Bengal and Punjab officers as arranged. All satisfactory so far.'[42] The next communication was long for a telegram, and was sent on 30 September. The version given, followed by an official communiqué to the press, which formed the master narrative of all official accounts,[43] was later held up by the *Report of the Komagata Maru Committee of Inquiry*; they exonerated the colonial government. The official position on the 'incident', subsequently described as the 'Budge Budge Riot' in the press and police accounts, projected the massacre as an unavoidable confrontation between the colonial state and ungrateful, restive migrants bent on an insurrection. Historical evidence strongly suggests that coercive tactics by the British officials led to a gunfight, which then took on the form of a full-scale massacre, resulting in the death of twenty-one passengers. Two European officers and two police constables from Punjab were also killed. Two Indian residents at Budge Budge, a Bengali middle-class onlooker and a shop assistant from Orissa were killed by bullets fired by the troops.[44] Rukmini Kanta Mazumdar, an East Bengali resident of Noakhali who was visiting his relative at Budge Budge, and Dinabondhu Uriya of Bhadrak in Orissa, who worked as a cook in an eating joint close to the railway station, were trapped in the wrong place when the firing began. According to an official account composed immediately afterwards,

> ten of the Sikhs died from .303 bullets fired by the troops; two probably by .450 bullets fired either by the police or by the officers of the troops; one Sikh by a bullet fired from a .380 weapon which could only have been fired by one of the rioters as neither police nor troops had a weapon of this calibre. One Uriya died from revolver wounds (a servant); one Bengali outsider was killed by misadventure by a .303 bullet from the troops; one Sikh died from drowning. . . . Another body was brought up to the bank from the river about four days after the riot. The body was so decomposed as to be unidentifiable, but the local police officers said that it was the body of a Sikh, because it had long hair and a beard.[45]

He had 'met his death by drowning in the Hooghly river.' Eighteen Sikhs were killed at the railway station at Budge Budge, two died in hospital from fatal injuries, and one from drowning while trying to escape the carnage. Later, the drowned man with long hair was identified as Indra Singh.[46] The post-mortem reports cited death from bullet wounds as the dead Sikhs, the two Indian bystanders, were dissected one by one by Lieutenant Colonel Newman, Civil Surgeon of 24 Parganas and Indian Medical Service. His scalpel touched smashed jaws, perforated and broken clavicles, fatal injuries in the upper parts of the bodies, mostly the head, the chest, the face and the stomach.[47] The clinical descriptions were regulated by an official purpose to register the physical causes rather than the social or political conditions of death. They concealed the circumstances that could have been avoided and separated the dead from the living. Yet they held up a visceral portrait of the extent of violence committed by the colonial state.

The pathology of state has not escaped the notice of historians. Darshan S. Tatla has pointed at the sharp contrast between the official version, which found final embodiment in the *Report of the Komagata Maru Committee of Inquiry* (1914), and the counter-version offered by Gurdit Singh in his *Voyage of the Komagata Maru or India's Slavery Abroad* (1927).[48] The passengers as victims of racial exclusion were blamed for being thrust into the most violent chapter of their exhausting journey of victimization. Successively refined through telling and retelling, the imperial officialdom advanced the argument that despite the consideration shown to them from Vancouver to Budge Budge, the assistance rendered and benevolence extended, the passengers remained suspicious of white authority, were unhappy with the arrangements and chose a path of hostile non-cooperation followed by violent disobedience. The police officials on the ground, while recording their defensive–aggressive statements, repeatedly declared that they had remained calm in the face of 'insolence' instigated by extremist elements, and that the Sikhs were the first to fire at the colonial forces at Budge Budge Railway Station. They also freely admitted of having prepared in advance to use force and mobilize troops from Fort William and elsewhere. Further, they inadvertently revealed that the passengers, despite their suspicions, were peaceful; they had put up with colonial authority, including searches. They had obeyed the orders to turn back from the road to Calcutta and had remained herded in the railway station at Budge Budge. The officers acknowledged having underestimated the ability of the emigrants to unite as victims of prolonged persecution, and to defend Gurdit Singh when they realized that the British authorities had special plans for him. David Petrie reported the mood of resistance soon after the incident. Along with the rest of the colonial bureaucracy, as far as he was concerned, the battle line was already drawn:

> Most of the Sikhs, too, were men who had been abroad in the colonies and elsewhere – Hong Kong, Shanghai, Manila, and so on. It is a matter of common experience that Indians too often return from abroad with the tainted political views and diminished respect for their white rulers. . . . On an examination of all the circumstances, it is difficult to avoid the conclusion that Gurdit Singh's deliberate resolve to pursue his own way in defiance of authority must have led, sooner or later, to the same result.[49]

The official versions, compiled in a confidential Bengal Home Department dossier entitled 'Riot by Passengers of the S.S. Komagata Maru at Budge Budge', offered imperial insiders' accounts and insights into the way monitoring and repression were carried out as strategy, and the victims blamed for the sanguinary outcome of their journey. The 'event' reconstructed through official statements projected the passengers as initially 'docile' and 'anxious' to return home, followed by signs of dissent expressed by generally 'secretive' behaviour and a 'closing of ranks'. In the eyes of the figures of authority heading an organized and armed force sent to suppress them, the fact that the targets were capable of emerging as a counter-collective was a source of extreme disquiet. Inspired by revolutionary ideas and impatient with racist persecutions, the migrants were willing to resist the imperial order. They were no longer convinced by claims of paternalistic concern, supplemented by regular doses of verbal abuse, threats of coercion and an intrusive, all-encompassing regime of surveillance. They were daring to defy the long-established relationship between the master race and subject populations deemed as naturally inferior. This was recorded by Petrie:

> . . . among the more intelligent of the passengers to whom one most naturally turned for assistance, I found little disposition to listen to reason or argument. On one occasion, when I was trying to persuade two or three boorish individuals that all Government wanted to do was to befriend and assist them, one of the 'leaders' intervened and said that, although this might be the intention of the Government, it was unwise to place reliance on loose talkers like myself. Another 'leader' refused to tell me his name, and many conversations were broken off because the parties addressed turned away and declined to listen

further. The demeanour of most of the active participants in the conversation was very offensive and insolent, and I can't quote other instances or rudeness because they happened so frequently as to obliterate the details of individual cases. There was hardly a man one spoke to who had not thrown off completely the courtesy one is accustomed to meet with from the Sikh in his own country. The native police officers on board were no more successful.[50]

Petrie also spoke of the difficulty of implementing the prior strategy without use of force. Separating Gurdit Singh from the others proved to be difficult as he was guarded zealously by his companions: 'In particular, a huge Sikh, called Amar Singh, stood over me the whole time. He was in black *nihang*'s clothes, with a knife slung over his shoulder. He appeared to act as a sort of personal body-guard to Gurdit Singh.'[51] When the passengers started marching out of the ship, symbolically placing the *Guru Granth Sahib* at the head of the procession as a sign of obeying a parallel and spiritually superior authority, the officers felt interfering with marchers carrying a holy book and its removal could be 'a somewhat sticky business'.[52] Cumming, also directed like Petrie by the twin benefits of colonial foresight and hindsight, took the myth of sinister natives and their customs even further. He claimed that the *Guru Granth Sahib* was being carried around by the Sikhs not just as an act of faith but with strategic cunning since it was large enough to hide, and probably contained, contraband firearms. In the perception of their armed escorts, by the time the passengers reached the moonlit station-yard having submitted to all official directives, 'The Sikhs were in a sullen and ugly temper.'[53] To discipline and control them, the deployment of overwhelming force as a strategy was now converted into baton-charges, followed by orders to open fire.

To ward off charges of official culpability, the victims were criminalized before and after the massacre. Though existing evidence does not suggest that the massacre was premeditated, there is ample indication in the secret official records that recourse to force was always entertained. The passengers had travelled across half the world enduring a strenuous voyage that thrust them into penury, uncertainty and, finally, to extreme violence. The central role of repression in the imperial strategy of containment revealed that they were wading through imperial and racial authority that was not just distributed across seas and lands, but was an ever-present force regulating their lives and labour. They were navigating a bureaucratic climate and official mind-set that was in no mood to accommodate democratic dissent

from below. Conversations with officers and constables on duty revealed
the self-perception of the passengers as victims of imperial racism. Sardar
Sukha Singh, Deputy Superintendent of Police, CID, Punjab, who had
gone aboard the *Komagata Maru*, reported that Gurdit Singh had criticized
the British government; he had said that His Majesty did not rule other
colonies the way he ruled India. As an example, Gurdit Singh had cited
the treatment meted out to the ship's passengers at Vancouver, and had
spoken of the restrictions imposed on Indian traders and labourers across
the British empire. He had pointed at the legal right of British subjects to go
anywhere within the empire, which in practice had meant being prevented
from entering Canada even if the British flag was flying there. According
to Sukha Singh, the passengers had their minds 'poisoned' by such 'anti-
government talk'. Probably anticipating the government's plans, Gurdit
Singh had allegedly incited the passengers along with Amir Mohammad, his
'Munshi', Daljit Singh, his secretary, and Amar Singh Nihang, his orderly;
he had led them to believe that they were probably not being taken to

Ships at Chandpal Ghat, 1912 (Courtesy Royal Commission on the Ancient and Historical
Monuments of Scotland [RCAHMS])

Punjab but to some unknown destination. However, Sukha Singh admitted that the 'rioting' by the passengers was 'unexpected'.

After the massacre, Petrie acknowledged that the government had deputed the officers to meet the *Komagata Maru* with 'a definite view'. When the ship arrived at Budge Budge, the officers explained to Gurdit Singh that the ship was to be searched in conformity with the new wartime regulations. Gurdit Singh lived in his office room with Amir Mohammad Khan and Daljit, his secretary, occupied the room where the safe was located. Gurdit Singh did not object and the search immediately began. Petrie personally examined Gurdit Singh's room and safe, using keys handed over by Daljit Singh. Nothing 'objectionable' was found, though some papers were collected for further inspection. Gurdit Singh's office room contained a dressing table with drawers full of documents related to the commercial aspects of the voyage. Petrie ordered the room to be locked up for future examination. Through this measure, he probably ensured that the passengers would not have access to the documents if compensation claims and complaints of racist harassment within the empire ended up in court. The two Sindhi brothers, Jawahar Mal and Narain, who had boarded the ship at Kobe 'under suspicious circumstances', also had their first-class cabins and effects searched. After the cabin passengers, the rest of the ship was also inspected. Only one copy of Ghadar literature was found, from 'a dull-looking fellow, Mastan Singh, an inoffensive fellow'. In fact, there was nothing to indicate that the passengers were 'in the grip of extreme feelings'. Though 'a little surly during interrogation', after 'friendly chaff' they became 'cheerful' and opened up to the officers. The police also met the members of the ship's 'committee', ten or twelve passengers elected by the rest to look after their comfort and secure rations. All were civil except Dhan Singh, who was 'sullen' and 'insolent'. The rest were 'somewhat out-talked by Mir Mohammad Khan, who spoke volubly, giving utterance to expressions of loyalty of a rather fulsome type'. The native police officers were left on board for the night to mix freely with the passengers and pick up 'any scraps of information likely to help us'. On 29 September, Petrie stated, when they again went aboard,

> Gurdit Singh asked to speak to Humphreys, who took him apart into a deck cabin. He spoke, however, loudly enough to be overheard by the Sikhs, who were by this time crowding around in large numbers. I did not catch the whole of his conversation, but I heard his assertion that none of them would go ashore at Budge Budge; he also said if they had done anything wrong, a Judge

should be sent for to take their statements, after which Government could shoot them or do what it chose; if there was a question of dying, they would all die together, and so on. There was more inconsequential talk of this nature and I heard the same thing repeated ad nauseam by different passengers I talked to. After Gurdit Singh's pronouncement, which seemed to find almost universal acceptance, a complete dead-lock resulted. Halliday and Slocock, who had come out from Calcutta to meet the steamer, had by this time come on board, and they in common with all of us moved about freely among the passengers arguing, persuading and coaxing. Some of those I talked to professed fears as to their getting to their homes from the wrong side of the river, and said that perhaps Government's benevolent intentions concealed some design to send them into captivity in Assam or some such place. Such fears may have been genuinely entertained by some of the more ignorant passengers, although, I do not believe that even in their minds they were of spontaneous growth. Others said they desired to land at Howrah and march in procession to the Gurudwara there.[54]

When the passengers defied orders to turn back and started marching, Petrie and the other police officials sent from Calcutta suspended dialogue and issued open threats. Petrie claimed the official side was outnumbered, and, fearing resistance, he sought armed reinforcements:

[The passengers] streamed down the road to Calcutta, the Granth Sahib being carried in triumph at the head of the procession. After a hasty consultation, I gathered about 10 or 12 Punjab constables. . . . I reached the head of the procession. . . . Two of the party, both in nihang's clothes, advanced as if to attack me. One of them was Gurdit Singh's body-guard Amar Singh, and I had to cover him with my pistol to get clear of him. Seeing that the Sikhs were in a temper, on which reason was little likely to make any impression, and as any attempt to use force could only have ended in disaster to our small party, I gave a hasty order to the constables with me to do nothing, and hurried back to explain the situation to Donald. He immediately telephoned to Calcutta, asking for a sufficient force of police or military to be sent out to intercept the Sikhs. I should mention that when I was passing along the procession . . . I saw the Sindhi Jawahar Mal in the middle of it; he seemed pale with excitement, and with his right hand held aloft was shouting 'Quick march! Quick march!'[55]

In reply to the criticism as to why the ship was not searched thoroughly for weapons, Petrie claimed that the officers relied on 'tact and reconciliation' rather than 'pure force'. Body search and minute check of the 'passenger's kits' could have bred great resentment. He also admitted that the implementation of the official plan would have led to some form of violence: 'To separate Gurdit Singh from his followers would have been followed by a riot, either in Calcutta or in Ludhiana.'[56] He also justified the strategy of repression over dialogue on the ground that there had arisen, in the course of interactions, a pressing need to demonstrate the triumph of racialized authority to the returning subjects: 'In fact, the officers pursued this policy to a point where they must have almost made themselves ridiculous in the eyes of men who, by their conduct in Vancouver, had shown that they were prepared to listen to no argument save that of armed force.'[57]

On 28 September 1914, the day after the ship's arrival and before the massacre next day, Captain Yamamoto's statement was recorded with the aid of Captain Cardew, a British official, who acted as the translator and interpreter. Yamamoto recalled the pre-history of his ship, 'formerly employed in the China coastal trade and in voyages to Java'.[58] She was chartered by Gurdit Singh from Hong Kong with plans to return there in future and pick up more passengers as part of a business venture. Yamamoto thought that guns were picked up by the passengers from Yokohama on the way back. He also claimed that Gurdit Singh was rude to him. Keen to project himself as an ally of the colonial authorities, Yamamoto declared that though the British Consul at Kobe had told him not to pick up the two Sindhi brothers, Gurdit Singh had welcomed them. The captain called them 'young bloods' who delivered incendiary lectures to instigate the passengers against British authority on the voyage from Kobe to Calcutta. Yamamoto accused Gurdit Singh of personal involvement in hiding arms. He labelled Gurdit Singh, his secretary Daljit Singh and Jawahar Mal as 'dangerous men', and declared that 'if they were in the hands of the Japanese Government these three and a good many others would have been executed'. He considered Jawahar Mal, 'the elder young blood', to be even more dangerous than Gurdit Singh. The captain reported a few occasions of fighting between the Indian passengers and the Japanese crew. The latter, armed with an iron bar and butcher's cleaver, had split open the head of an Indian. The captain proudly proclaimed that after this lesson, the Indians were shy of crossing the Japanese. Yamamoto complained that twenty dangerous persons were on board, and his mate could furnish a full list of names since he only knew the prominent ones. The captain's account of the voyage, designed to suit colonial requirements, was still suspected of deliberate omissions. The British officials thought Gurdit Singh had been in communication with sympathetic Japanese imperial officials at Moji, and that this information had been suppressed by the Japanese crew. The Japanese held that the Indians had secured five pistols, which they threw overboard as the ship approached the Bengal coast. They also claimed that Gurdit Singh distributed guns when required; Daljit possessed one and Mir Mohammad Khan was 'a bad man and a ringleader'. The Sindhi brothers from Kobe were branded as the most dangerous, for they believed that war afforded them the opportunity to make trouble for the British government.[59]

On the basis of the *Report of the Komagata Maru Committee of Inquiry*, all responsibility was deflected from the shoulders of colonial officialdom and the army of repression they commanded. Effectively, the victims were held as solely culpable for the massacre unleashed upon them. Cumming, Chief Secretary to the Government of Bengal, went so far as to say that Punjabi Head Constable Mal Singh's death as explained by Gunner H. Facer, formerly a Sergeant of Calcutta Police, was not acceptable; Facer had claimed that the soldiers irresponsibly shot the hapless policeman who was on active duty. Cumming claimed that it was impossible to reconstruct how Mal Singh had died; he had been accidentally shot and the Royal Fusiliers were not to be blamed. The Governor General in Council agreed with this position, and pointed out with much satisfaction that the Committee of Inquiry also did not regard the conduct of the authorities as worthy of blame in any way.[60]

A decade later, in the course of the 1920s, Gurdit Singh was keen to offer a rebuttal. He was unaware of the details of these statements carefully wrapped away in an intelligence dossier. Some of the details that emerged from his version were the exact opposite of the statements which formed the basis of the official 'truth'. According to Gurdit Singh, after the stranded passengers were forced to loot water from the Japanese crew, the Canadian authorities had allowed the latter to procure firearms to control the Indian migrants. Later, the Japanese sailors started selling them secretly to the passengers to turn a quick profit. Gurdit Singh claimed that the committee led by him and Jawahar Mal ensured these illegal weapons were got rid of before the ship reached Bengal. He had instructed the captain to prevent his crew from selling revolvers and ammunitions to the migrants. When the ship reached Kulpi in the Bengal coastal region, local boatmen who wanted to sell their wares to the passengers were prevented by the British authorities from approaching the ship. This generated a feeling of 'unease' among the returning migrants, and stoked their suspicion of colonial authority. Gurdit Singh was also surprised that his cables had not reached India from Singapore; and that no friend was present to greet them, only a hostile police force. He suspected that the European Custom Officer had either pocketed the 'paltry sum' of thirty dollars and did not send the telegram, or 'the government stopped these wires, which fact, never came to my knowledge'.[61] He felt that if the telegrams had been received, the massacre at Budge Budge may not have occurred. He insisted that the government was less than transparent in dealing with him and the passengers. This was revealed when the 'notorious hound' Sukha Singh came aboard on 27 September as the ring leader of the twenty Punjabi policemen in plainclothes to trick them: 'like theatre actors the same men came the next day now clad in police uniform and searched the persons of the passengers'.[62] He complained of being subjected to racist verbal abuse from the white officers when he tried to find out the government's intentions vis-à-vis the passengers; he had stated before them that the passengers were ready to die, but needed to know the charges against them.[63] Gurdit Singh claimed that they were repeatedly threatened, pushed, kicked, clubbed and beaten before the final confrontation and massacre at Budge Budge Railway Station.[64]

Voices from the Komagata Maru

Though the counter-versions emerging from the passengers in 1914–15 were not allowed to reach the public, they constituted an unofficial negation of the state's account of the events. Imprisoned and tracked down after the massacre, the survivor-passengers revealed the precarious world they had been thrust into in their statements before the police and through correspondence. They represented the suppressed voices from the Komagata Maru. Fragments from the voices of the soldiers also survive. They conducted the manhunt for the missing passengers who had run away from the scene of shooting. Their statements exposed the perils and predatory character of the repressive measures, which took on the form of a full-scale counter-insurgency operation. When the troops fired, the passengers attempted to escape their captors. The troops, led by British military officers, surged through the crops; they found the countryside to be a swampy marshland, a difficult terrain where few paths intersected. They started stopping and interrogating local villagers to close down on their quarry. A passenger was captured from one of the villages. Sixteen prisoners were taken, though some escaped through the fields by crossing a stream. Lieutenant F.J.O. Hume-Wright of the 16th Rajputs, in his statement before the authorities on 2 October 1914, reported that the soldiers had fired upon the Sikhs while trying to capture them from the marshy crop-covered countryside: 'We found no arms or ammunition on any of the prisoners, but these they had most probably thrown away into the crop, or into the water before they were captured.'[65] In April 1915, a revolver, supposedly belonging to the '*Komagata Maru* Sikhs', was recovered from a fish tank in Budge Budge.[66]

On 8 October, a reward of Rs 100 was announced by the Inspector General of Police, Bengal, for information that would lead to the arrest of 'Sikh emigrants who belonged to the assembly present at the Budge Budge riot, who are still at large'. On 13 October, he offered a reward of Rs 1,000 for clues leading to the arrest of Gurdit Singh, pinpointed as the leader of the Budge Budge 'affray'. By 10 October, several Budge Budge fugitives had been captured. At Dakshineswar, driven by desperation, a Sikh, along with four or five others, had barged into the house of a local resident, Kapil Biswas. Kapil chased the Sikh, and while he was plunging into a tank and then again into another, struck him in the head. By this time a large crowd had gathered, and he was caught. When he told them that he was a fugitive, they took him to a doctor's house where he was given food and a change of clothes, and his wound was 'attended to'. He was then handed over to the officials of Baranagar Police Station. Though his companions remained untraced, another was captured from Belghoria, a few miles east of Baranagar, near Calcutta, on 5 October. On 15 October, the Inspector General thanked all ranks of the armed forces deployed at Budge Budge during the confrontation with the passengers of the *Komagata Maru*. The Howrah and Alipore Armed Reserve forces and the Dhaka military police under Captain MacPherson's command were especially praised for their actions.[67]

Among the 211 passengers, mostly Sikhs along with several from Muslim and Hindu backgrounds, who were arrested immediately after the massacre, the vast majority were unarmed;[68] those who possessed guns did not use them. The captives contested the voices of repression, representing a clash of affinities that had taken centre stage when the ship finally ended its journey. They countered the interpretations of their situation furnished by the colonial officials, the contentions of authority figures of different ranks such as Cleveland, Duke, Petrie, Cumming and Hume-Wright. Since historians have already delved into the massacre and its aftermath in detail,[69] it will be productive to examine the neglected voices of some of the passengers. They uncovered the experiential world of migrant workers on the *Komagata Maru*, turned away at every port and finally overwhelmed by pre-planned repression in the country of their birth, the only land-mass willing to receive them. The detained passengers recorded their ill-treatment and exhaustion. They were brought to Calcutta, not under circumstances of their own choosing, and incarcerated at Alipore Jail. They had travelled far from rural districts and native states of Punjab – from Ferozepur, Lahore, Hoshiarpur, Amritsar and Nabha, only to end up as prisoners aboard the ship and later in the more dismal surroundings of the colonial prison. Watched and subjected to continuous imperial monitoring, they spent short, relatively peaceful breaks in Japanese ports such as Kobe, Moji and Yokohama. The passengers claimed they were harassed at every turn, at every British port they passed. Stranded for two months at Vancouver where the court turned down their demand to disembark, they suffered prolonged privations and were refused entry at Singapore. As mentioned, their statements, taken down in police stations and prison cells, offered counter-claims of abuse, clashing with the narratives of events furnished by their captors. Handwritten statements in Punjabi, written in the Gurumukhi script, were recorded and translated into English for official proceedings. The interned travellers recorded a desperate journey through an unknown topography of terror – of escaping from Budge Budge Railway Station as 'fugitives'; of being chased and shot at by the troops; of crossing rivers, trekking through marshes, fields and roads, hiding in forests, begging for alms and seeking asylum in nearby villages, adjoining districts, suburbs and finally in the neighbourhoods of Calcutta.

Individual statements testified to a passage of persecution which had ended in resistance and aborted attempts to evade colonial authority. Tara Singh began by stating on 4 October 1914: 'I am a Sikh. I was on the steamer "Komagata Maru". We landed at Budge Budge.'[70] He then furnished a description of a harrowing journey. He had boarded the ship from Manila where he used to work, convinced that better opportunities waited in Canada. He claimed that he did not participate in a riot. When the confrontation began, he fled with others but soon lost his companions. After the firing at Budge Budge, he remained concealed in a jungle at night. In the morning, he crossed the river by a small boat. The boatman ferried him free of charge. Then he came near a station below Howrah, on the Bombay line. The police deduced that it was probably Shalimar. From there, he walked through the jungle keeping the railway line in view. He did not know the name of any village or place he passed on the way: 'After passing 2 or 3 miles from Midnapur towards Bankura, I was near a *nala* (ditch) when I met the Babu who gave me clothes and money. I came through Midnapur town road.'[71] The unknown Bengali gentleman (babu) travelling in a bullock cart was halting at the roadside when they met; this anonymous benefactor warned him that the British government could execute him if he was captured, gave him money, and provided a fresh set of clothes and disguise. The Bengali babu told him: 'You had better change your appearance and address, or the Sarcar will hang you.' He 'got scissors from somewhere and cut my hair and gave me a change of dress. I don't know the name of the Babu.'[72] The gentleman also threw away the clothes Tara Singh had been wearing. Tara Singh again started 'walking by the road, sleeping under the tree and begging food'.[73] He met another escaped passenger from the ship, and they thought of making their way to Kashi (Benaras) together. With the money given by the Bengali gentleman he purchased a train ticket, and his companion did the same. They reached Bankura Railway Station, walked for a while and, at night, slept near a liquor shop. Next day, they started walking again. On the road, they met and were arrested by another babu, a police sub-inspector, Hari Das Mukerji, to whom he initially gave a false account out of fear. His left thumb print and signature were attached to his statement. A physical examination revealed a scar on the left side of his ribcage, a little above the waist. He claimed to have acquired it from sleeping in the jungle. Some old scars were also found, but no other mark of injury was detected. When asked how the clothes he was wearing came to be torn, he replied that the 'Babu gave me torn cloth'. When asked how his shirt sleeve had got torn, he said, 'The shirt got torn by my sleeping in the jungle by resting my arm under my head.'[74]

Surain Singh, later convicted under the Arms Act of 1878, also spoke of local assistance and complained of being beaten by the constable who arrested him. He claimed that revolvers procured by Gurdit Singh were on board and were to be made use of when necessary. Like Tara Singh, he had also 'stepped away' and crossed the river by boat. On the other side of the river-bank he was joined by nine others, including Hakim Singh, Narain Singh, Dalip Singh and Thakar Singh. Thakar Singh had sustained a bullet injury on his arm. They walked on foot passing a village and crossing a river again by boat, and were joined by twenty-five Sikhs. Thirty-five of them were lying in the jungle when a regiment turned up at 2 a.m. and started firing. Surain ran alone to one side, did not fire any shot from his pistol and did not know if anyone else was armed. He stopped at a house on the road where he ate bread and drank water. A police sub-inspector soon arrived there and questioned him, and took him to the local police station. Surain Singh handed over his revolver with the cartridges. He was repeatedly searched, his garments were torn from his body and he was beaten. Another captured passenger, Inder Singh, implied that trouble broke out when the British tried to arrest Gurdit Singh: 'The Sikhs who were standing close by, had sticks with them and so had the European police. European sergeant struck a *danda* (baton) and . . . fighting commenced. Then the firing commenced. I ran away.'[75] Bhagwan Singh from Jalandhar also claimed: 'When the firing commenced I ran away and swam across the river – I got my head hair clipped off on my way to village . . . where a *chowkidar* (guard) arrested me.'[76] Complaints of physical abuse were not entertained. The complaint of ill-treatment of a captured passenger, Mangal Singh, was dismissed on the ground that he was dangerous, eccentric and had to be forcibly restrained.[77]

Those who cooperated with the forces of authority received better treatment, but could not hide that they were in the minority among the ship's passengers, who were determined to follow Gurdit Singh and seek some form of justice in the face of racist persecution. Bhagwan Singh had provided a clue regarding the disagreement between Gurdit Singh and his critics on board. Pohlo Ram and Bhan Singh, who sided with the ship's doctor Raghunath Singh, wanted the deposit money collected from the passengers to be paid back to them, but Gurdit Singh felt that the money was required for the civil suit. This was echoed on 3 October 1914 by Pohlo Ram, son of Rama Mal Khatri of Hoshiarpur, when he reached Ludhiana. He was among the 59 persons who had readily boarded the special train on 27 September to Punjab soon after the ship had arrived, thereby avoiding the confrontation and massacre. Pohlo Ram had left from Calcutta to study engineering in the USA in 1913, but he could not proceed from Hong Kong on account of immigration restrictions imposed by the American authorities. From Hong Kong he had travelled to Manila, 'a colony belonging to the US'. From there, he communicated with Gurdit Singh and boarded the *Komagata Maru* to head towards North America. According to Pohlo Ram, at Hong Kong Gurdit Singh did not have much following among the passengers; but almost all had gone over to his side by the time they reached Vancouver. He claimed: 'There was a secret society on board headed by Gurdit Singh. I was not a member of it myself, but I could name some of them. Nearly all the men of Amritsar, Lahore and Gurdaspur

District were members, and some of Ferozepur and Ludhiana District.'78 However, he had not heard Gurdit Singh inciting the passengers as the ship approached Budge Budge. He thought the Japanese crew may have hidden the arms since they were not searched when the ship reached Budge Budge.

Bhan Singh, a 27-year-old passenger, recorded his statement on the same day. He provided details of a life of privation aboard the ship, the experience of being welcomed in Japan with banquets and dances organized by émigré Indians and their Japanese contacts, and the 'seditious' aspects of the last stretch of the ship's journey when Gurdit Singh and the Sindhi brothers openly expressed anti-colonial views. Very critical of Gurdit Singh and his anti-imperialist politics, he had sided with Raghunath Singh and Pohlo Ram. He claimed: 'Prem Singh . . . learnt the Gadar-di-Gunj by heart. I believe one other passenger . . . knows it by heart, but I do not know his name.'79 He was implying what the colonial officials feared and suspected – the Ghadar tendency had indeed moved some of the passengers to confront colonial authority at a time of a face-to-face encounter with imperial repression.

In Custody

The effects of the passengers were taken from them during official searches; these were carefully listed and designated as 'offensive' material to justify repression. The police sifted through newspapers and their contents, telegrams, diaries, letters and poems to uncover the political, emotional and literary world of dissent which had germinated among the migrants. Some of the newspapers, letters and documents found on board were labelled as 'seditious'. *The Hindustani*, an anti-colonial English newspaper found with passenger Narain Singh, was marked in pencil by the police to pinpoint the passages against the British government. A report of a mass meeting at Vancouver attracted special attention; it was held on 31 May 1914, when the *Komagata Maru* was docked there, and was presided over by Rahim Bhai. Speakers had delivered militant, anti-imperialist speeches – Bhai Balwant Singh had told the audience that the British government must collapse in the near future; Bhai Munshi Ram had observed that the British government took away from India thirty million pounds each year and in return brought 'fancies, drink habits and insolence'. An Englishman, probably a Socialist, also spoke in the same vein. Funds for the harassed passengers were collected on the spot in response to Gurdit Singh's appeal for assistance. The police concluded that if the paper was read out and explained to the passengers, they could not be expected to remain 'peaceful' or 'loyal' to Britain's authority over India. A Punjabi copy of *Ghadar* (14 July 1914) in Gurumukhi script was also found, and immediately classified as openly 'seditious'. A diary belonging to Kehar Singh, a pocket book belonging to Pohlo Ram with dates and daily notes, and a notebook of Bagga Singh containing poems in Punjabi were also collected. The poems were ordered to be translated in order to understand their content.[80] A poem in Punjabi found in the notebook of Lal Singh combined older Muslim millenarian and rebel strains evident during the Revolt of 1857–58, and a pan-Islamist position on the need to wage a *jihad* against the British empire, with the fervour and emotions invested in the Ghadar Movement. A voice of violent revenge against white authority and emphasis on the rising power of the racially subordinated shaped the lines – 'We will cut out the tongues of the *Feringhis* in order to teach them not to use the word "tum".'[81] The poem proclaimed Hindu–Muslim unity to destroy 'the *Feringhis*, root and branch', and identity was expressed in the following terms: 'We are the children of the old Ghazis; we will take revenge on behalf of Turkey and Persia.'

The telegrams exchanged between Hong Kong and Manila sent by Gurdit Singh, Pohlo Ram and Harnam Singh, a 'seditious' Granthi of the Hong Kong Gurudwara and close to Gurdit Singh, were found and taken away. A notice in Punjabi regarding the ship and signed by Gurdit Singh in Gurumukhi was translated. Gurdit had written that he would fight the ship's cause in court and before the British government, and publish the result so that Indians came to know about the voyage and its outcome. He had also announced that the ships of the company (the Guru Nanak Steamship Company) were to be registered at Vancouver in future, and would travel all over the world to transport passengers. A Punjabi letter in Gurumukhi script written by Gurdit Singh claimed that if the ship was not allowed to dock at Vancouver, it would sail to Brazil or to some port in South America; from there, various routes existed to travel to North America. Two letters to Gurdit in Gurumukhi, a letter from Gurdit to Pohlo Ram, also in Gurumukhi, and a ticket of the Sri Nanak Company signed by Gurdit in favour of Nur Khan to sail from Hong Kong to Victoria, British Columbia were discovered by the police. A letter from Labh Singh, engaged by the Timber Company in Vancouver, to passengers Mohan Singh and Bhagwan Singh, regretted that they were not allowed to land and deplored the Canadian judiciary as unjust. Sukha Singh, who had drawn up this inventory, felt that 'Other papers are not worth mentioning.'[82]

During the early months of their internment, the *Komagata Maru* prisoners were subjected to severe prison conditions that they tried to resist. In January 1915, Dayal Singh, after a period of separation, was permitted to associate with other prisoners. Others were also segregated from the rest of the prisoners for three months; their special confinement was deemed necessary by J. Mulvany, Superintendent, Alipore Central Jail. Mulvany was so worried by their less-than-docile conduct that he urged his superiors, 'May I ask that you will press for early orders for the removal of these prisoners as their demeanour causes me increasing anxiety and I am apprehensive of trouble.'[83] The ten Sikh prisoners kept apart from the rest were Badwa Singh, Kahal Singh, Santa Singh, Uzir Singh, Dan Singh, Dayal Singh, Japuram Singh, Amar Singh, Chandan Singh and Nabkaul Singh. The last three continued to be detained even after the others were sent to Punjab. On 12 January 1915, the Chief Secretary to the Punjab government wrote to his counterpart in Bengal that nine ringleaders of the *Komagata Maru* and twenty-three followers of Gurdit Singh were likely to be dangerous, and should remain confined; he quoted the official report on the *Komagata Maru* to emphasize this point. Of the 211 originally interned, 90 prisoners were released and permitted to return to their homes. The two Sindhi brothers, Jawahar Mal and Narain Das, were handed over to the Bombay government. The remaining prisoners were to be sent back to Ludhiana in batches of eight, with the exception of thirty-two passengers who were considered particularly dangerous. In late January 1915, J.G. Cumming thanked the jail authorities for the 'tact' and 'skill' with which the 'troublesome' Punjabis, the detained passengers of the *Komagata Maru* who had been lodged there for four months, had been handled. On 31 January, it was noted that several could not be sent back to Punjab for specific reasons: Dilip Singh for displaying 'maniacal symptoms', Bahadur Singh because he was in Medical College Hospital, and Nan Singh since he was carrying a large sum of money in his possession. On 11 February 1915, Dilip and Bahadur recovered and were prepared to be sent to Punjab.[84]

Nine prisoners still remained after the others had left as the Punjab government was extremely reluctant to take them back in a climate of local insurrection. Under confinement at Alipore Central Jail under the Ingress into India Ordinance (V of 1914), they were considered 'most dangerous' and temporarily detained in Bengal. Their physical conditions were regulated in keeping with rules imposed upon political prisoners held without trial. They were photographed and fingerprinted. It was decided that they would be permitted to wear their own clothing. If they had none, clothing was to be supplied by the authorities, but they could not wear convict uniforms as they were being held under wartime emergency provisions. Regarding interviews by visitors from outside, the colonial government decided that these were only to be granted by individual orders issued on the basis of each application. The prisoners were to be given ordinary jail food, and extra provisions could be purchased by the detainees if their funds permitted this. Letters to and from the detainees would be submitted to the authorities, who could withhold them at their discretion. In all such cases, reports were to be submitted to the government. An internment order from Cumming on 7 March 1915 revealed the decision to send the prisoners to different district jails. Amir Mohammad Khan from Ludhiana, the chief among the 'active mischief-makers' and Gurdit Singh's close aide, was to be confined at Mymensingh Jail along with Harnam Singh of Lahore; Amar Singh Nihang from Lahore district was to be confined at Rangpur Boalia along with Sundar Singh of Ferozepur; Surain Singh, who was from Amritsar, was also to be kept at Rangpur; Sucha Singh from Lahore was to be jailed at Dinajpur; Nabkaul Singh of Nabha State was to be sent to Darjeeling; and Chandan Singh of Ferozepur was to be sent to Bankura.[85] An order regarding a *Komagata Maru* prisoner, probably Sucha Singh, instructed the prison authorities of Dinajpur Jail that he must be separated from other prisoners and placed in an individual cell, but not kept in solitary confinement.[86] The internment orders of these prisoners were probably not carried out or implemented with immediate effect. They were still in Alipore Central Jail during July 1915,[87] when it was decided that fresh orders were to be issued to continue holding the *Komagata Maru* prisoners there.[88]

Letters from Prison

Those incarcerated for a long stretch in prison recorded their desperation by writing to officials and family members, and appealed to be set free. In their letters, the jail emerged as a state of being and a physical condition, a continuation of prolonged confinement that had started when the ship had been kept in the harbour and turned away from Canada. Amir Mohammad Khan, also referred to as Mir Mohammad Khan, described in police parlance as a 27-year-old Pathan from Ludhiana of fair complexion with a flower tattoo on his right forearm, had been charged with murder and rioting. He was a trader with knowledge of Arabic, and was regarded as a prisoner of

'good character'. Though he was a Muslim, he was classified as a 'Sikh detenu'
from the *Komagata Maru*. Amir carried no disease and was perfectly healthy
upon admission to prison, weighing 134 kilos. Reduced to 123 kilos and
unable to perform any labour in jail within a few months, he complained of
rapid loss of weight. He interpreted this as a symptom of impending death,
an outcome of being condemned 'without trial in violation of all laws
divine and human', and separated without being informed of any charge
'from wife, child and friends'. In May 1915, a signed petition from Amir
Mohammad Khan was sent to the Governor of Bengal; it was forwarded
by J.A.L. Swan, District Magistrate, 24 Parganas, to the Chief Secretary,
Government of Bengal. Amir wrote he was 'worn down with cares and
anxieties and the climate of the country ha[d] tolled very heavily upon him',
and he was 'perceptibly hastening to a premature grave'. He claimed to have
been a peace-loving, loyal subject from a well-to-do family, and one of those
men who 'in the history of all the nations' enjoy 'substance and importance
in the society', unlike those who cause 'commotions' with the intention to
'raise themselves if possible'. However, he also declared that he 'd[id] not
mean by this that persons of wealth never commit crimes'. He was clearly
writing as an organizer, having actively mobilized the passengers on the
ship; he expressed surprise that he and the remaining prisoners from Punjab
had not been released even if others had returned to their home province: 'it
will not be out of place if your memorialist adds here that Suren Singh was
. . . convicted under Arms Act and sentenced . . . but on the expiration of
his sentence he has been added to the number . . . not released.' He wished
to be reunited with his family and declared that he 'solemnly protest[ed]
in the face of God and men against the violation . . . of his person and
liberty.'[89]

Letters from other prisoners to their relatives and colonial officials drew
a similar portrait of their uncertain situation. Sucha Singh wrote to his
brother that he was anxious to meet him again, and that he was confined at
Alipore Central Jail. Indra Singh, addressing his elder brother, also hoped
to see the latter and sent respects to their mother. Sundar Singh, addressing
the priest of Howrah Gurudwara, wrote: 'Please do pray to God that I may
be released from confinement, that my troubles may be redressed and that
I may meet my wife and children soon.'[90] During March 1915, Nabkaul
Singh solicited the 'kind attention' of Maharajah of Burdwan to their case,
drawing attention to his plight and that of others still in detention. Amar
Singh, in a private letter addressed to his brother, observed that though

he was free of criminal charges, he did not know the reason for continued incarceration. He was also keen to learn how his family was faring. Indar Singh, posted in a Hong Kong regiment and brother of Surain (alias Ratan) Singh, wrote that he was much grieved to learn of the latter's imprisonment. He was hoping Surain will return to his family soon. Surain had informed his brother that he had been sentenced to two years' imprisonment, having been implicated in a criminal case. On appeal, his sentence had been reduced to six months. He was hoping to be reunited with his family at the end of the term.[91] This was not to be, for he was detained under the Ingress into India Ordinance, 1914 and 'Foreigner's Act', after his sentence under the 'Arms Act' expired in April 1915. Nabkaul Singh wrote to the District Magistrate, 24 Parganas in April 1915 from Alipore Central Jail, that he was a poor man and that the full amount of his money taken by the arresting officer, a European, at Budge Budge Railway Station, was yet to be returned to him.[92] Pilfering and misappropriating the money of those arrested was not an uncommon practice. On 5 December 1915, *The Statesman*, a Calcutta daily under European ownership, had found an 'Echo of the Budge Budge Riot case' when Bombardier Haslem, a European soldier and wireless operator at Fort William, was sentenced to three months' imprisonment. He had tried to encash Japanese yen notes under different names from Indian moneychangers and European banks, such as The Hongkong and Shanghai Banking Corporation (HSBC). Police suspected that the money was stolen during the violence at Budge Budge; Nunda Singh, a Sikh arrested at Bhawanipore in connection with the incident at the railway station, possessed similar notes.[93]

In May, the District Magistrate withheld three telegrams by Nabkaul Singh addressed to Sardar Daljit Singh (a member of the Komagata Maru Inquiry Committee), Lieutenant Governor of Punjab, and the Viceroy. Nabkaul had wanted to know when the Sikhs who were still in jail were to be released, since the enquiry was long over and the rest of the prisoners had been set free. He had requested an 'urgent reply'.[94] At the end of the year, it was officially claimed that all *Komagata Maru* passengers had been sent back to the region of their origin. In November 1915, a Bengal government order in the form of a secret letter reached the Post-Master General, informing him that the interception of all correspondence of the *Komagata Maru* prisoners stood cancelled as they had been transferred to Punjab.[95] Dearth of records prevents the emergence of a detailed account of their forced repatriation.

Conclusion

A careful reading of colonial intelligence sources reveals that a coercive strategy was built into the scheme of receiving the *Komagata Maru* long before the passengers reached the shores of Bengal. Peaceful protest in the form of public condemnations of imperial racism and legal proceedings was an intolerable prospect in the corridors of power. Wartime Calcutta, seen as a crisis-ridden metropolitan hotbed of anti-colonial feelings and opinions, was debarred to the migrants. Their local allies, affiliated with *The Bengalee*, a moderate nationalist newspaper, were not allowed to receive a telegram from the passengers, so that the arrival of the ship and the containment of those on board could be carried out in utmost secrecy. The local turmoil in the city and the region was cited to legitimize the repressive actions of a beleaguered imperial authority at wartime. Aggressive strategy was manifested in verbal abuse and application of force towards the passengers of the *Komagata Maru* with catastrophic results. The racial stereotype of Sikhs as members of a subservient 'martial race' was overturned by the actions of the passengers, and came to haunt the top, middle and lower rungs of imperial governance. By challenging colonial authority, the passengers rudely jolted the colonial perception of Sikhs as a loyal ethno-racial subject population who could be exploited at will from the top as a cheap reserve of military and manual labour in the service of British and other empires. The massacre of survivors-turned-prisoners constituted the repressed voices from the *Komagata Maru*. They contested the official version of events by drawing attention to the imperialized condition as a prison house in the concrete and abstract sense. Though violent coercion triumphed, and ships carrying Punjabi immigrants from the eastern seas came to be monitored, the news of the massacre spread and the journey of the *Komagata Maru* found an echo in the public sphere and the revolutionary underground in ways that were to surprise the colonial authorities. The lost ship and the resistance of its passengers metaphorically reappeared like spectres to repeatedly confront them in the immediate and distant future.

NOTES AND REFERENCES

[1] Sumit Sarkar, *Modern India 1885–1947*, Delhi, 1983, pp.147–49. D.C. Ellinwood and S.D. Pradhan, *India and World War I*, Delhi, 1978.

[2] *Report on Native Papers in Bengal 1914*. For sources of more such reports, see Suchetana Chattopadhyay, 'War-time in an Imperial City: The Apocalyptic Mood

in Culcutta (1914–1918)', in *India and World War I: A Centennial Assessment*, edited by Roger D. Long and Ian Talbot, London and New York, 2018.

[3] Ibid.

[4] Ibid.

[5] Ibid.

[6] Ibid.

[7] *Weekly Reports of Intelligence Branch, Bengal Police 1914.*

[8] *Report on Native Papers in Bengal 1915.*

[9] See Upendra Narayan Chakravorty, *Indian Nationalism and the First World War (1914–1918),* Calcutta, 1997.

[10] *Report on Native Papers in Bengal 1914.*

[11] Ibid.

[12] *Weekly Reports of Intelligence Branch, Bengal Police 1914.*

[13] Ibid. '*Sala*' is a swear-word in Bengali and Hindustani, and may be literally translated as 'brother-in-law'.

[14] *Weekly Reports of Intelligence Branch, Bengal Police 1914.*

[15] Ibid.

[16] See Hew Strachnan, *The Oxford Illustrated History of the First World War,* Oxford, 2014.

[17] *Weekly Reports of the Intelligence Branch, Bengal Police 1914.*

[18] Hugh Johnston, *The Voyage of the Komagata Maru: The Sikh Challenge to Canada's Colour Bar,* Vancouver, 1995, p. 96.

[19] Randall J. Metscher, 'Emden', in Spencer C. Tucker, ed., *The European Powers in the First World War: An Encyclopedia,* New York, 2013, pp. 239–40.

[20] Cornelis Dijk, *The Netherlands Indies and the Great War 1914–1918,* Leiden, 2007, p. 183.

[21] Johnston, *The Voyage of the Komagata Maru,* p. 96.

[22] *The Statesman,* 7 November 1914.

[23] *The Statesman,* 21 November 1914.

[24] *The Statesman,* 6 November 1914.

[25] *Weekly Reports of Intelligence Branch, Bengal Police 1914.*

[26] *The Statesman,* 6 November 1914.

[27] Amiya Kumar Bagchi, *Private Investment in India 1900–1939,* Cambridge, 1972, pp. 275–76.

[28] Home (Political) WBSA 322/1914. (WBSA stands for West Bengal State Archives.)

[29] *Weekly Reports of Intelligence Branch, Bengal Police 1914.*

[30] Home (Political) WBSA 322/1914.

[31] Ibid.

[32] Ibid. For an understanding of the militarized colonial state apparatus in Punjab, see Tan Tai Yong, *The Garrison State: Military, Government and Society in Colonial Punjab, 1849–1947,* Delhi, 2005.

[33] Intelligence Branch of Bengal Police 1105/1914(57/14).

[34] Ibid.

[35] Home (Political) WBSA 322/1914.

[36] Colonial control exercised upon the Sikh passengers of the *Komagata Maru* after they had landed has been analysed by Darshan S. Tatla. See Darshan S. Tatla, 'Introduction', in Baba Gurdit Singh, *Voyage of Komagata Maru or India's Slavery Abroad*, edited by Darshan S. Tatla, Chandigarh, 2007, p. 20.

[37] Home (Political) WBSA 322/1914.

[38] Ibid.

[39] *Weekly Reports of Intelligence Branch, Bengal Police 1914.*

[40] Home (Political) WBSA 322/1914. Michael O'Dwyer also presided as Lieutenant Governor of Punjab during post-war repression over the Jallianwala Bagh massacre at Amritsar in 1919.

[41] For a socio-linguistic understanding of 'event', see Claudia Maienborn, Klaus von Heusinger and Paul Portner, *Semantics*, Volume 3, Berlin, 2013, p. 2585.

[42] Home (Political) WBSA 322/1914.

[43] Ibid.

[44] Darshan S. Tatla, ed., *Report of the Komagata Maru Committee of Inquiry and Some Further Documents*, Chandigarh, 2007, pp. 74–75.

[45] Home (Political) WBSA 322/1914.

[46] Ibid. Also Tatla, ed., *Report of the Komagata Maru Committee of Inquiry*, pp. 74–75.

[47] Ananda Bhattacharyya, ed., *Remembering Komagata Maru: Official Reports and Contemporary Accounts*, Delhi, 2017, pp. 20–25.

[48] Darshan S. Tatla, 'Introduction', in Tatla, ed., *Report of the Komagata Maru Committee of Inquiry*, pp. 1–28.

[49] Home (Political) WBSA 322/1914. Also quoted, in part, by Tatla, 'Introduction', in Tatla, ed., *Report of the Komagata Maru Committee of Inquiry*, p. 21. Petrie's presence during the *Komagata Maru* incident and other exercises elevated him to the post of Director, Criminal Intelligence in Delhi, during the 1920s and Director General of MI5 during the 1940s; his tenacious service to imperial surveillance and policing was to earn him a knighthood.

[50] Home (Political) WBSA 322/1914.

[51] Ibid.

[52] Ibid.

[53] Ibid.

[54] Ibid.

[55] Ibid.

[56] Ibid.

[57] Ibid.

[58] Ibid.

[59] Ibid.

[60] Home (Political) WBSA 80/1915 pp. 20–23.

[61] Baba Gurdit Singh, *Voyage of Komagata Maru or India's Slavery Abroad*, edited by Tatla, pp. 141–42.

[62] Ibid., p. 142.

[63] Ibid., pp. 144–45.

[64] Ibid., pp. 146–52.
[65] Home (Political) WBSA 322/1914.
[66] Home (Political) WBSA 26/1915 p. 63.
[67] *The Statesman*, 8, 13, 10, 15 October 1914.
[68] Tatla, ed., *Report of the Komagata Maru Committee of Inquiry*, pp. 105–34.
[69] Johnston, *The Voyage of the Komagata Maru*, pp. 95–115.
[70] Home (Political) WBSA 322/1914.
[71] Ibid.
[72] Ibid.
[73] Ibid.
[74] Ibid.
[75] Ibid.
[76] Ibid.
[77] Home (Political) WBSA 80/1915, pp. 20–23.
[78] Home (Political) WBSA 322/1914.
[79] Ibid.
[80] Home (Political) WBSA 322/1914 KW.
[81] Bhattacharyya, ed., *Remembering Komagata Maru*, pp. 11–12.
[82] Home (Political) WBSA 322/1914 KW.
[83] Home (Political) WBSA 26/1915, pp. 1–39.
[84] Ibid.
[85] Ibid., pp. 40–41.
[86] Ibid., pp. 45–57.
[87] Home (Political) WBSA 26/1915 KW.
[88] Ibid., pp. 70–75.
[89] Ibid., pp. 64–68.
[90] Ibid., pp. 42–44.
[91] Ibid., pp. 45–57.
[92] Ibid., pp. 58–62.
[93] *The Statesman*, October–December 1914.
[94] Home (Political) WBSA 26/1915, pp. 64–68 and 69.
[95] Ibid., pp. 88–89.

CHAPTER TWO

Closely Observed Ships

The *Komagata Maru* set a template of colonial strategy to suppress Punjabi Sikh labourers and other returning emigrants. What were the social components of political control imposed? How did the repressive state apparatus actively seek and receive help from European-owned monopolistic business interests? Were various forms of colonial authority and interest interlocked in the process? How did the police authorities from Bengal, Punjab, Delhi and Simla collaborate and draw support from an inter-imperial geography of surveillance? What was the impact of colonial surveillance on vessels and travellers during the weeks, months and years that followed? Finally, did the passengers resist, and if so, what were their ways? Drawing on the official voices traceable in reports, circulars and correspondence, this chapter examines the unknown facets of repression in the wake of the *Komagata Maru's* journey.

After the resistance shown by the *Komagata Maru*, all ships sailing to India from America and East Asia came to be watched closely. The British authorities in India were haunted by a spectre of return: the return of the repressed as a rebel underlined official imagination, strategy and action. Punjabi Sikh emigrants became formal targets of the colonial repressive state apparatus as an ethno-linguistic-religious segment, and represented a distinct class fraction. Imperial control was pitted against a migrant body of officially recognized 'semi-destitute' workers, their racialized subjecthood identified as a challenge to the colonial order. Potential and actual radicalization of the Sikh workers made them collectively 'suspect'. Labelled as capable of sowing discontent and rebellion in the colonial army, in rural and urban Punjab as well as in Bengal, where anti-imperial nationalist and pan-Islamist networks were active, the 'threat' they represented was both real and imaginary, and, accordingly, described with precision as well as exaggeration. The British empire's paternalistic strategies of rule were set aside in favour of openly coercive measures. This policy projected those returning as 'insiders' as the ones who had become 'outsiders', having unlearnt racial and social subservience to their colonial rulers by absorbing anti-imperialist political currents through travel in the wider world.

As mentioned in the previous chapter, repression was central to the strategy of containment adopted in relation to the passengers of the *Komagata Maru*; it was continued after the confrontation and massacre at Budge Budge. The Ingress into India Ordinance (V of 1914) introduced in early September was enforced on future arrivants to project coercion as the lawful product of a wartime colonial 'rule of law'. The use of the police, with military support, was automatically justified as necessary for the preservation of state security in the face of 'Ghadar' (Revolt). Cooperation with consular and colonial officials in different Asian ports was already in place. Ports and harbours in the Bengal delta were kept under scrutiny. Officers with knowledge of Punjabi continued to be deployed for examining the passengers. Police in plain clothes boarded ships once they reached Bengal to discreetly gather information. The majority of the Sikh passengers, especially those coming from North America, were forced to board the 'special' train to Punjab, a prison on wheels. In October, with the widening of the surveillance network, a composite strategy incorporating other measures was put into place. A direct link with colonial capital was established to bolster and further intensify surveillance procedures. The shipping companies were taken into confidence to gather prior intelligence on those arriving, especially the indigent. Legal measures were applied whenever deemed necessary to supplement the Ingress into India Ordinance (V of 1914). Baggage and bodies were subjected to rigorous searches to detect arms and seditious literature. Yet, resistance could not be wiped out and surfaced in unexpected ways.

Watch on the Hooghly

'The solitary Sikh "labourer" from Victoria who is bound for Calcutta must transship into a boat bound for this port at Penang or Singapore. Which boat he comes up in is not known.'[1] This poetic observation came from a surveillance report circulated in November 1914. The top echelons of the imperial officialdom became exceptionally busy during the autumn and winter months. The 'honourable gentlemen' were flooded with 'confidential' telegrams, letters, instructions and suggestions. Exchanging logistical ideas between themselves and with others on an emergency basis, they remained on their toes, ever-anxious to invent, evolve, supervise and implement the devices of surveillance and repression. Together, they constituted the official side and voice of repression.

The private interests of European monopolistic business firms synchronized functions of different departments and hierarchies and the pervasive ideology of colonial governance to suppress 'lesser races' converged in the process of repression, and were embedded in an inter-imperial geography of surveillance. Stretching from the ports of the western seaboard of the Americas to Bengal and South India via East and Southeast Asia, the map of colonial control drew on trans-regional movements of metropolitan capital and facilitated the institutional imposition of rapid, well thought-out repressive measures. With tense and systematic efficiency, a vast coordination of intelligence gathering and coercion was undertaken. Surveillance on Sikh emigrants by the British colonial state in India encompassed the Central Intelligence Department (CID) headquartered in Delhi and Simla, the provincial governments of Punjab and Bengal, and the armed forces. An array of personnel from Bengal – linked with the Home Department, Intelligence Branch (IB), Special Branch, city and district police, the port and customs – were pressed into service.

On 7 October, eight days after the massacre, a high-powered meeting was held at Writers' Building to chalk out logistics. In the headquarters of imperial authority in Calcutta, a state of high alert prevailed. The impending threat to Britain's Indian empire in the form of ships and emigrants was assessed; ways of containing opposition through an effective plan of action were of primary concern. J.G. Cumming, Chief Secretary, Government of Bengal, attended the meeting with Sir William Duke, Member of Council, R.B. Hughes-Buller, Inspector General of Bengal Police, R.H.S. Hutchinson, Deputy Inspector General, Bengal Intelligence Branch, and F. Anley, Superintendent of Port Police. They decided upon rigorous physical search of the ships, 'each and every passenger' and effects, 'as was done in Karachi and Bombay';[2] continuing the practice of stopping and searching ships from the east before they reached Calcutta; leaving the practical details to the Bengal Police; and gathering advance information on the passengers, including those of 'superior class'. It was pointed out that the large inflow of passengers necessitated 'effective enquiries' by gathering 'previous knowledge of persons who were coming'.[3] This position led to an immediate secret collaboration with shipping companies, upper-class cabin passengers, as well as officers on board, who were seen as 'natural' allies cemented by bonds of social location and race. Being poor, the majority of Sikh deck passengers were targeted as carriers of a rebellious strain. A revised set of instructions in 1915 reiterated: 'Enquiries will then be made amongst the other passengers having special regard to persons of superior status.'[4] In November 1914, a further tightening of the search procedure involved sifting through the meagre worldly possessions of the migrants. The Punjab CID instructed its Bengal counterpart that containers, pails and boxes belonging to the returning emigrants were to be inspected by customs officers to determine if false bottoms existed. Tins of ghee and baskets of food required 'special' attention.

The *Komagata Maru* cast a long shadow on the deliberations. The officials realized that 'great objections' would arise if the ships were detained at Kulpi where the *Komagata Maru* was stopped on its way to Calcutta. Probably fearing public outrage over any step which echoed the action against the *Komagata Maru*, the government decided that in the 'existing circumstances', it was best to stop and search the ships moving from Diamond Harbour upwards. The plan survived the zealous assertion of petty bureaucratic authority by the Calcutta Police. The latter initially rebuffed, on grounds of territorial integrity, a suggestion made by the Bengal Police that Lowman (Special Branch) and Anley (Port Police) should board all ships as supervising officers since other officers might not be always available. F. Halliday, Commissioner of Police, Calcutta, stiffly informed F. Roddis of Bengal Police, also headquartered in Calcutta: 'I am sorry to appear disobliging but I think Lowman and Anley must stick within their own jurisdiction. . . .' Cooperation between key departments soon began. A system of shared authority was put in place. In November, the Home Department, Government of Bengal, entrusted senior police officials with exercising the powers of supervising officers under Ordinance V of 1914. They were R.H.S. Hutchinson, Deputy Inspector General, Intelligence Branch; C.A. Tegart, Superintendent of Police; L.H. Colson, Superintendent of Police; F.J. Lowman, Deputy Commissioner, Special Branch, Calcutta Police; and T.S.R. Anley, Deputy Commissioner, Port Police, Calcutta. Hutchinson, Tegart and Colson were initially empowered as supervisors in October, and were replaced by Lowman and Anley in December. Later, various police officials including an Assistant Commissioner from Calcutta were delegated this responsibility.[5]

All ships coming from the east were detained at Diamond Harbour or at Calcutta. At the high-profile meeting held on 7 October, 'special difficulties' were registered in dealing with ships from the east; these were 'rarely' tied up at a jetty and were harder to search than those in a shed. Outram Ghat, one of the main disembarkation points in Calcutta, was favoured as a spot to thoroughly comb the vessels. In the course of 8–9 October, it was formally resolved that ships and steamers would be stopped at Diamond Harbour. There, supervising officers from the Bengal IB would go on board to conduct searches and investigate if the Ingress into India Ordinance (V of 1914) was applicable to any of the passengers. Sir Charles Cleveland, Director of Criminal Intelligence, endorsed this view from Simla in his correspondence with Slocock. In the case of Calcutta, the city police was entrusted with primary responsibility.

Acting as Cleveland's eyes, ears and long arm, F.S.A. Slocock, Inspector General of Police, Central Provinces, had been assigned by the Central Intelligence as Officer on Special Duty in Bengal while preparing for the

Ships in Calcutta docks (Photo by Indranil Roy, June 2014)

arrival of the *Komagata Maru*. Ensconced in the luxurious, racially exclusive surroundings of Bengal Club, he was the Director's man in Calcutta, receiving comments and instructions from Simla almost every day. The micro-correspondence between Cleveland and Slocock revealed the paradoxical relationship between the colonial strategies of paternalism and repression as the month progressed. Referring to a telegram from America received via London on 14 August, Cleveland noted that the Ghadar Party was persuading Indian emigrants to return at a time of war since 'the present crisis was favourable for trouble'. Observing that 'an unusually large numbers of Indians' were on their way back to India from Canada, US and the Far East, he stressed on drawing up a reliable list of Sikh rebels to suit 'our purposes'. Choked under an avalanche of native names, the Director complained:

> As you know, certain names are very common among Sikhs and in the lists are repeated over and over again. We have no guarantee that a conspicuous Sikh seditionist leaving Vancouver to come back to India to give trouble would give his name, father's name etc. correctly to the people who compile lists for us.[6]

The native's deceitful cunning had to be taken into consideration while affixing identity by separating 'the dangerous from the innocent'.

Cleveland felt 'the case of "Komagata" . . . was a very special one', since it had been chartered by Indian interests. Indians returning from America and Canada normally changed their ships at Japanese and Chinese ports, boarding vessels controlled by the British colonial capital. The Director regarded the passenger list of a ship from San Francisco to Yokohama to be an unreliable guide for detecting the identity of travellers from Yokohama to Calcutta. He insisted that all returning passengers must be treated as potential rebels: 'we practically know . . . a large number of Indians, including among them some really dangerous people, may be expected to return to Calcutta during the next two months. I cannot think of any sure means of picking out the dangerous from the innocent when the ships arrive in Calcutta.'[7] Having unlocked the floodgate of victimization, he was uncomfortable with the possible political consequence of such an action. His 'personal view' was leniency towards those who survived the search unscathed.

The Director's cautionary words were effective. An intelligence 'note' circulated on closely observed ships (12 October) revealed the strategy of attaching a safety valve, in the form of occasional freedom of movement, to the general policy of stifling repression. When Tegart, Colson, Hutchinson and Boyd travelled by *Nancy*, the police launch, to Diamond Harbour, with officers and constables from Punjab, the Bengal IB, the Preventive Services personnel and the Gurkha military police who followed by train, they found only a few emigrants from the east who had travelled on the *Choi Sang* and *Yat Sang*; the passengers were then allowed to proceed to Calcutta.

The captains of the two vessels had forewarned the officials that another vessel, the *Nam Sang*, would bring 'trouble'. After resistance was reported, Cleveland advocated iron-fisted repression:

> It looks to me as if a number of Sikhs who may quite possibly have been upset over the 'Komagata Maru' incident are leaving British Columbia, and a lot of them may stay in Hong Kong or Chinese ports. I feel very doubtful about the policy of treating these men as suspects on their arrival in India. Hopkinson does not, I think discriminate much between Indians who give trouble to the Canadian authorities over immigration restrictions, and Indians who are plotting against the Government of India. And, though Sikhs who went to Canada as loyal subjects of the Raj, may, unfortunately leave there in a rather different mood, I must say I am inclined to discount the value of the label 'Seditionist' when affixed in Canada by subordinate officials.
>
> While sympathizing with this kindly view of the character and intentions of the Sikhs now on their way back to India, we must remember that these unfortunate people for some time past have been subjected to the most inciting and provoking exhortations of the 'Ghadr' party. We have seen from numerous letters sent by Sikhs in the Far East, in Canada and in the United States of America that the 'Ghadr' poison had worked on them and converted them, at the time of writing at least, into blood-thirsty fanatical revolutionaries: and in view of the history of the 'Komagata Maru' we must fear that on their way back these Sikhs have been preached at by selected orators of the 'Ghadr' party.
>
> The practical sedition of the Gurdit Singh party has shown that the ravings of the Far Eastern Sikhs, who have been converted to the 'Ghadr' doctrines, are not mere froth.
>
> It would be advisable to take the above considerations into view when issuing directions regarding the treatment of these returning emigrants.[8]

In a note to Hughes-Buller (17 October), Cumming succinctly summarized the Director's position: 'It is obviously impossible when there is no previous knowledge as to the nature of the passengers, to combine the two incompatibles of extreme strictness and friendly tenderliness. Sir Charles favours the more strict policy.' As vigilance mounted, Slattery,

Superintendent of Punjab CID, was sent to Calcutta. His job was to keep the Punjab government 'fully informed of all particulars obtainable regarding the number, identity and character of doubtful Sikh emigrants returning to the Punjab in the near future'.[9]

Regional surveillance was supported by the transcontinental intelligence gathered from North America, East Asia and Britain. Surveillance as day-to-day practice revealed imperial control over ships on a war footing. Though no one in Bengal was even contemplating such an action, Cleveland, having received further intelligence from Canada, instructed Slocock (14 October): 'I do not think it wise to slacken off reception arrangements.'[10] The departure of Punjabi migrants to North America also caused disquiet. On the same day, a list of emigrants heading to Canada was sent to Bengal from Punjab via Simla. The physical manifestations of keeping watch criminalized the passengers. Bengal, especially the network of ports and docks in and around Calcutta, was formally identified as the receiving zone of floating sedition from the east. From September, the provincial administration had been prepared to monitor those returning. As early as 19 September, Cumming had instructed the Commissioners of Police and District Magistrates of southwest Bengal, Chittagong and Darjeeling on the procedures to be applied on Sikh travellers should they pass through various harbours and routes. On 5 October, in the backdrop of rising tensions generated by the shooting of the *Komagata Maru* passengers at Budge Budge, the British Consular officials at Kobe, Shanghai, Hong Kong and Singapore were requested by Central Intelligence to send information about 'objectionable individuals' sailing to India. Authorities from Simla sent surveillance reports gathered from Canada via London. These were laced with the palpable fear of a revolutionary multitude drawn mostly from Sikh workers, but also Indian students, organized by émigré leaders in North America. The imperial surveillance network suspected 'five or six thousand Indians, mostly Sikhs' on the Pacific Slope, and living in the USA and British Columbia, of being 'affected by anarchical doctrines'. The revolutionary diaspora had 'devoted much attention to these classes in recent years with a view to creating trouble in India through returning emigrants. In addition Sikhs in the police etc. at Hong Kong and Shanghai are said to have been worked on by the revolutionaries'.[11] Among the numerous 'possible undesirables', it was difficult to obtain substantial intelligence from 'the mere mention of a few names'. Cleveland asked the Inspector General of Police, CID, Punjab, 'for necessary action, lists, in duplicate, of Punjabi passengers who left Victoria, British Columbia, by "S.S. Shidzukao Maru" on 25th August, by "S.S. Empress of India" from Vancouver on 22nd August, and by "S.S. Kwang Sang" on 1st October from Hong Kong.'[12] A telegram from the Colonial Secretary, Hong Kong, to the Secretary to the Government of India, Home Department, provided a list of returning immigrants who sailed on 24 and 25 October for Calcutta on *Kamsang* and *Sanuki Maru*; this list was forwarded by J.W. Nelson, Criminal Intelligence Office, Delhi, to J.G. Cumming. The great majority were, unsurprisingly, labourers. Other passengers were also of the plebian and 'middle' sort: watchmen, tailors, students and police personnel. Two deportees from the United States were also mentioned. Sometimes, hitches were recorded in the trans-imperial travel of intelligence material. On 2 November, the Intelligence Branch in Calcutta complained that the list of seditious Sikhs sent by the Canadian government through the Secretary of State could not be found in the office file. Within days, this was followed by a rapid compilation of names. A fresh list of 'Canadian suspects', with names of thirty-one Sikhs, on their way back to India, was circulated in December.[13]

Inter-imperial surveillance was also vigorously pursued from 1914 onwards. Information-sharing between different empires led to suppression of rebels. During 1915–16, the voyages of *SS Japan* from Singapore to Bengal represented expanding inter-colonial cooperation. In early 1916, sixteen men (fifteen Sikhs and one Muslim), two women and three children (twenty-one in total) expelled from Sumatra, who had landed via Singapore in Calcutta on *SS Japan*, were detained at Presidency Jail under Ordinance V of 1914 and sent to Delhi Jail on suspicion of sedition. The ship had been kept under a tight watch from 1915, and many passengers had been criminalized. Khuda Bux, an Indian Muslim who had travelled to Bengal on the same ship, was deported to Bombay and handed over to the local police authorities. Ladha Singh and Chait Ram, also detainees from *SS Japan*, were sent under escort from Calcutta to Rangoon in February 1916, to give evidence in a conspiracy case in Burma. The Dutch authorities had informed their British counterparts that the twenty-one adults arrested were collecting funds to subvert the colonial order in India. Their claim of raising money to build a place of worship was disregarded. The two women, Mussamat Prem (with her 12-year-old son) and Narain Kaur (with two small children), were also branded as 'undesirable persons' alongside the men. David Petrie had advised Straits authorities[14] to keep the detainees under armed guard. In Singapore, they were made to board *SS Japan* and brought to Bengal.[15] Cleveland had informed Hutchinson after the arrival of the *Komagata Maru* that Indian emigrants from the Far East should be prevented from disembarking at Burma on their return journey 'unless they could show really good reasons for being allowed to do so'.[16] Yet vigilance, including on the borders of eastern Bengal, yielded little. Rather than conspiracy, it exposed enfeebled circumstances of migrant labourers in remote regions. In reply to queries, the Chittagong Police Office informed Hutchinson that very few ships called at the port and there were 'no passengers of late from the Far East'. If they arrived, they were to be scrutinized 'without any harassment'; this treatment had been extended to the Sikh workers who had passed through Chittagong. They came from Calcutta by rail to engage in railway construction, and returned home in 'fever-stricken' conditions.[17]

The supervisory role thrust on the Bengal police continued to be a source of strain. No weekly intelligence report had been filed during the last week of September 1914, when the *Komagata Maru* had arrived, owing to the 'Budge Budge riot case', demonstrating that the police authorities were under extreme pressure.[18] Despite the steps adopted to help Bengal authorities by amassing information from Canada, London, Punjab and elsewhere, the pressure associated with keeping watch was voiced from time to time. Hughes-Buller, in a confidential letter (26 October), complained to Cleveland that the Home Department and Central Intelligence had not supplied the Bengal IB with 'complete information'. He differed with the Director on the processing of inter-continental, inter-regional information through the Central Intelligence network headquartered in Simla and Delhi, advocating direct communication with Bengal: 'Arrangements should also be made with Canada, Japan, Hong Kong, and Singapore to wire us the number of passengers which may be proceeding by different boats, and if any of them are known to be suspicious or dangerous, their names, father's name and residences should be given.'[19] He pointed to the heavy burden shouldered by the Bengal IB, since the ships with large numbers of passengers were its responsibility. He had managed to convince Halliday that Calcutta Police will only have to examine those vessels from the Far East which contained not more than fifty passengers. In addition, the Calcutta Police had been offered assistance by the Punjab officers who were working with the IB staff.[20]

The practice was formally adopted in early 1915. The Deputy Inspector General of Police, Intelligence Branch, remained in charge of all arrangements in connection with the enforcement of the Ingress into India

Ordinance (V of 1914) with reference to ships arriving from the Far East and America. In the case of vessels containing not more than fifty returning Indians coming from beyond Singapore, the examination was taken over by the Commissioner of Police, Calcutta. In all other cases, the examination was conducted under the orders of the Deputy Inspector General, Intelligence Branch. Punjab officers present in Calcutta continued to assist the Calcutta Police or the IB officers whenever the need arose. The Deputy Inspector General, Intelligence Branch was responsible for keeping himself informed, by communication with the shipping agents and the port authorities, of the names of ships arriving from America and the Far East, and informing the port authorities the details of particular vessels being anchored at Diamond Harbour to wait for the supervising officer. The Deputy Inspector General arranged for steamers or boats to take the supervising officer to the ships. The supervising officer boarded each boat coming from the Far East at Diamond Harbour. He was accompanied by an escort of one *havildar* and ten armed men, provided by the Inspector General of Police. Also present were men in plain clothes (one or more Indian officers from the Punjab, an Indian officer from the IB and two orderlies) who could blend in and spy on the passengers; with their assistance, he obtained names of all Indian travellers from the ship's officers and 'quietly' questioned the Indian cabin passengers to secure information on them as well as on impoverished co-passengers. The officers consulted 'Indian Agitators Abroad' and 'Indian Agitators in America', surveillance handbooks on Indian political activists, in case any of the passengers featured in the pages. The officers of the Custom Preventive Service continued to board ships below Garden Reach. The supervising officer decided whether a passenger's effects or person were to be specially searched. If it was deemed necessary to enforce the provisions of Ordinance V, the passenger was detained in the Calcutta Police lock-up after landing, and the matter promptly reported in writing to the Bengal government. The division of surveillance duties on ships among the Calcutta Police and the Bengal IB was aimed at formally recognizing and slightly reducing the sense of being overburdened while having to maintain watch on the Hooghly.[21]

At the insistence of Cleveland, Hughes-Buller and other high-ranking officers, regular stocktaking of ships and passengers continued. They periodically sent notes to subordinates, enquiring how many ships and passengers had arrived from the Far East in the wake of the *Komagata Maru*'s voyage, the kind of people the ships carried and the way they were dealt with. The names of vessels arriving in Calcutta and the approximate dates of their arrival were recorded in advance. The Shipping Telegraph list was published daily and read by Intelligence officers to spot vessels sailing from the Far East and America with 'undesirable passengers'. The Director General of Post and Telegraphs, Calcutta, received Hutchinson's pressing request to be spared additional expenses on 26 October. Seeking exemption from having to pay Rs 30 per quarter for the Indian Telegraph Gazette, Hutchinson sourly noted: 'I obtained from the Superintendent Central Telegraph Office the first issue of the Indian Telegraph Gazette in ignorance of the fact that a payment would be insisted upon.'[22]

After several months of intensive surveillance, the flow of passengers from the east declined and policing arrangements were modified. On 21 January 1915, the Chief Secretary, Punjab, informed the Chief Secretary, Bengal that Punjab wished to recall Slattery as the 'rush' of emigrants from the Far East and America 'ha[d] ceased for the present'. Slattery left in February. However, the two Sub Inspectors of the Punjab police were retained to assist the Bengal authorities to deal with Punjabi emigrants.[23] In October 1916, deployment of 'a lady Inspectress' to search Punjabi women, wives of Sikh emigrants from the Far East, was considered: 'The emigrants sometimes have their wives with them and may hand over articles to them.'[24] The plan was abandoned by the officialdom, probably in anticipation of another round of public outcry. The inspectress was allowed to go on leave and lower-grade officials noted with evident relief: 'We are not, I understand, to do any searching.'[25] Surveillance probably deterred many who feared harassment, persecution and imprisonment on returning. Nevertheless, the authorities continued to expect them.

To Deal with Floating Sedition

Shorn of its hegemonic claim of representing the interests of all imperial subjects, colonial law became the instrument of open coercion. The Ingress into India Ordinance remained the favoured tool of repression. On 3 October, Sir William Vincent of the Legislative Department from Simla spelt out to Cumming that the Foreigners Ordinance was applicable to foreigners, and the Ingress into India Ordinance (V of 1914) was intended for persons not defined as foreigners in the Foreigners Ordinance. The implication was that the latter would provide the most appropriate mechanism, sanctioned by law, to curb passengers from the east. The Writers'

Building meeting (7 October) considered the best ways of implementing Ordinance V of 1914 on Punjabi Sikh emigrants. In April 1916, it was noted that in practice, Ordinance V of 1914 had been jointly applied with the Foreigners Ordinance through an official notification issued in October 1914.[26] Ordinance V of 1914 remained in operation against the Punjabi migrants as late as 1919. All ordinary Punjabi passengers had to report to the police authorities upon their return to India.[27]

Following the confrontation and massacre at Budge Budge, special attention was paid to the future import of firearms by emigrants to resist colonial authority. Surain Singh, one of the passengers on the *Komagata Maru*, was tried and sentenced under the Arms Act of 1878. Hughes-Buller wrote to Slocock (7 October):

> Are revolvers procurable without license in Hong Kong, Shanghai, Penang and Singapore and can a passenger on board a ship take his revolver with him, if he possesses one, without a license? We understand that facilities exist for Indians to obtain revolvers in Japan and possibly in China and also in America. Is there any possibility of getting any information from those places of arms in the possession of Indians leaving for India?[28]

The same day, Hughes-Buller attended the secret meeting at Writers' Building to improve ways of detecting gun-smuggling by Indian passengers arriving at Calcutta. The assembled officials felt that the searches for firearms undertaken on the Indian side of the eastern border were 'lax' compared to the practice followed on the western border, and 'entirely different' to what had been done in Karachi and Bombay. The system needed to be improved 'at least to the standard of those places'. Boyd, Superintendent of Calcutta Police, was entrusted with this responsibility. A.B. Kettlewell wrote to Cumming on behalf of the Punjab Government (14 October):

> . . . in view of the information now available regarding the probable attitude and intentions of these expected arrivals and of there being reason to believe that many of them will be in the possession of arms and some possibly bombs, the Lieutenant-Governor would be glad if adequate precautions are taken thoroughly to search . . . these people before they are allowed to entrain for the Punjab.[29]

Cumming observed in his confidential note to Hughes-Buller (17 October): 'The letter of the Punjab Government evidently desires that the search for arms should be continued. Sir Charles Cleveland has sent to me a copy of private correspondence on the subject.'[30] The vigil on the eastern border was no longer relaxed.

Coopting Colonial Capital

The strict regime of watching the passengers from the east linked colonial policing with colonial capital. The cooperation with shipping companies began in earnest from early October 1914. These enterprises, owned by the monopolistic 'Managing Agency' houses, formed the commercial pillars of the British colonial capital in Asia.[31] In Calcutta, Mackinnon-Mackenzie, Jardine Skinner and Andrew Yule controlled the shipping traffic in the docks of South Bengal. As official agents of British India, Indo-China and the Nippon Yusen Kaisha lines, they facilitated the transport of travellers to various destinations between eastern India and the west coast of America. Their interests as the most profitable firms in the waters of East Asia were protected by the territorial and informal empires. In return, they readily accommodated the needs of imperial governance.

On 7 October, the high-ranking officials at Writers' Building decided to seek the formal collaboration of shipping companies. On the same day, steps were taken to methodically incorporate the colonial firms in the process of surveillance. The Indo-China Steam Navigation Company readily furnished Hutchinson with the details of its ships arriving 'around sunset' from the east in Calcutta on Monday, 12 October. A 'confidential' communication also reached Mackinnon Mackenzie's headquarters at 16 Strand Road, Calcutta, from the headquarters of the Intelligence Branch, CID at 11 Camac Street. Tegart enquired:

> I should be much obliged if you would let me have the names of any of your steamers which will be arriving in Calcutta during the next fortnight from the Far East, together with the dates on which each steamer is expected to arrive here. As the matter is urgent I would be very grateful if you would let me have a reply by the bearer of this letter.[32]

Only the shipping agents, Anley pointed out, were recipients of telegraphic advice when a ship left the last port of call, and were in a position to inform the police when a vessel was expected in Calcutta.

As promised over the phone, the Hong Kong authorities of Jardine Skinner agreed to send passengers in batches of fifty in their ships so that the numbers were 'manageable' for search purposes by the Calcutta Police.

In a confidential note to the Chief Secretary on 26 October, the Inspector General of Police confirmed that some ships will be carrying no more than fifty passengers.[33] The network of special relationships yielded immediate practical results. The names of vessels sailing to Calcutta, the number of passengers including those sleeping on the deck and the approximate dates of arrivals were systematically recorded. It was noted that the *Tosha Maru* (Andrew Yule's vessel) was expected on 25 October, the *Hang Sang* (Jardine Skinner) on 27 October and the *Kut Sang* (Jardine Skinner) on 29 October. Among the ships due to arrive, prior intelligence recorded that the *Fan Sang* contained thirty-five Indians including two Sikh watchmen who had been 'declared bad characters'. With the help of the shipping companies, the lists of Sikhs to be detained under the provisions of Ordinance V of 1914 were drawn up. Three persons – including Sohan Singh, one of the principal Ghadar leaders – were arrested on the *Nam Sang* (12 October), three were detained from the *Foo Sang* (15 October) and two were rounded up from the *Kwang Sang* (19 October). The Bengal IB started compiling its own list of suspects with the help of shipping agents, the Central Intelligence having informed L.N. Bird, Special Assistant to Deputy Inspector General, Intelligence Bureau, Bengal, that they had neither composed nor possessed any list of 'undesirable Indians' living in the Strait settlements.[34] When the *Tosha Maru* was searched in late October 1914, the ship's doctor, Binod Bihari Adhya of Calcutta, who was employed by Andrew Yule, handed over a hand-case placed in his cabin by unknown persons, containing four revolvers, two automatic pistols and some papers in Gurumukhi. Some 'seditious' literature were also discovered in the personal effects of one of the passengers, Dant Singh.[35]

The deck passengers were specially marked for surveillance. The Indo-China Steam Navigation Company Limited (with Jardine Skinner and Company as agents) informed the IB on 3 November that the *Kut Sang* left Penang on 2 November and was due to reach port on 7 November. She was carrying 115 deck passengers on board. Bird directed G.W. Dixon, Superintendent of Police, Chittagong (22 October) 'to examine Indian deck passengers by the B.I. Boats coming from Rangoon especially Sikhs.'[36] He suggested that they should be 'quietly' questioned as to where they were coming from, and the names and addresses of the passengers from the Far East were to be forwarded to the IB. He also wanted to know whether many Sikhs travelled to Chittagong from the east and if they were to proceed to their homes by train. He advised deployment of 'tact' and instructed that the passengers must not be harassed. On the same day, the Bengal IB sent the following missive to Cleveland: 'I am trying to arrange with the Agents concerned to inform us by wire the number of Indian Cabin and Deck passengers leaving Penang.'[37] Unobtrusive surveillance along paternalistic lines was interspersed with the necessity of determining the class background and political attitude of the travellers.

The top bureaucrats were not entirely satisfied with the information at their disposal. Cumming informed C.A. Barron, Chief Secretary to the Government of Punjab (1 February 1915):

> The officers of this Government also keep themselves informed by communicating with the shipping agents and the port authorities, of the names of the ships coming from America and the Far East, but the Agents are usually able to give only the total number of passengers and the names of the ports at which they have embarked. I am to say that in spite of these limited resources of information, every effort will be made to comply with the request of the Government of Punjab.[38]

In 1915, as the number of passengers from the east dwindled, modification of the previous policy was urged within the police bureaucracy. It was felt that colonial capital had cooperated sufficiently with the colonial state and needed relief from having to share the strain of carrying out surveillance. Clarke, officiating Commissioner of Police, Calcutta, conveyed to Cumming in early April that the government needed to adopt a relaxed attitude regarding private colonial enterprises, as the interests of shipping companies had to be considered. He favoured vigilance in individual cases rather than following a hard-and-fast rule, since 'shipping companies are helpful and cooperative to customs and police'.[39]

The police authorities continued to receive advance intelligence on the arrival of ships in the coming years. The shipping agents faithfully furnished details of ships belonging to the Indo-China line, the Nippon Yusen Kaisha line and the British India line that were expected to reach Calcutta from East Asia.[40] The cooption of colonial capital, whose conservation was of foremost concern to the colonial state and which formed the reason for the state's existence, played a crucial and indispensable role in organizing and implementing surveillance on vessels and passengers. The entwined interests of commercial and administrative institutions of colonial power were repeatedly demonstrated.

To Return

> . . . all officers may understand that these people are a potential source of
> danger to peace, and that it is necessary to keep the strictest surveillance
> over any of them who may halt at any place in their districts. In such cases
> the greatest care must be taken to observe any communication of any kind
> between them and local persons whether suspect or otherwise.

At the end of October 1914, the wider aim of surveillance was thus
outlined. What was the impact of surveillance on passengers? As the closely
observed ships sailed in, one after another, the vessels carried resistance in
the form of 'defiance'. This mood was influenced by the Ghadar tendency.
However, it was also a response to surveillance and repression, an aspect that
remains underinvestigated. The perspective of the colonizers was countered
at a quotidian level and inadvertently revealed the experiential world of the
targets of repression.

Clandestine and possible return of Indian organizers at large in North
America and East Asia caused anxiety. Slocock warned Hughes-Buller (12
October) that H. Rahim, the well-known Indian dissident from Vancouver,
might slip into India; he had played 'a prominent part in the Komagata
business there' and edited *Hindustani*, an anti-imperialist paper. He also
pointed out that Bir Singh, Gurdit Singh's Secretary and one of his 'chief
lieutenants' on the voyage to Vancouver, had got off at Yokohama or
Kobe on the return journey. Adrift in Japan, he was suspected of trying
to return by another boat in future. The confirmed returnees were also
treated as fugitives from colonial law. Those with prior political records
were imprisoned under the Ingress into India Ordinance and the rest were
speedily deported by train under armed escort to Ludhiana, where they
were subjected to further screening.[41]

The closely observed ships continued to arrive and the passengers were
compulsorily 'entrained'. The last stretch of their journey to Punjab on
railway tracks was completed under the guise of a 'free' ride for which the
officials demanded their gratitude. From official descriptions, clues can be
found about the motivations and feelings that turned passengers into resisting
subjects. During their prolonged ordeals as an officially criminalized group
of people, they defied the complex of racial and imperial authority through
a range of expressions and actions. Though the colonial authorities accused
them of being 'readymade' carriers of subversion, the colonial records indicate

a process of self-organization among the passengers in the decks and railway compartments as they dealt with authoritarian restrictions at close quarters.

On 13 October, the *Nam Sang* reached the docks at Diamond Harbour near Calcutta. Commander Gilroy and First Officer Falk complained of the insolent and violent conduct of the Punjabi migrants. The Sikh deck passengers from Hong Kong, 'a party of 75', inspired by 'instigators', were accused of having 'given a considerable amount of trouble on the voyage'. They had shown 'an extremely independent spirit, quarrelling frequently among themselves and using foul abuse in English' with the ship's officers.[42] They had demanded various privileges to which they had 'no right whatever and in spite of most considerate treatment by the officers of the ship, had displayed a mutinous and unruly spirit throughout'.[43] The officers alleged that the migrants had terrorized white passengers, chased the ship's crew, including a fitter, and had tried to prevent the rescue of a European woman who had gone overboard, injuring Falk in the process. Three Sikhs – Bhaktawan Singh, Jhawan Singh and Sohan Singh – were arrested from the ship as ring leaders 'who led these disturbances', after being pointed out by the First Officer. Gilroy, Falk and Boyd from the Preventive Services immediately bonded as representatives of besieged racial authority, and proceeded to articulate, support and reiterate what became the official version of life on board. Boyd claimed the ship's officers were relieved to see the armed force of the colonial state accompanying him. The description of the search procedure by Boyd revealed the treatment meted out to the passengers. Boyd separated and lined up those travelling from the east of Singapore on deck, thoroughly searched them and found 'no arms or ammunition of any sort'. Only one copy of the revolutionary organ, *Ghadar*, and a few pornographic photographs were found. All Punjabi correspondence discovered on them and their belongings were inspected.

The ship's arrival was noted in *The Statesman* (15 October 1914), a leading voice of colonial capital. The newspaper recorded the arrival of *Nam Sang* and praised police arrangements against returning emigrants: 'The proceedings were very quietly and expeditiously got through without a single hitch.'[44] The officials were pleased with this report, but offered a somewhat different picture of the reality on the ground in a confidential report. After the arrest of the three 'leaders' under Ordinance V of 1914, the rest were sent under armed escort to Howrah Railway Station and made to board the special train to Punjab. Tegart, Colson and Hutchinson followed them to the station:

We had previously explained to these men the circumstances that had arisen on
the arrival of the 'Komagata Maru' and that if they went ashore and broke up
into small parties, there would be every prospect of their being arrested either
in Calcutta or when travelling up country. . . . We had considerable difficulty
in getting them into the train, but this was satisfactorily accomplished.[45]

Despite demonization of the passengers by the ship's officers and
the colonial administrators, it was evident from the official statements
that distrust was mutual and antipathy was not one-sided. The tension
generated among the passengers by the behaviour of those in positions of
petty authority managed to surface even in the official versions; for instance,
the descriptions offered by First Officer Falk during the attempted rescue
of the 'European lady saloon passenger' indicated that the passengers may
have become desperate, suspecting the white officers and crew of trying
to abandon ship when they lowered lifeboats to the sea. During the entire
procedure after landing, the passengers were kept under armed guard, a
confirmation of their near-complete criminalization by the state.

The *Foo Sang*, a ship of the Indo-China Steamship Company, also
arrived on the same day (15 October). Colson led the police search and was
accompanied by Slattery. Among the deck passengers were found Meher
Singh, Puran Singh and Basant Singh. Regarding Meher and Puran, the
Punjab Police had 'reliable information' from Canada via London and
Simla, that they had left Victoria, British Columbia in August 'with bombs'.
Instead of explosives, the detectives discovered Savarkar's 'Indian War of
Independence (1857)', a 'proscribed book', and a leaflet entitled 'Jahaj
Parsakar', 'recently' prohibited under the Sea Customs Act, in Puran Singh's
baggage. Slattery informed the company that an individual named Basant
Singh had been dismissed in May from the Government Press at Singapore
for having sent into India a copy of the banned *Ghadar*. When envelopes
addressed to him as a book binder in the Singapore Government Press
were found, the officers interrogated and learnt from Basant Singh that he
had indeed held that position; he claimed he had left his work voluntarily
in April. Seen as fitting subjects for enforcing Ordinance V of 1914, the
two 'dangerous' but unarmed emigrants from Canada and the 'seditious'
bookbinder from Singapore were detained and sent to the Lalbazar lock-up
with all their personal effects 'for necessary action'.[46]

A month after the *Komagata Maru*'s arrival in the dying evening light
of 29 October, the *Tosha Maru* anchored with Sikh passengers from North

America and East Asia at Kidderpore (Khidirpur) docks. Captain E.D. Dallas-Smith, Assistant Commandant, Dhaka Military Police Battalion, who was put in charge of accompanying the passengers under armed escort by train, complained of inadequate food and water provisions which inflamed their feelings. Unhappiness with the lack of support he received from those above him, the 'indefiniteness of the instructions' which prevented an application of 'overwhelming' force, having to deploy diplomacy and good humour in the face of abusive conduct and 'wild talk' from those beneath him, being reduced to quivering anxiety at the prospect of mass resistance and stripped of the language of command, left their mark on his report. No warrants or other special papers had been issued to deal with the 'suspect' passengers in his custody, some of whom he described as 'prisoners' and 'detenus': 'Thus I was compelled to proceed with a train full of turbulent persons, some of the worst of them, in open compartments, who were not prisoners and the using of force against whom in the event of defiance of orders would be a matter of very doubtful legality.'[47] There were 79 'detenus', 4 'prisoners', 100 'free pass travellers'. Though 'a guard of 100 rifles' was on board, Dallas-Smith regarded the force as inadequate in the face of a violent confrontation, which he dreaded but did not occur. Slattery and Sub Inspector Indar Singh of the Punjab Police, with their insider's knowledge on dissent from Punjab, also accompanied him; he drew comfort from their presence while travelling with 300 persons. He relied heavily on their 'tactful handling of the passengers', to which 'the absence of disturbance en route was largely due'. The armed escort was strengthened at Delhi by fifty men of the Delhi Police, at the request of the Inspector General of Police, Punjab. He was relieved to hand over the train to the Punjab Police, present with a guard of 108 men from the Lahore Reserve Force. One hundred of the passengers, he later learnt, were selected for internment in the Montgomery and Multan Central Jails, and the rest were allowed to proceed to their homes. Dallas-Smith's account bears an imprint of shocked offence at the expressions of anger by the migrants, locked into compartments without basic amenities. He was furious with them for being an 'unceasing cause of anxiety'. He admitted that they became quiet after the first twenty hours. Nevertheless, their 'attitude . . . left no doubt as to the frame of mind in which they were returning to their country.'[48]

The *On Sang* of the Indo-China line arrived on 3 January 1915, carrying soldiers of the Indian army who were on sick leave, 'distressed' seamen, three Sindhi shopkeepers and eleven Muslim labourers from Bombay and Bengal working in Panama. 170 Punjabi migrants, including one woman and two children, mostly from Canada and the United States, were on board. Two passengers, described as 'dangerous characters', were detained. The rest, with the exception of those allowed an 'extension of stay' in Calcutta, were promptly sent to Punjab, again 'quietly and expeditiously'.[49] A report on the ship by Slattery demonstrated the deep-seated fear of an uprising from below. The Punjabis returning from America were suspected of being closely in touch with the Ghadar Party and of returning to India in the hope of starting a revolution. The routine of containment was already in place. An armed force of troops and police was present at the dockside when they landed; and a large staff of customs officers searched the person and baggage of all the passengers carefully. The names of all Punjabi men were registered by gazetted officers of the Calcutta and Bengal Police under the personal superintendence of the Police Commissioner; they were given written orders to leave Calcutta before midnight on 7 January 1915 and report themselves at Ludhiana before midnight to an officer appointed by the Punjab government. One of the Punjabi officers on duty got into conversation with an emigrant, who happened to be a man of his own village, returning from Shanghai. Suram Singh, of village Padhana, Lahore, reportedly said that 'from the time this batch of emigrants had touched at Shanghai, they had been very careful in their demeanour'.[50] Up to that point they had 'indulged in fiery seditious language' and were in 'a state of exaltation (*josh mein hue*)'. Since all ports from Shanghai onwards were British-controlled, and the officials were largely Indian or spoke Indian languages, the emigrants were deliberately inoffensive so that 'their entry into India might not be barred'. Suram Singh gathered from them that their leaders had been approached by German 'spies', who predicted the downfall of British rule and the coming victory of the Germans. The Indians in America had been persuaded by these agents to return to India and 'wrest its sovereignty from the British for themselves'. 'Take it and hold it,' they had warned, 'otherwise we shall soon be coming and your chance will have gone.' It was in this hope, Suram Singh said, that these Sikh emigrants, 'forfeiting lucrative employment', were returning to India. They were also under the impression that Canada was soon to be absorbed into the United States of America, and future emigration of Indians to North America would no longer be obstructed.[51]

Suram Singh's account indicates that the migrants inhabited a 'polycultural' world.[52] Their confidence that they could go back and forth between continents and countries freed of imperial subjecthood was evident in their changed appearance, independent behaviour, awareness of entitlements and experience of surviving in the wider world. Slattery noted with alarm their distance and disaffiliation from the 'little traditions' of essentialized community identities which the colonial state could so far map, classify, embellish and control:

> The passengers appeared to be in affluent circumstances, though they did not have very much luggage. They were all well-dressed in American-cut clothes. Some of them, while still calling themselves Sikhs have shaved their beards and cut their hair; and a few of them were even observed smoking. At the dock side they had no objection to purchasing refreshments from Muhammadan vendors. To such an extent were they imbued with Western ideas that many of them had forgotten to what sub-caste they belonged; and they had most lordly ideas as to the amount of accommodation they required on the train.
>
> They are due to arrive in Ludhiana on the evening of the 5th January 1915. Reports regarding them have been sent in advance of them both to the special officer at Ludhiana and to the C.I.D. at Lahore.

Once the 'special train' was in motion, the polite and compliant demeanour of some of the passengers underwent an abrupt sea change. Occupants of one of the carriages shouted 'Bande Mataram', 'called it to one another, to the Bengali railway men, and to a small knot of European police officers who were on duty at the time of departure.'[53] A man made a gesture of 'hatred and contempt' throwing something with open hands at the officers and intoning soundless words with a 'grimace', his 'pantomime' interpreted as 'I throw dust on your head.'[54]

Seditious conversations by Sikhs continued to be reported. The Sikh labourers from East Asia, considered less dangerous by sections of colonial officialdom and treated less harshly in Calcutta, were also showing signs of resistance. The Delhi Police noted in November that five Sikhs on their way from Hong Kong via Howrah to the Punjab broke journey in Delhi for a few hours on the night of 14 November 1914. One of them, a man from Ludhiana, in conversation with an informer, remarked: 'I am not in a position to tell you anything just now. You will soon come to know all that is shortly to happen here.' He said that the Ghadar Party had united Hindus and Muslims in islands of Southeast Asia. The Indians working there were returning to their country to spread word in the ruined villages that the 'firinghis' will be overpowered by the Germans. Har Dayal had gone to Germany and Mian Abdul, 'a venerable old man', was visiting Turkey to seek assistance, taking some Sikhs with him. Turkish help was on its way. The Sikhs were taking lessons in aviation and bomb-making at the behest of Ghadar. Almost all Sikhs and Pathans in the islands were on their way back, and three months after their return, 'new events' would take place in India. He was a party to this secret programme but refused to divulge details since he did not wish to end up in prison. He told the informer that over 200 Indians were returning from the islands and travelling in small batches in accordance with a pre-arranged plan. In an indication of the spirit of rebellion, which would culminate in the aborted Singapore Mutiny in 1915 and which was spreading among the troops, he claimed that the Sikh regiment and a battery at Hong Kong had refused to go to the front; the regiment at Singapore would soon follow their example. With regard to the 'Budge Budge riot', he believed more than a hundred Europeans had been killed by the Sikhs in revenge. He felt the sacrifice made by the *Komagata Maru* Sikhs was going to bear fruit. The report sadly noted: 'Unfortunately the informer failed to obtain the names of the party. They complained that their names had been taken at nearly all stations along the line, and the informer's impression was that they had been giving false names.'[55]

As repression and surveillance intensified, the passengers tried to evade authoritarianism and harassment by changing their travel route. Their attempts to bypass the official 'reception arrangements' in Bengal was noted in October 1914: 'A steady stream of Punjabis, the great majority of whom are Sikhs, has lately been entering India by various ports.'[56] They tended to arrive in groups varying from a few individuals to more than 200 in size. An increasing number entered India via Colombo and Dhanushkodi. They came from America, Canada, Hong Kong, Shanghai, Japan, Manila and the Straits. Intelligence reports suggested that money had been collected among Indians in Manila as early as August to raise the banner of revolt in India at wartime, and that the local Indian society there was being kept under close watch.[57] The police predicted with alarmist zeal: 'the number who may possibly arrive under present conditions run into many thousands'.[58] The reason for the 'unusually' large influx of 'these men' was identified as:

> the restriction of employment on account of the slackness of trade due to the war, but the chief cause is a wide-spread unrest among the whole class. This has been fostered by the Ghadr Party in America and by other agitators, including, it is suspected, German agents, and the majority of the men now returning to India are doing so with the deliberate intention of assisting in a revolt, which

they believe will shortly be started or is already going on in the Punjab. Plenty of proof of this has been furnished by the action of the men who have already returned to the Punjab, a large gang of whom has been recently broken after killing a Sub-Inspector of Police and others, and by others who have made a deliberate attempt to raise the people against Government.

With reference to dates and numbers, it was recorded that 'several parties have already passed through the Madras Presidency'. According to police calculations, on 27 October, 51 men, 6 women and 8 children, on 19 November, 16 men, 3 women and 1 child, on 9 December, 28 men and on 13 December, 94 men had arrived. The movements of the party of 51 men, 6 women and 8 children were considered 'particularly instructive'. Having reached Dhanushkodi on 27 October, they had proceeded to Madura and halted. The same night, 48 of them went by train to Madras, leaving 3 at Madura who arrived a day later. At Madras, they split up, though they were bound for the Punjab; 28 went away by the Bombay line to Delhi and Amritsar, and some went up by the East Coast line as far as Bezwada, where they entered the native state of Hyderabad. Subsequently, they tried to purchase revolvers at Nanded. They were dealt with under the Ingress Ordinance of 1914 'to ensure a proper search for arms and seditious literature, and due intimation to the Punjab authorities if they journey to the Punjab'.[59]

The tendency to resist flowed through other channels. Connections and solidarity were sought with the pan-Islamic anti-colonial network in Calcutta and South Bengal. They were met with strict censorship. On 22 October 1914, citing 'inflammatory elements' active in wartime India and abroad and their motivation, akin to 'Komagata Maru Sikhs . . . returning to India', intelligence reports held that 'ill-disposed persons . . . flocking from America with the avowed purpose of stirring up trouble' had to be curbed. This was mentioned by Hughes-Buller to Cumming alongside the distribution of *jihad* leaflets and other pan-Islamist literature, and accordingly, a strong case for muzzling the anti-colonial press sympathetic to these tendencies was made.[60] In November 1914, a letter reached Abdul Ghaffur, a rural resident of Hooghly district from New Orleans. Written by his brother Abdul Zahur, it was sympathetic to Turkey and scathing in its criticism of the British empire; it claimed that Britain was not 'great' and the soldiers 'from our country' who had come to fight in Europe, namely 700 Sikhs mobilized from Punjab, were decimated in a single day.

Zahur's letter held that the war news circulated by newspapers in India was 'completely false' and was cited by the authorities to advocate rigid postal censorship.[61] In January 1915, Ghadar leaflets from San Francisco were sent to *Al Hilal*, an anti-imperialist paper edited by Maulana Abul Kalam Azad. The envelope, with postmark dated 8 December 1914, was intercepted by the Postal Censor; it contained the Urdu leaflets *Bande Mataram* and *Ghadar ka Shagom*, issued and printed by Yugantar Asram, San Francisco. While the first leaflet claimed that Indians in Canada had been treated so cruelly that they had resisted with arms, the second leaflet called for killing all white tyrants; it was a call for mutiny to overthrow British rule at wartime. Ghadar leaflets were also sent to one Haji Gul Muhammad Khan of 11 Tiljala Road in Calcutta. Munshi Abdur Rauf of Hooghly was also sent five copies each of the Ghadar leaflets, dated 27 and 30 October 1914, in a plain cover from Republic del Ecuador. His acquaintance, Munshi Abdul Rahman, while making domestic references in the covering letter, echoed Zahur and informed him that the material, printed in California, would equip him with a correct perspective on the war. The Postal Censor continued to remain busy as references to Ghadar and the *Komagata Maru* continued to flow in from the Americas, and contacts were sought to forge an alliance between different anti-colonial militant streams.[62]

Following the aborted Singapore Mutiny (1915) in which Pathan soldiers had participated in large numbers,[63] connections between Sikh and Muslim opponents of the empire increasingly worried the colonial authorities. In March, Abdul Rahim, a resident of the United Provinces, who boarded the *Tosha Maru* from Singapore, reported close friendship between Sikh and Pathan passengers. Though the latter occupied a separate quarter of the ship, they ate with the Sikhs and sympathized with their political aims to overthrow colonial rule in India. The Sikhs were 'orderly', probably because they saw themselves as activist-organizers, had friends in every port, bargained with Japanese shipping agents and procured compensation when forced to remain for four or five days in Penang, and raised funds for the Ghadar Party and held meetings regularly on board. Rahim's statement suggested that under the influence of Ghadar, the Sikh activists stood up to confront various forms of authority. This capability earned them respect, and they gained a following among other Indian passengers who identified with their circumstances.

In August 1915, a Muslim trader in Swatow near Hong Kong, accused of engaging in anti-British intrigues with Germans, and 'a Turk' who was staying at the German Vice-Consul's house were brought to Bengal on *SS Japan*. Haroon Omar, a Gujarati shopkeeper, allegedly kept seditious literature in his shop and was friendly towards all Indian visitors, acting as a 'father' to them. Sikhs and Muslims regularly visited the premises. Among his Sikh acquaintances were watchmen employed in the Standard Oil Company. Haroon was described by the local British police as 'an uneducated, fat, happy-go-lucky Mahomedan' capable of writing and reading Hindi and Gujarati, though never having attended school. He was kind despite being in debt: 'He owes a good deal of money. . . . He appears to be a man of generous impulses.' From Swatow, Haroon was brought by the British police to Hong Kong and deported to India. Haroon admitted of having heard the word 'Ghadar' in conversations among Indian visitors at his shop, but never thought of reporting them as he was never asked to do so. He had helped destitute Muslims and Hindus travelling in ships; they were brought to his shop by Sampan men, and he paid for their passage money to Hong Kong. He claimed that penniless Sikhs never visited him. The British authorities were convinced that he was a sympathizer of Germany, though he denied connections with German businesses or with the Consul.[64] Sixty-one Punjabis and thirteen North-West Frontier men also arrived on *SS Japan*. They were asked to proceed to their home provinces and report to police authorities in Ludhiana and Peshawar. Haroon Omar and Niranjan or Narang Singh, the two deportees from Swatow, were detained in Lalbazar Central Police lock-up and later interned at Alipore Central Jail under Ordinance V of 1914. Haroon was ultimately delivered to the Commissioner of Police in Bombay under police escort in December 1915. Narang Singh was sent to Ludhiana and handed over to the Deputy Commissioner of Police, CID, Punjab.[65]

As mentioned, assisted by Dutch authorities, twenty-one passengers, the majority being Sikh men, women and children, were also detained and deported to Bengal by *SS Japan*.[66] In December 1915, the Government of India issued an order effectively preventing travel through the eastern seas from India; passports to the Far East, Japan and America were to be refused altogether except to those who had 'definite business' there or were 'beyond all suspicion'.[67] In March 1916, Hughes-Buller pointed out to the Chief Secretary the pressing need to register passengers once they embark at a port. Citing the examples of *Komagata Maru* and *Tosha Maru* passengers, he argued that if such a system had existed in 1914, the authorities could have used the knowledge 'in locating and tracing antecedents of these men who eventually caused so much trouble here and in the Punjab.'[68] Upholding the model of issuing official passes to people seeking to leave Britain as the ideal system to follow across the empire, official control over the movement of Indians travelling between India, East Asia and the Americas was proposed. Fomalization of repressive checks on travellers through a system of registration was legitimized on grounds of state security,[69] and eventually led to widespread and compulsory adoption of the passport in the inter-war years.[70]

Meanwhile, the colonial officialdom congratulated itself on warding off the looming threat to the empire by sea. Their success was demonstrated in the subsequent voyages of the closely observed ships. The *Tosha Maru*, for instance, continued to connect Calcutta with colonial and semi-colonial port-cities lying to the east, carrying cargo and people.[71] By May 1916, the Punjabi Sikh passengers were significantly absent in the narratives of those travelling to Japan by the *Tosha Maru*. They were not to be spotted on the vessel's wide deck washed diligently with hosepipes every day, where one could 'easily ride a bicycle' and observe Venus shining overhead at night while projecting a luminous reflection on the dark waters.[72] To a less impressed traveller, the ship's awning could also be perceived as a gigantic shroud, a symbol of death on an industrial scale, signalling an impending apocalypse by enveloping the dying sky.[73]

Conclusions

The colonial authorities took pride in being able to control shiploads of rebels. For the officers in charge of implementing imperial logistics, the days were not sufficiently long. Their strenuous objectives made them turn in different directions at once: from writing reports, dispatching telegrams and sending enquiries to boarding ships anchored in the docks, supervising searches and arrests, and arranging for armed escorts. They drew on all the modern technologies of transport and communication at their disposal, developed in the course of the nineteenth and early twentieth centuries: railways, steamers, motor cars, telegraph and telephone. They could also fall back on the inter-imperial geography of surveillance with its overlapping zones of spatialized focus and control. Ideologically, they could easily shift from 'benevolent' paternalism to paternalistic repression to iron-fisted repression in keeping with the needs of the imperium. A century later, while reading the documents they generated, the tedium accompanying official voices of colonialism stands exposed. Their counterpoints, the voices of passengers arriving from the east, were not recorded in detail. Only glimpses of their resistance and details of their repression survive. They also served as experimental subjects. The process of surveillance was expanded, and the techniques were refined and distilled in relation to them.

This micro-surveillance prevented the Ghadar network from becoming effective within India through diasporic reinforcements. The colonial perspective bred its counter-perspective. In the closely observed ships and upon embarkation, the migrants often responded to imperial authority with everyday acts of fleeting and organized resistance. Occidental pride registered a blow. The sign of defiance among the natives at a deeper level was interpreted by colonial officials as a sign of confidence, a step forward in a war from below. Holding the fort by drawing on the usual east–west boundaries to control a racialized subject population proved difficult. The codes of accepted behaviour imposed on the natives were challenged continuously. By rejecting the codes and the regime behind it, a segment of the criminalized subjects not only defied authority but sought regime change through a range of attitudes and positions, words and gestures, programmes and actions. The aspirations that turned the impulse of revolt into revolutionary plans, local actions inspired by the Ghadar tendency, or the development of a long-term anti-imperialist current among Sikh workers were shaped in the backdrop of surveillance and repression imposed from the top. Though the 'external' entry of revolutionary actions in the form of dissidents and arms was successfully suppressed, self-aware militancy among a segment of the Sikh diaspora surfaced in Bengal through wartime and post-war anti-colonial movements. The echo of the *Komagata Maru* could not be erased and other closely observed ships influenced the trans-terriorial efforts of Punjabi migrant workers against oppressive conditions imposed from above.

NOTES AND REFERENCES

[1] Intelligence Branch of the Bengal Police (IB) 1105/1914, pp. 57/14. By Victoria is meant Victoria in British Columbia (BC), Canada.

[2] Ibid.

[3] Ibid.

[4] Ibid.

[5] Ibid.

[6] Ibid.

[7] Ibid.

[8] Ibid.

[9] Ibid.

[10] Ibid.

[11] Ibid.

[12] Ibid.

[13] Ibid.

[14] A cluster of British colonial territories in Southeast Asia.

[15] Home (Political) WBSA 80A/1916.

[16] IB 1105/1914 (57/14).

[17] Ibid.

[18] *Weekly Report of Intelligence Branch, Bengal Police 1914.*

[19] IB 1105/1914 (57/14).

[20] Ibid.

[21] Ibid.

[22] Ibid.

[23] Home (Political) WBSA 322/1914.

[24] IB 1105/1914 (57/14).

[25] Ibid.

[26] Ibid.

[27] Home (Political) WBSA 58/1919.

[28] Ibid.

[29] Ibid.

[30] Ibid.

[31] To grasp the entwined world of the colonial state and colonial capital, see Amiya Kumar Bagchi, *Private Investment in India 1900–1939*, Cambridge, 1972.

[32] IB 1105/1914 (57/14).

[33] Ibid.

[34] Ibid.

[35] *Weekly Reports of the Intelligence Branch, Bengal Police 1914.*

[36] IB 1105/1914 (57/14).

[37] Ibid.

[38] Home (Political) WBSA 322/1914.

[39] Ibid.

[40] IB 1105/1914 (57/14).

[41] Ibid.; Home (Political) WBSA 322/1914.

[42] IB 1105/1914 (57/14).

[43] Ibid.

[44] Ibid.

[45] Ibid.

[46] Ibid.

[47] Ibid.; *Weekly Reports of the Intelligence Branch, Bengal Police 1914.* The *Tosha Maru* incident finds brief mention in Upendra Narayan Chakravorty, *Indian Nationalism and the First World War (1914–18)*, Calcutta, 1997, p. 113. Also, Hugh Johnston, *The Voyage of the Komagata Maru: The Sikh Challenge to Canada's Colour Bar*, Vancouver, 1995, p. 113.

[48] Ibid.

[49] IB 1105/1914 (57/14).

50 *Weekly Reports of Intelligence Branch, Bengal Police 1915.*

51 Ibid.

52 For an explanation of 'polyculturalism' from below, as opposed to cosmopolitanism and multiculturalism from above, see Vijay Prashad, *Everybody Was Kung Fu Fighting: Afro-Asian Connections and the Myth of Cultural Purity*, Boston, 2002.

53 *Weekly Reports of Intelligence Branch, Bengal Police 1915.*

54 Ibid.

55 IB 1105/1914 (57/14).

56 Ibid.

57 *Weekly Reports of Intelligence Branch, Bengal Police 1914.*

58 IB 1105/1914 (57/14).

59 Ibid.

60 Home (Political) WBSA 312/1914.

61 *Weekly Reports of Intelligence Branch, Bengal Police 1914.*

62 *Weekly Reports of Intelligence Branch, Bengal Police 1915.*

63 Sho Kuwajima, *Indian Mutiny in Singapore*, Calcutta, [1915] 1991.

64 Home (Political) WBSA 368/1915. Shantou or Swatow, on the west coast of the Pacific Ocean was a treaty port in southeastern China, collectively controlled by the western powers.

65 Home (Political) WBSA 368/1915 (5–14). Home (Political) WBSA 368/1915(22–24). Home (Political) WBSA 368/15(29–31).

66 Home (Political) WBSA 80A/1916.

67 Home (Political) WBSA 26/1915 K.W.

68 Home (Political) WBSA 332/16.

69 Ibid.

70 See John Torpey, *The Invention of the Passport: Surveillance, Citizenship and the State*, Cambridge and New York, 2000.

71 IB 58/1917. In 1917, Chakraborty, Chatterjee and Company, a firm selling books in Calcutta, and suspected of transacting in 'seditious' literature and employing revolutionaries, was sent copies of a book (*Chinese Religion through Hindu Eyes* by Binay Sarkar) from Shanghai via Singapore on the *Tosha Maru.*

72 Mukul Chandra Dey, *Japan theke Jorasanko: Chithi o Dinalipi, 1916–1917* (Japan to Jorasanko: Letters and Diary, 1916–1917), edited by Satyasree Ukil, Calcutta, 2005, pp. 14, 7, 13.

73 Rabindranath Tagore, *Japan-jatri* (Voyager to Japan), Santiniketan, 1974, pp. 10–12. Cited by Satyasree Ukil in the first note to the second letter of Mukul Dey. See Mukul Chandra Dey, *Japan theke Jorasanko*, edited by Satyasree Ukil, pp. 127–28. Accompanied by Mukul Dey, a young artist, and others, Rabindranath travelled to Japan by the *Tosha Maru* in 1916. In the backdrop of the Ghadar-inspired uprisings and resistance, the route taken by the poet's entourage attracted the attention of British intelligence. See index 8 (C.J. Davidson, 'Memorandum on the attitude of Japan in regard to Indian unrest/secret copy'), cited by Satyasree Ukil in ibid., pp. 287–300.

CHAPTER THREE

In the Public Sphere and Underground

The voyage of the *Komagata Maru* received extensive and emotive focus in the public sphere and generated controversy and questions. The migration of impoverished labourers and the conditions in which they travelled to meet the demands of the labour markets of territories within the formal boundaries of the British empire came to be emphasized; racist restrictions dominating the white settler colonies and the colonial government's collusion in the process, as evident in its reluctance to confront them, were highlighted. Following the massacre, the demand for an independent enquiry free of government interference was voiced. While middle-class expressions of civil outrage were registered in public, a cross-class underground connection was also developing in Calcutta and its surroundings. The secret society networks of middle-class Bengali Hindus were strategically stepping beyond their elite confines to establish links with the Ghadar and pan-Islamist activists. This was a part of a wider programme to get arms from Germany, and trigger rebellion in the ranks of colonial troops from Lahore to Calcutta to Singapore.[1] The intersections of anti-colonial strands in Calcutta and its suburbs during 1914–16 can be understood more fully by examining the actions of the scarcely noticed Punjabi Sikh political diaspora. This chapter attempts to do so by treating the public impact of the *Komagata Maru*'s journey on the world of print and its subterranean effect on the local underground revolutionary world through the mediation of those sympathetic to the Ghadar tendency.

Ship, Migration and Race

Immigration within the British empire and to the Americas generated controversy in the urban public sphere long before the arrival of the *Komagata Maru*. The treatment of Indian labourers working overseas and of Indian migrants in South Africa had attracted mounting criticism against British authority, one of the factors prompting the wartime colonial administration to prevent the ship from reaching Calcutta. Race and livelihood as terrains of discrimination and exploitation received concentrated focus alongside the journey of the *Komagata Maru*. The ideas of economic self-sufficiency and self-government to ward off colonial drain, propagated by the Swadeshi and Boycott Movements during the first decade of the twentieth century in the region, were extended to the sphere of migration.

Between March and August 1914, while the ship navigated its way towards Canada, its passengers were prevented from landing and the vessel was turned back; members of the local Hindu and Muslim, Bengali and non-Bengali intelligentsia in Calcutta avidly followed the ship's passage in print. Mostly, they advocated counter-responses to overcome discriminatory hurdles against migrants through a boycott of white personnel and the products of countries pursuing policies of racial exclusion. In March 1914, *Prabashi*, a quality Bengali literary journal with an interest in Indian migration, observed:

> Lord Bryce in a recent speech expressed the opinion that the best way of preventing black men and white men from coming into conflict with another is to make the latter remain in their own countries. But how are the plantations, mines and factories of white men in the colonies to go on without black labourers? Again, if black men are not to go out of their own countries, why should not the same rule apply to white men as well? . . . white men do not mind having black men working as coolies in the colonies, but they can never brook the idea of the latter standing up as men . . . and competing with them in their trade and commerce.[2]

This analytical perspective stemmed from an understanding of the international racial hierarchy regulating the supply and flow of labourers whose origins lay in non-European colonies. This position, underlined by a feeling of outrage, found an echo across the spectrum of critical voices in print. The otherwise 'empire-loyalist' and moderate *Moslem Hitaishi* wrote on 17 April: 'Honesty and truthfulness are fast disappearing from among the so-called civilized races, with whom the one obligatory duty seems to be to oppress the weaker nations. Practising oppression, cruelty and robbery is now the sole means of making a name on earth.' Pointing at the United States which had 'recently passed an Asiatic Exclusion Bill', the paper argued that Indians should not 'go to a country which does not want us'. Pointing at the mesh of colonial drain, racism and international capital, the paper observed:

> But why do we leave our country at all for foreign climes? We are driven by hunger to pass our days in exile under the oppression of uncivilized boors and it is those boors who are freely robbing our country of its crops and valuables, giving us in exchange trifles. . . . Those men are robbing us of our bread and yet would not give us anything even if we labour for them. We are weak and it is useless to waste words to point these things out to men who recognize money-making as the sole aim of life, who are strangers to honesty and gratitude.

While identifying the need to migrate as a compulsion built into the desperate living conditions of subject populations by the colonial state, the paper sarcastically held that there should be 'no objection to America excluding Asiatics utterly and without reservation. But before they enforce such exclusion, let all Americans in Asia clear out bag and baggage.'[3] Angrily predicting that 'a flame will ere long be kindled in the East which will consume all America', it called for commensurate retaliation: 'If Indians are excluded from America, Indians would be forced to boycott all American goods. Hence, we warn the American Government to proceed with due circumspection.' Its appeal to 'all Indians' was non-violent counter-attack:

> without being activated by any animosity, to give up the use henceforth of all American articles like Dietz Lanterns, nibs, pencils and other steel and iron goods. Let each Indian community undertake such a boycott as a sacred duty. . . . If they do shirk it, the world in future will have no place for them.[4]

The proposal of boycotting white settler colonies, their imports and citizens as means of a preventive strike against racism continued to be voiced in newspaper pages. Referring to the decision of the Government of British Columbia's refusal of entry to the '500 Indians' travelling from Shanghai, the *Samay* observed on 24 April that 'colour prejudice' present in British colonies should be countered with effective steps to combat such persecution. It advocated that this could be done by stopping the entry of all articles manufactured by the colonizers into India. The *Hitavadi* of the same date, also referring to the racism of the Canadian authorities, wrote: 'Unless the British Government stops this kind of arbitrary conduct on the part of the colonies, the problem of imperial rule will become increasingly difficult.' On 22 May, the paper wrote: 'The Government of India can, if they wish, take adequate retaliatory measures against the Canadians and we hope they will do it.'[5]

'Asiatic immigration in British Columbia' continued to attract attention, and the colonial government repeatedly asked to take responsibility through 'retaliation'. The *Bengalee* publicized the plight of the stranded passengers of the *Komagata Maru* and observed, in May:

> . . . things are coming to a head so far as the right of Asiatics to enter British Columbia is concerned. The Japanese steamer Komagata Maru with six hundred Hindu emigrants will shortly arrive at Victoria and the Canadian authorities are determined to prohibit their entry. Most of these passengers embarked on the vessel apparently at Calcutta to comply with the condition of continuous journey imposed by the immigration law. In the mean time a council order, which imposes an absolute prohibition on the entry of all artisans and labourers, has been revived. It is not known how to characterize this conduct of the Canadian Government. The only remedy left is retaliation and the paper is confident that His Excellency Lord Hardinge will not shrink from it.[6]

The *Amrita Bazar Patrika* remarked that the attitude of the British Columbian authorities towards the 600 Indians travelling on the *Komagata Maru* showed the 'length' of 'the anti-Asiatic bias of the white races'. Referring to the 'humiliating' laws enacted by the Canadian authorities, the inaction of the British imperial authorities in this matter, and the poverty of Indians which compelled them to seek work overseas despite harsh conditions, ill-treatment and sacrifice of all self-respect, the paper insisted that imperial authorities should be held accountable:

> Either they must see that the economic conditions of this country are so improved as to enable all Indians to eke out at least a bare subsistence here without being put to the necessity of courting humiliation and oppression abroad, or if they confess their inability to do that, they should at least see that those Indian subjects of His Majesty that do go abroad for seeking livelihood, are treated like British citizens.[7]

Strongly anti-racist pronouncements, meant to put pressure on the government, indirectly influenced the colonizers to seek the route of repression. Rather than yield to demands of ending racial segregation, which was blended into the ideological and social fabric of imperialism, a covert strategy of coercion was chalked out to deal with the migrants.

Meanwhile 'Indians in Canada', along with Gurdit Singh, were defended in the press. Opinion-makers of the European capital felt that he possessed 'ingenuity and courage' even if he had failed to move the Canadian authorities from their implacable opposition to Asian immigration.[8] They defensively added that Canada was independent in all but name, and that Indian politicians should not be 'clamouring' for British intervention as Britain had little influence or authority: 'the sooner this is realized in India, the better for the peace of the Empire'.[9] The claim of exasperated helplessness and passing the blame on to the Indian subjects were already being contested on the ground that a hidden motive of racial solidarity simmered beneath the surface. The *Bengalee* (12 July 1914) observed that Gurdit Singh had lost 14,000 pounds, and claimed that the British as well as the Ottawa government knew that a steamer had been chartered for Canada; if any prior warning had been given, the 'heavy loss' could have been prevented. The paper thought such 'friendliness' was not to be expected from colonial authorities who treated Indian subjects like pariahs. The *Bengalee* did not think that the country should quietly accept the rejection of the India Council Bill on the treatment of Indian immigrants who wanted to enter Canada. The bill's rejection was a triumph of the extremist Europeans in India, and their agitation had been engineered from Simla, the summer capital of the Viceroy, by persons whose tactics were beneath contempt.[10] *Samay*, *Darshak* and *Bangabasi* were 'indignant' during July 'at the refusal of the Canada Government to allow the Indians on board the Komagata Maru to land in that country',[11] and repeated the demand that the authorities in India should 'retaliate by prohibiting the entrance of Canadians into India'.[12] The papers were 'confident that if the people of India unitedly ask the Government to pass a law in this connection it will accede to their request'.[13] The *Barisal Hitaishi* of 13 July hailed Gurdit as a *swadeshi* (national) hero and strongly criticized European newspapers for attacking him:

> The Statesman, The Englishman, The Times and some other papers have described Gurdit Singh's act as silly, but they do not for a moment think why an Indian has spent such a large sum as two lakhs and ten thousand rupees for protecting the rights of his countrymen in a foreign land. The people of India

hesitate to buy Swadeshi cloths because they are dearer than foreign-made cloths by a few annas only. But the fact that an Indian has spent such a huge sum of money shows that a great awakening has taken place in this country. *The Statesman* and *The Englishman* may not relish the idea, but the day is sure to come when the doors of all British colonies are sure to open to the Indians' knocks.[14]

The police noted in July that one of the 'burning questions' influencing the 'advanced section of Bengali society' was the treatment accorded to Indian emigrants who wanted to enter Canada. The *Komagata Maru's* journey was taking on the form of a campaign against racism, and was being related to the rights of immigrants from India and the wider questions of governance and material conditions within India. To this was added the demand for self-government and freedom from racial domination of Europeans. On 10 July, at a public meeting held at College Square, equal rights to migrate to different parts of the British empire, including Canada, were demanded by moderate and extremist nationalists. Speakers contested the one-way free flow of capital, personnel and goods. They pointed out that many foreigners visited India to earn their livelihood, and that Indians should not be debarred from seeking the same within the different countries of the British empire. Widespread poverty, which drove people to migrate, was also highlighted. Sasanka Jiban Ray, one of the orators, felt only self-government in India could earn Indians equality and honour in the other colonies, and praised Gandhi for securing certain concessions in South Africa. Gnan Chandra Ray, 'said to be a pleader', proposed raising subscriptions to assist Gurdit Singh in tiding over his losses. The police agents noted that '300 persons of all caste and creed' had attended the meeting.[15]

The journey of the *Komagata Maru*, depicted in the pages of the local newspapers, led to comparisons between the campaigns launched by Gandhi and Gurdit Singh. Through discussions on their efforts, racism in white settler colonies was dissected. In May, the *Amrita Bazar Patrika* remarked that

the incidents connected with the Komagata maru bid failed to develop into another South African affair and, perhaps, to work out another Gandhi in Sardar Gurdit Singh, who seems to be a leader of almost equal determination and force of character, but of more pecuniary resources which he is ready to stake for the sake of obtaining victory in the cause he has taken up.

The incident, fuelled by the forces of racism, had perhaps unintentionally succeeded in 'beating out so many sturdy heroes on the anvil of oppression and persecution'. The pathology of imperial racism was commented upon. The quarantined physical state of the vessel's passengers was emphasized with the observation that the migrants were being treated as small pox or plague patients. Moral arguments on the position of migrants as worthy subjects with values conforming to the capitalist ethic, and victimized by unworthy administrators of the British empire, were articulated to expose racial double standards: 'And what is the fault of these Indians? Their first fault is that their skin is not white; their second fault is that they are thrifty, sober and industrious; and lastly, that they honestly confide in the assurances given to them that they have the right of British subjects.'[16]

The *Bengalee*, observing that the Canadians were determined to prohibit the landing of the immigrants on board the *Komagata Maru*, also compared Gurdit Singh's efforts on behalf of Indian migrants with those of Gandhi in South Africa:

> No Indian has been permitted ashore, even to buy stores, and hundreds of Vancouver Hindus who attempted to reach the ship in boats were turned back, even their presence on the wharves being objected to. When this attitude of the Canadian authorities is compared with that of Gurdit Singh, the rich Hindu leader who chartered the ship to test the immigration lanes, and is prepared to fight to the finish if his countrymen are deported, it becomes perfectly clear that this time Indians must hear the last word on their right to enter the different parts of the Empire without any let or hindrance. In Gurdit Singh the Canadian Hindus have got their Gandhi, and the sacrifice and single mindedness of which he has given examples leaves no doubt that it will not be at any rate smooth sailing with the Canadian authorities.[17]

As the call for a material retaliation against imperial capital was combined with contesting racism on moral grounds, the question of citizenship within the British empire and the dilemma of living within colonial jurisdictions came to the forefront. The *Bengalee* observed in June that after the experience of the *Komagata Maru*, Indian emigrants would find it difficult to enter Canada on chartered ships, but the incident could not be accepted as a final settlement: 'Whether in Canada or elsewhere, whenever the British flag flies, Indians must insist on an open door for themselves and agitate unceasingly till they get what they want.'[18] The *Prabashi* announced that racism will spell the doom of empire:

The British Empire will be a mere name unless all its subjects can travel and reside freely in all its parts. And if Indians are to be excluded from any part of the colonial Empire, India should have authority to enforce a similar exclusion against colonials. Let a resolution be moved repeatedly in the Supreme Legislative Council at Delhi urging such exclusion.[19]

The *Hablul Matin*, a moderate nationalist Muslim newspaper printed in Persian and English, offered solidarity to the ship's passengers and their leader in July:

. . . the last act in the drama of the Komagata maru incident is over and the curtain has fallen over an episode which reflects the greatest discredit upon a most important colony of the British Empire. The gallant Sikhs will have to return to Hong-Kong. They have suffered a loss of more than two lakhs of rupees. But it is certain that the matter will not be allowed to drop at this stage, and more will be heard of it in the future. The heroic conduct of Gurdit Singh reminds one of the patriotic courage shown by Hampden when he refused to pay the illegal tax of Ship money. The courts decided in favour of the Crown, but the principle for which Hampden fought triumphed in the end. Gurdit Singh and his friends are returning after having suffered the greatest humiliation, amidst the exultation of their enemies; but the sympathies of their countrymen, Hindus and Moslems, will cheer them in their hour of trouble. The Indian people, irrespective of religious and sectarian differences, should support this gallant band of Sikhs, because they have suffered for a great principle. The real question at issue is whether the Indians are to be treated as outcasts or subjects of a great empire. That must be decided, and the Indians must take up the cause of Gurdit Singh and his friends, if they want the verdict to be favourable to their national aspiration.[20]

The *Samay* (31 July) urged every District Association in Bengal to agitate for a redress of the humiliation to which Indians had been subjected in Canada over the *Komagata Maru*: 'When an extreme moderate like Babu Bhupendra Nath Basu has moved in the matter none need to hesitate to join in this agitation. If Government does not do anything, the Indians must have recourse to boycott to teach the Canadians that the Indians have a sense of self-respect.'[21]

The *Komagata Maru* passengers and Gurdit Singh were honoured as warriors against racism in the nationalist press, and the ship's passage was vested with a symbolic challenge to the claims of racial supremacy advanced by the white communities both within and outside India. The collective experience of the stranded passengers was repeatedly commented upon alongside the Gandhi-led movement of South African Indians against racist discrimination, and local incidents of sexual abuses and assaults on Indians by European soldiers and civilians. Just before the arrival of the ship at Budge Budge, the town gained notoriety in the press for sexual harassment of an Indian woman railway passenger by European soldiers who had boarded the train from there after a football match.[22] The *Komagata Maru's* voyage as an event made many Calcutta journalists question the foundations of the British empire and call for a need to go beyond religious identities to resist oppressive practices underlying colonialism. They did not know or realize that the journey of the passengers was far from over, and would ultimately bring them to the doorstep of the city under violent circumstances.

After the Massacre

Immediately after the massacre, the European print media was utilized by the government. The official version of the events was published in the *Empire*, a Calcutta-based newspaper, and in the Associated Press. This was done in a social climate of popular indictment of government action, and was expressed through rumours and informal acts of defiance towards European authority from below. 'Some malicious rumours', the government noted, were being circulated to the effect that British soldiers at Budge Budge killed several Sikh women and children, and that their bodies were thrown into the river.[23] Beyond Calcutta, rumours were also floating in the mining town of Raniganj that Sikh troops had refused to fight in France. When they returned, they had been set upon and killed.[24]

Even more disturbing to the white householder in the imperial metropolis was the attitude of the predominantly Muslim domestic workers. A month after the massacre, a regular columnist noted in *Capital*, the voice of colonial capital published from Calcutta: 'at the time of the "Komagatu" trouble there was so much agitation that we were afraid that we would have no servants left'.[25] The impact of the event was felt not just inside European homes, but in colonial prisons too. Nalini Kishore Guha and other incarcerated revolutionaries from a bhadralok (Bengali upper-caste Hindu) background, upon learning of the confrontation at Budge Budge and the massacre of the *Komagata Maru* passengers, were gripped by a wild hope that the moment of a national revolution had finally arrived, and wondered: 'Will the impenetrable walls of the colonial prison collapse?' Not allowed to read newspapers, the political prisoners depended on scraps of news conveyed by others. At the time of the *Komagata Maru*'s arrival, followed by the shooting, Guha noticed that jail security was increased even though he failed to guess the reason. Later, he was to observe the grim faces of the 'sahibs'.[26]

The authorities were clearly defensive. The police initially held as follows:

> While a number of educated Indians consider that the Sikhs after all the sufferings they had endured should have been allowed to do as they wished, and not have been restricted in any way, discussion mostly centres round the treatment that is to be meted out to those who have been captured.

The government, nevertheless, was relieved to find that 'remarkably little notice has been taken by the Indian Press of the incident. It is, perhaps, fortunate that for the first few days there were no issues of Indian papers, owing to the Durga Pujas.'[27] By deliberately ignoring their own reading of the submerged currents, the police was satisfied that the press approved of official action, and remarks were confined to the search of Sikhs before they landed. The sole exception, *Bengalee*, argued that the passengers should not have been restricted; if they had not been prevented from reaching Calcutta, the incident could have been averted. They would have consulted the local leaders and quietly gone home. While admitting the incident led to 'a very large amount of discussion by the general public', the custodians of law and order were happy that there was little evidence of 'actual panic in the city'. Rumours of possible looting at a time of acute war-induced scarcity and hunger made some shopkeepers down their shutters for a while, but the order of colonial normalcy was soon restored.

The Marwaris of Barabazar, the centre of the Indian trading capital in Calcutta, were the only community to be apprehensive of looting in the area by the poor. Two days after the incident, they responded with class panic and left the city in large numbers. The Marwari businessmen thought the withdrawal of the police to the southern suburbs will damage their property, and they hired a large number of thugs to come to Calcutta and protect their assets. Though 150 constables of the 'Calcutta Scottish' were deployed in the neighbourhood, the traders were not satisfied. The police suspected that they were exploiting the situation to ensure an increase in the European police force in the area, a trained reserve which frightened Indians. Apparently, this was a demand they had made repeatedly.[28]

The colonial state enjoyed little popular support in the public sphere in relation to the *Komagata Maru* incident. Even the official hope that the press will not cause a stir over the massacre was short-lived. The Calcutta print organs quickly became vocal after the festive break in autumn. The police reported in early October:

> The Budge Budge riot has been the chief topic of conversation during the last week. The general impression in Calcutta appears to be that the offensive was first taken by the military whilst the Sikhs here lay the blame on Sirdar Suka Singh, Deputy Superintendent of Police, Punjab, who was specially deputed to escort the immigrants to the Punjab. It is said that he used abusive language which was not understood by the Europeans present, and so insulted the immigrants and roused them to a state of fury.

The widespread opinion was that the government had not taken the press and public into its confidence; that the public should know who was responsible for allowing the Sikhs to land with arms without being previously searched; and that the riot occurred at a particularly 'unfortunate moment' as Sikh soldiers were assisting the British war effort in Europe. The *Bengalee* felt a lack of cooperation between the authorities and the people was plainly visible, and hoped that the government would offer material support to the families of the Sikhs who were killed and clemency to those arrested. The role of the CID, the official surveillance apparatus which often spent time 'shadowing innocent persons', was questioned, since it was 'not able to scent the presence of arms amongst the Sikhs!'

A deeply loyalist meeting at Bara Sikh Sangat by some Punjabi residents of Calcutta supporting government action vis-à-vis the passengers of the *Komagata Maru* was also reported. That the gathering was not acceptable to many was noted by a police official: 'I am given to understand that many of the Sikhs did not wholly associate themselves with the resolutions passed, saying that the meeting was an official one. They keenly desire an impartial enquiry into the matter with non-official members from their own community.'[29] Though the colonial officials did not openly admit that they had organized the loyalist meeting from behind the scenes, one of their assistants resurfaced later, stirring up embarrassing memories and claiming formal recognition for past service. On 10 February 1919, Amar

The Bara Sikh Sangat as it appears now

Nath Sharma, a Punjabi Hindu auctioneer who operated in Calcutta during 1914, wrote to Cumming from Lahore. He was pleading for a letter from the government acknowledging the 'services' he had rendered in connection with 'the Budge Budge Riot Affair'. He claimed that he had arrived in Calcutta at the behest of the government, held several meetings with Cumming and penned the resolutions supporting the government at a meeting held at the Bara Sikh Sangat on Harrison Road. He was assisted in his efforts by his 'caste-brother' Sundar Mal, an Honorary Magistrate of Calcutta. They had to 'labour very hard' to convince the Secretary and Mahant of the Sangat to let them hold a loyalist gathering. The aim of the meeting, as desired by the government, was 'to pacify the feeling of the Sikhs and other Hindu Public of the Punjab'. At the direction of Sardar Sukha Singh, the Punjab CID officer posted in Bengal at the time, he had also stopped an attempt to hold an anti-government meeting by 'mischief making people' at the Howrah Gurudwara. He boasted of having received a silver watch and a 'gold' certificate from the Punjab CID for his continued assistance to colonial intelligence. In late April 1919, in the month of the Amritsar massacre, Cumming, as Chief Secretary, hastily issued a brief letter officially recognizing Sharma's help and 'his influence with the Sikh community of Calcutta to allay the excitement which followed that regrettable occurrence'.[30]

Despite hasty attempts to pacify the Punjabi diaspora and local opinion, the government stood indicted in public. On 3 October 1914, the Bengali paper *Nayak* accused the police authorities headquartered in Calcutta of making 'a mountain out of a molehill' at Budge Budge. Recognizing the massacre as an 'event' with far-reaching consequences, it was difficult to believe that the arrival of 300 Sikhs would have led to anarchy in the city and predicted serious repercussions of the incident in future. Since the white community did not mix with the 'illiterate' and 'bewildered' common people, and spent their days signing papers, meeting each other in clubs and attending dances and plays, they were going to be reviled in every fair (mela), road, bathing place in Punjab, and the colonial system would be stigmatized in all the towns of India, especially in upper India where 'serious untruths' would be spread. In a sarcastic vein, the paper felt that there was no point in explaining this to the authorities as it may invite trouble.[31] Demands for state compensation and freedom of movement were reiterated in this context.

Noting the Governor of Bengal's gesture of 'condolence' to the relatives of bystanders killed at Budge Budge, the *Hitavadi* (16 October) held that the Governor of Bengal has shown great magnanimity by sending letters of condolence to the relatives of the innocent outsiders who have been killed by shots in the Budge Budge riot. It will, however, be a matter of great satisfaction if His Excellency provides for the indigent families of the deceased.

On the same day, the *Muhammadi* (Calcutta) re-emphasized that the Sikhs who tried to enter Canada were upholding the rights of all Indians and the colonial government had interfered harshly with their liberty of movement when they returned to the homeland.[32] In December, the *Amrita Bazar Patrika* pressed the government to compensate shopkeepers, wayfarers and others in Budge Budge who had 'suffered injury for no fault of their own in consequence of the disturbance'.[33]

Loyalist and counter-loyalist views clashed, showing the wide divergence between the government-affiliated and the independent press. The *Indian Mirror*, in a loyal vein, observed in early October:

> There were troubles enough in Canada, but the tragic business at Budge Budge shows that the Canadian authorities were after all wise in not allowing these dangerous fanatics to land on their shores. . . . Gurdit Singh has a lot to answer for. The Komagata maru voyage should never have been undertaken. The Bengal authorities acted with great discrimination. Sir William Duke was on the SPOT himself to reason with the men. Further leniency will be a mistake.

The *Amrita Bazar Patrika*, on the other hand, pointed out the follies of depending on the state. It had praised the Viceroy 'only the other day' for kindly thinking of the passengers of the *Komagata Maru* who were lying stranded in Japan and undertaking to repatriate them at government expense. Looking at the outcome, the paper wished that 'the ill fated' ship had remained in Japan rather than face 'a tragedy of such a grim nature at Budge Budge'.[34] The *Calcutta Budget* remarked that the 'tragic' incidents that occurred at Budge Budge might have been anticipated by the authorities, and the loss of life avoided.[35] The *Dainik Bharat Mitra* wrote: 'The public would have been better pleased if a non-official enquiry had been held. As the Bengal Government is directly concerned in the affair, it would be better if the Government of India takes over the enquiry in its own hands.'[36] The restrictive conditions under which the colonial 'civil society' functioned were demonstrated during the demands for a public enquiry. Though some newspapers questioned the government's action, almost all positions were couched in subservient tones as Indian opinion-makers of all shades were supporting the imperial war effort or were keen to avoid colonial censorship.

The European press, in contrast, adopting an aggressive position in favour of the government, tried to downplay the controversy over racism. In the pages of these newspapers, the Sikhs were projected as either violent trouble-making migrants engaged in lawless chaos or loyal providers of military labour serving the empire abroad. News reports and photographs conveyed implicit approval and disapproval. *The Statesman*, a conduit of European colonial perspectives in the city, reported on 24 October that a Commission of Enquiry had been formed 'to inquire into the occurrences at Budge Budge on the occasion of the landing of the Sikhs who went to Vancouver by the S.S. Komagata Maru', and had met at the old legislative department of the Government of India at Esplanade West. Its proceedings were to be secret and conveyed as communiqués to the public once the committee was ready. On 28 October, the paper carried a press photo of Sikh soldiers arriving in France. The 'loyal' character of the troops from Punjab was emphasized through photographs. On 15 December, a press photo of wounded Sikh soldiers was printed: they were sedate, calm and contented by all appearances, reading newspapers at an unknown location. Paradoxically, the Sikh diaspora from Canada to Calcutta were depicted as riot-prone and eager to disrupt peace and order. On 5 November, the murder of Inspector Hopkinson of the Immigration Department in the Court House at Vancouver was interpreted as a culmination of serial murder and a shooting spree by Sikhs. While observing the 'tragic' character of these incidents, the Sikhs were presented as a community seething with violence. This was in keeping with their 'local' image. On 10 November, *The Statesman* reported that the Sikhs had engaged in serious rioting at Calcutta's Collin Street and had been sentenced to varying terms of rigorous imprisonment.[37]

Once the official Committee of Inquiry was formed to enquire into the Budge Budge affair, its aim and composition were critically analysed by the Indian press. Referring to its appointment, the *Nayak* observed:

> . . . it is necessary for us to put a few questions now:
> (1) Which party did first open fire at Budge Budge? And why did it open fire?
> (2) It is rumoured everywhere that on the platform of the Budge Budge station an English official kicked a Sikh of position in the gang. Is this rumour true? If not, it is necessary that it should be contradicted without delay. For it has spread far and wide, and many Sikhs and up countrymen believe it.
> . . . The Sikhs who have been arrested and are now in hajat should be

released and assured of safety, and then their deposition should be taken. Gurdit Singh should be sought out and his deposition also taken in public. Why has a hue and cry been issued against him? And why have the other Sikhs, who fled, wounded or otherwise, from Budge Budge after the riot, been hunted down like dogs and jackals and arrested?

The *Bengalee* (22 October 1914) called for an open, unbiased enquiry, and implied that the findings may go against the government if the truth emerges before the public. The paper reported receiving letters about the riot which it had abstained from publishing, thereby complicating the situation. It held that a considerable body of independent evidence was available and should be recorded, as they may prove valuable to the commission: 'In any case, let the enquiry be thorough and sifting and let the fullest publicity be given to it, so that the public may form their own conclusions and may, if possible, see their way to support the findings of the commission.'[38]

The *Sanjivani* on the same day criticized the victimization, demonization and harassment accompanying imperial vigilance on the Punjabi Sikhs:

... strict steps are being taken by the police to arrest the Sikhs who disappeared after the Budge Budge riot: every train passing out of Bengal is being rigorously searched by policemen. In some stations armed police have been detailed for this duty. They look into every passing train and wherever they meet a Sikh, make him alight. It is certainly not adding to the contentment of the ordinary Sikhs. The ordinary passenger also is being subjected to annoyance.[39]

The *Bangavasi* (31 October) also felt the proceedings of the committee should be published in newspapers and satisfy the public more than an official 'communique'.[40]

The fate of the passengers who had survived the massacre and were subjected to incarceration was criticized. The *Prabashi* summarized 'the action of the Government which led to the severe oppression of the ill-fated Sikh passengers'. The periodical repeated the counter-narrative that had emerged in the public sphere after the massacre as the official investigation progressed towards a defence of the colonial state's actions:

The passengers of the ship went to Canada to earn their livelihood, but they did not kill anybody; nor was any of them killed. But a worse fate awaited them in their own country. When they returned to Budge Budge they killed some men, and many of them were also killed. That was not all. Most of them were arrested, while others are hiding themselves to avoid arrest.

While praising the statesmanship and spirit of sympathy of Lord Hardinge whose influence enabled the passengers to return to their native land, the official decision not to allow them to land in Calcutta was condemned. It was argued that a 'serious blunder' was committed in handing over the charge of the Sikhs, after their 'bitter experience in Canada', to 'officials who are accustomed to behave in a high-handed manner towards Indians'.[41] The *Prabashi* wondered how 'those poor people who were on the point of starvation from shortness of funds and were being brought home with Government help and money' could purchase arms, 'where they bought them and which party used arms and in what circumstances'.[42] Focusing on the suppressed components of the event, the official account that the Sikhs were suddenly excited and fired was questioned. Having deciphered the ill-concealed official strategy of containment, the paper wondered aloud if they had been mistreated by the police upon arrival, and picked up the mistaken idea that they were being sent to prison or transported. It requested Lord Hardinge to grant the Sikhs who were under arrest or absconding an amnesty, and appoint an independent commission to investigate the matter, as they were 'no *goondas* (thugs) or inveterate *budmash*es (evil-doers) and have had enough of punishment, even death.'[43]

Samay (18 December) demanded the release of Sikhs arrested in connection with the *Komagata Maru* and the end of a 'crop of rumours' generated by their continued detention.[44] The condition of political prisoners along with the *Komagata Maru* incident and the Ghadar tendency created inter-provincial solidarity and concern. Protesting against the death sentence handed to a Bengali revolutionary in Punjab on 13 February 1915, the *Dainik Basumati* remarked:

> The enhancement by the Punjab Chief Court of the sentence of transportation for life, imposed by the Delhi Sessions Court on Basanta Kumar Biswas in the Delhi Conspiracy case, to a death sentence, seems improper to us. We are in favour of anarchists being severely punished, but still, sentences ought to be commensurate with offences. . . . We are of the opinion that extreme severity of punishment often produces a bad result. Specially, when the lower court thinks that death sentence would be improper, should not the higher court desist from imposing it? When man cannot give life, he ought not to take it away lightly.[45]

The metaphysical pessimism of press analysis was followed by prosaic public predictions of uprisings in Punjab. In September 1915, the Lahore Conspiracy Case became 'the subject of much comment'. The punishments were considered 'too severe' and the proceedings seen as 'a court-martial'. The political repression in Punjab evoked empathy and disturbed the police authorities: 'Many people think that the result will provoke further disturbances in the Punjab. It has become so much the custom in Bengal to look upon persons tried in any conspiracy case as patriots, that any conviction in such cases . . . is looked upon as an oppression of innocent men.'[46]

It must be observed in this context that the image of the model Sikh soldiers fighting in Europe for the British empire also underwent transition in the course of the war, as its counterpoint, the image of Sikh labourers as victims of racist abuse within the British empire, was also circulated. The rumours of 'mutiny' accompanying the Budge Budge massacre could not wipe away the established perception of Sikh regiments as 'loyal' and indispensable to the British military cause, and was evident in the pages of *Sandesh*, a Bengali children's magazine, in 1915. In its pages, the comfortable stay of Indian troops in England was reproduced from an account by a Sikh soldier.[47] The image of the 'content' and obedient Sikh soldier continued to be distributed by newspapers and literary journals, such as *Modern Review* (1916). Yet, the mournful eyes and sombre visage of the wounded could be spotted in the group photographs. They may have conveyed different impressions to discerning readers.[48]

The transcontinental flow of critical political literature held up counter-versions, carefully sorted and suppressed by imperial surveillance in Calcutta. In April 1915, the Postal Censor discovered a 'plain cover' addressed to Ramananda Chattopadhyay, editor of *Prabashi* and *Modern Review*, from 68 Tranby Avenue, Toronto, by Sundar Singh, an organizer who had been active against Canada's immigration laws in Vancouver, and who was known to the imperial authorities as a difficult opponent. Inside were found newspaper cuttings on Indian emigration and Sundar Singh's letter to Chattopadhyay urging the latter to visit Canada, study the conditions of the immigrants and place them before the people of India. The content of the envelope that most annoyed the authorities was a pamphlet, 'The Sikhs in Canada – An Appeal'. Its author, Mrs Anna Ross mentioned that 90 per cent of 'East Indians' living in British Columbia were of Punjabi Sikh origin. Mixing eulogy with a plea for egalitarianism, she praised them as disciples of gurus who had rejected the hierarchical Brahmanical Hinduism, abolished idolatry, erased caste differences and granted 'equal rights to women'. She held that 'they look like heroes and walk like kings'. She insisted that they were highly valued as labourers by their Californian employers. Referring to the *Komagata*

Maru's passage in the concluding portion of the pamphlet, she indicted the Canadian government. Instead of receiving the immigrants who had politely claimed admission as British subjects, the Canadian authorities had heaped upon them 'indignity after indignity': 'It is almost inconceivable the lengths to which official insolence went in the treatment of these strong, proud, independent men.' Eventually, after being prevented from setting foot on the shore, 'the guns of the Rainbow were trained on the little Komagata Maru' and the ship sailed away: 'It is a sad story; it is a shameful story.'[49]

Into the Underground

While criticisms were voiced by a predominantly middle-class local intelligentsia in the public sphere, a tiny segment of Sikh workers joined the revolutionary underground. Influenced by the Ghadar Movement, their submerged activities were interwoven with the climate of wartime colonial repression that had led to the firing and imprisonment of stranded passengers of the *Komagata Maru*. The minute and predominantly working-class Sikh migrants in and around Calcutta were chiefly visible in the neighbourhood of Bhawanipore (Bhabanipur), in the Kidderpore (Khidirpur) dock area, and in Calcutta's industrial twin-city of Howrah.[50] In these spaces of labour concentration, Punjabi Sikh activists who joined the underground lived, earned their livelihoods and developed a degree of social support. Drawn from the ranks of cab drivers, chauffeurs, janitors and tailors, they were of de-rooted agrarian background; some of them possessed military experience as former soldiers. Their consciousness from below was shaped by the migratory appeal of Ghadar as a movement of labour and popular revolt stretching from

Slum at 100 Bakulbagan Road, Bhabanipur

Burma to China to the Pacific. While moving back and forth from one region to another, they had become familiar with individuals, literature and ideas advocating a revolutionary programme to overthrow the colonial regime. Through their efforts, Calcutta and Howrah became connected with the diasporic revolutionary movement brewing in the British port-cities, colonies of Southeast Asia, and further east in China, Japan and North America.

At the centre of the minute Sikh revolutionary underground were Dewan Singh, a Granthi (ceremonial custodian or guard) of the Howrah Gurudwara, and Chait Singh, a taxi driver from Bhawanipore. Sikh travellers with

Old house at Bakulbagan Road, Bhabanipur

Ghadar sympathies were harboured by the Howrah Gurudwara. Committee members of the Gurudwara were regarded by the authorities as 'in some way involved in the Komagata Maru affair'. They and other Sikhs living in the vicinity of Calcutta were perceived as sympathetic to Gurdit Singh's scheme of transporting Punjabi labourers to Canada. They saw those killed at Budge Budge and the fugitive Sikhs as victims. They were participants in a network that received and distributed seditious Ghadar literature. Though they could not be directly connected with the riot, they were labelled as having been inspired by the voyage of the *Komagata Maru* to 'take interest in politics'. The Granthis of Howrah Gurudwara, from an official viewpoint, were 'a very undesirable lot'. Among them, Dewan Singh, originally from Ludhiana, was pinned down as the figure linking the Sikh revolutionaries with the *Jugantar* revolutionary cells that were active in Kidderpore and Howrah. While these cells had 'old' connections in Bengali Hindu middle-class circles, the participation of Dewan Singh and the Sikh revolutionaries in their activities was recognized as a new development.

Dewan Singh, 'a fluent Bengali speaker', was singled out for his 'close terms of friendship' with Bengali revolutionaries and for being 'deeply . . . concerned in the plotting of the Revolutionary Party of Bengal'. Enquiries made in Punjab as to his background revealed he had been 'a man of anti-British aspirations'. He was criminalized in the dossiers of 1916 as a rootless wanderer of loose morals, whose seditious tendencies were not rooted in any political conviction or ideological belief but in a deviant nature expressed early in life for he had worked as a male child prostitute: '. . . a "pukka budmas" [seasoned evil-doer] and not an active revolutionist. Dewan Singh started life – he is now about 50 years old – as what is euphemistically known as a "bazar dancing boy".'[51] Elsewhere, he was described in the following terms: 'In his boyhood he joined the "Jalsa" and danced with them and sold his land and [the] proceeds he squandered in drinking and illegal connection with women. He left his village some 20 years ago and led a wandering life.'[52]

Dewan Singh had been living in Bengal for sixteen years. By his own admission, he had worked as a 'semi-permanent' ticket inspector in the railways. He tendered his resignation 'because he refused to arrest

Old house at Manoharpukur Road, Bhabanipur

respectable people' for trespasses. He had also 'quarrelled with his superiors'. He was suspected of having direct connections with the *Komagata Maru* fugitives – suspicions that were strengthened when his nephew, Sher Singh, was arrested in possession of Ghadar leaflets, supposedly hidden in the ship and deposited at the Howrah Gurudwara with his uncle.[53] Sher Singh, a chauffeur, had previously served in 'a cavalry regiment', and was identified as 'a man of anti-British tendencies and suspected of propagating seditious literature and dealing with such matters'. He had resigned from the colonial army in 1911 and found work as the 'driver of a private motor car belonging to one Mr. Blackburn of Dum Dum and 2 Fairlie Place'. Dewan Singh's son, Jaswant Singh, lived in Bhawanipore and worked as a taxi driver. However, no connection could be established between him and the revolutionary underground.

Dewan Singh's former colleague, Sardara Singh from Ludhiana, had travelled to East Asia in 1913 after having worked as a Granthi at Howrah Gurudwara for some time. He was officially regarded as 'by far the most important leader', and featured in 'the Ghadar Directory' prepared to list and curb significant activists. His voyage was traced to European treaty ports in China, Shanghai and Hong Kong as well as Burma. On 30 March 1914, before leaving for Mandalay, he had written from Hong Kong to his friend Pertab Singh, a tailor in Howrah:

> In case you get any telegram from Vancouver concerning Guru Nanak Steamer (i.e. Komagata Maru. . .) you must send its reply without fail as upon this steamer the question of our national honour depends. Whatever the treatment will be accorded to this steamer, you must understand it would share our country's honour.[54]

He was suspected of being in Bengal during the arrival of the *Komagata Maru*. Pertab Singh of Patiala, a 'permanent resident' of Howrah for '8 or 9 years', acted as 'a Post Office' for other Sikhs and his house was 'a rendezvous for Sikh undesirables'. A friend of Dewan Singh, he was familiar with Kidderpore in a professional capacity since the area had registered a concentrated growth of tailoring as a vast, unorganized sector of labour. He had handed over all his 'poor savings' and wife's jewels to Teja Singh, a Sikh activist he had met while in Shanghai and accompanied to Hong Kong. The police regarded his 'recalcitrant', 'child-like' ignorance of all intrigues to be a 'tissue of lies'. Bharpur Singh of Ludhiana, the Granthi of Howrah Gurudwara in 1916, was perceived 'as equally undesirable as his predecessors'. The Punjab police had reported he was 'the right hand man of Randhir Singh of the Lahore Second Conspiracy Case, and that many of his friends have been sentenced to transportation for life in that case'.[55] Attar Singh, another friend of Dewan Singh, reportedly shared the same political outlook. A *durwan* (guard) at one Dulachand's *bagicha* (garden), he had reportedly served '6 months rigorous imprisonment and Rs. 100 fine' in Punjab for gender violence before landing in Bengal. Kartar Singh of Ludhiana, previously employed by Andrew Yule, was 'a young man (aged between 18 and 20 years)'. He was also regarded as 'a very undesirable person and a quite likely recruit to the ranks of the Ghadr Party'. Many Sikhs passing through Calcutta stopped at his place and this, along with his 'anti-British' position, made him a suspect. Ratan Singh and Babu Singh, taxi drivers with connections in Bhawanipore, were also members of the network. However, the 'exceedingly dangerous' figure among them was Chait Singh, a 'typical "Ghadr" man' in his early thirties. Possibly Dewan Singh's closest associate, he spoke English and Bengali, and had resided in Calcutta for four or five years. A former soldier, he was labelled as 'fanatical and full of grievances' against the British empire, having served 'in the 15th Sikhs' at Ferozepur for nine years and dismissed over 'a quarrel'.[56]

Action

During 1914–15, the presence of Sikh revolutionaries within the anti-colonial underground was noticed for the first time. They connected with bhadralok (Hindu upper-caste), middle-class youth active in *Jugantar* cells. The bhadralok revolutionaries did not harbour the same level of disdain or suspicion which they directed at pan-Islamist activists; the Sikh revolutionaries inspired by the Ghadar Movement were accommodated by them within the greater Hindu fraternity. Kidderpore and Bhawanipore became the territorial bases of combined action within Calcutta. The dock area was considered a congenial working environment; the revolutionaries could easily procure arms through local denizens of the underworld. The congested conditions, with 'extremely narrow' lanes through which 'hardly two people could pass abreast', facilitated anonymity.[57]

Attempting to organize an uprising among the troops was one of the foremost strategies that was adopted. Sher Singh was arrested in possession of Ghadar literature in 1914; he was allegedly showing them to soldiers on their way to Bombay for trans-shipment overseas.[58] Dewan Singh was also accused of attempting to spread rebellion in the ranks of colonial troops. A Drum Major of the 16th Rajputs stationed at Fort William reported to the authorities that Chait Singh and another Sikh met him for a drink near Kidderpore Bridge, where the 'general plan' of an uprising with the assistance of soldiers was discussed. He also met some 'babus' (Bengali bhadralok gentlemen) on 5 August 1915 at a rented house in Durga Das Lane, Kidderpore, where he learnt that Bengali revolutionaries had received help from Sikh taxi drivers, namely, Chait Singh and his close friend Babu Singh.[59] The other strategy was to procure guns and money through 'revolutionary dacoities'. Though discernible from the second half of the first decade of the twentieth century, this mode of action gained momentum during 1914–15 with the outbreak of the First World War. The revolutionaries took advantage of the Sikh presence among service-sector workers and the increase in the volume of motor vehicles in the streets of the city. With the help of Sikh drivers turned rebels, several taxi-cab robberies were committed.

Narendranath Bhattacharya, later famous as M.N. Roy, chalked out one of the first 'motor dacoities' in the Calcutta suburb of Garden Reach. Motor traffic, leading to numerous accidents and causing panic among the public, was on the rise in the city from 1914. The automobile was regarded by pedestrians as a dangerous novelty, a harbinger of calamity and death: thirty-two people were killed by motor vehicles in 1914 and twenty-eight in 1915; 175 chauffeurs were successfully prosecuted, and fines collected from each (Rs 15 on an average) for rash and negligent driving. The police found this to be a quick, lucrative way of capitalizing on lack of road safety. At the end of 1915, 608 motor cars and 147 motorcycles plied on the roads as newly registered vehicles. The actual number of automobiles with registration certificates came to 4,782. Large, medium and small businesses thrived in the taxi-trade: 196 companies carried on taxi-cab business, the largest company owning 106 cars. One of the smartest fleets was owned by the Indian Motor Taxi Cab Company, employers of Chait Singh and Ratan Singh. Eleven companies owned more than three and less than ten cars; the rest owned less than three cars.[60]

The life of a migrant Punjabi Sikh taxi driver resembled the patterns set by other male migrant workers in a city filled with men from a rural background. The journey involved arrival in the city, settling within a social support network composed of others from the same village, district or province, and entering the world of labour. Sometimes they followed the directions of older siblings, relatives and neighbours, staying with and relying on them to find their way in the city. For Punjabi Sikhs in the motor trade, the character of their livelihood dictated learning to drive and applying for a private license. Some made the transition from being a driver to becoming a trainer. Babu Singh of Ludhiana described these steps in his statement to the police, briefly mentioning the process of learning 'gari work' (automobile driving) from Labh Singh, a trainer, when he arrived in Calcutta from Punjab in 1912.[61]

Taking advantage of the ongoing transport revolution, Narendranath and his *Jugantar* friends hiding in Kidderpore at the time successfully carried out a novel robbery in broad daylight. On 12 February 1915, at 2 p.m., when three employees of the British Managing Agency house, Bird & Co., were delivering Rs 18,000 in a horse-drawn carriage to a factory, they were stopped in Garden Reach by four armed Bengalis in a taxi. They were made to hand over the cash at gunpoint; then the dacoits speedily left the scene, throwing the driver out of the car. The Sikh driver, Ratan Singh, turned out to be an accomplice and was arrested. The police were initially surprised that he had not turned up to identify suspects and thought that 'there can be little doubt that he is in a state of abject terror and has probably run away'. Though the revolutionaries had absconded, they were later rounded up from Calcutta.

On 17 November 1915, six armed Bengali youth robbed the shop of L.M. Rakhit at 80/1 Cornwallis Street. Just before the shop was closing in the evening, they suddenly arrived in a motor car, threatened the proprietor and his employees with revolvers, and made off with notes and cash being counted on the floor. Though four arrests were made by the police, no one present was willing to identify any of the suspects and the men were discharged. Chait Singh was later recognized by the police as the driver of the cab used by the 'dacoits'. On 2 December 1915, Chait Singh helped the Bengali revolutionaries rob a pawnbroker's shop on a central and busy thoroughfare of Calcutta. At about 7.15 p.m., five armed Bengali young men travelling in a stylish red torpedo-shaped motor car, the type of vehicle

66 Corporation Street

used by the Indian Motor Taxi Cab Company, looted the shop of Fakir Chand Dutta at 66, Corporation Street. Around Rs 20,000 to Rs 25,000 worth of jewellery, 'consisting entirely of gold and silver ornaments', were taken away. Though this robbery was witnessed by a number of people, and it was stated immediately afterwards that the driver appeared to be a Punjabi, no one provided 'any clue as to the direction taken by the culprits who left in the car in which they had arrived'. Those arrested were paraded before eyewitnesses who refused to recognize them. Chait Singh was among the suspects released on bail.[62]

Repression

The spate of hold-ups with the aid of automobiles worried the authorities. To prevent them, alarms and barriers in 'suitable areas' and 'patrols' by armed police motor cars were introduced for the first time. The world inhabited by taxi drivers became precarious as police harassment mounted and new regulations were introduced. Implementation of new motor-car rules was approved by the government on 1 April 1915. The principal changes involved imposition of fees for renewing driving licenses and re-registration of taxi-cabs. A 'prescribed uniform' for all taxi drivers was made mandatory and generated resistance. All chauffeurs were to be photographed. The new rules were enforced from 1 November. A section of the taxi drivers struck work for a few days in protest but their opposition was 'speedily overcome'.[63] The government adopted a draconian approach towards the strikers, arresting them and intimidating a large section of the drivers to return to work without any promise of modifying the rules they had objected to.[64] Taxi drivers were also frequently fined on the charge of 'rash driving'. In December 1915, a Bengali driver-owner was fined Rs 50 and his license was cancelled when he avoided collision with a Brougham belonging to one Colonel Deare and applied all the brakes to prevent the car from mounting the pavement. A Sikh driver was prosecuted for driving without a tail light and refusing to obey the sergeant who ordered him to stop. He claimed that he had been carrying a raja who did not want him to stop, being apprehensive that the sergeant would 'have a peep' at his queen's face. This defence generated much laughter in court, and he was asked to produce a letter from his elusive passenger.[65] A social concern for roads free of accidents was used to legitimize government control over workers engaged in the motor trade.[66] This was followed by tracking down and incarcerating Sikh members of the revolutionary underground. In 1916, a general crackdown on pan-Islamist and bhadralok revolutionaries was unleashed by the colonial state. The Ghadar sympathizers working with them also fell into the net of repression.

Colonial surveillance became alert to the networks at Kidderpore and Bhawanipore, and their links with the Howrah Gurudwara in 1916. Suddenly, a Sikh collective comprising of a chauffeur to a Bengali doctor, a goods-shed *durwan* (guard), a coolie and several taxi drivers were perceived as a threat to the state, and came under investigation for their association with Dewan Singh and Ratan Singh. For instance, Mela Singh, an 'uneducated coolie', was interrogated and briefly suspected of being 'Myli hi, Sikh chair merchant, New Market, Calcutta', who was to receive revolvers through a Chinese intermediary entrusted with the task by revolutionaries in Shanghai. The 'points of enquiry' were clearly outlined:

> The connection of the Sikh taxi-cab drivers in Calcutta with the Bengal Revolutionary Party seems to be by far the most important and immediate subject for investigation. It is not merely the occasional use of Sikh taxi-cab drivers for political *dakaities* that is disturbing but the likelihood of organized use being made on a bigger scale of the Sikh drivers, should any big disturbance break out in Calcutta. From what one hears there seems little doubt but that many drivers speak Bengali and are on close terms of intimacy with members of the Revolutionary Party.[67]

As a preventive measure, a permanent office of a policeman 'who understands Sikhs' was deemed 'necessary' in Calcutta. This was an echo and a by-product of the colonial strategy to gather intelligence on stereotype and control potential subversives. Effective enquiries required policemen with 'a good knowledge of the Sikhs permanently residing in Calcutta, and those places where visitors most commonly put up'. It was felt that surveillance in Calcutta had a long-term significance for countering the activities of the Ghadar Party in the Punjab. Since the city received many Sikhs travelling between India, Burma and the Far East, serving as 'a convenient place for the exchange of information by members of the Revolutionary Party', it was a seditious contact zone. A staff of enquiry consisting of Punjabis was also suggested in March 1916. It was felt that Inspector Bhag Singh should be assisted by 'two good Head Constables, and his work should not be solely confined to Calcutta' since Howrah and Calcutta were 'inseparable owing to the permanent importance of the Howrah Gurudwara'. When the Punjab CID refused to spare any trained officer, Inspector Bhag Singh suggested recruiting Sher Singh and Tara Singh, constables from Punjab, who could be deployed to spy on taxi drivers of Calcutta by living among them and 'learn[ing] their secrets'. This was considered a 'sound' idea: 'if they prove efficient officers the money will be well spent'.[68]

The Howrah Gurudwara committee, its Granthis, Dewan Singh in particular and his associates were suspected of 'sedition'. In January 1916, Dewan Singh was arrested. Inspector Bhag Singh, deputed from Punjab, became 'friendly' with him to find out more about his connections, though he refused to admit his 'guilt'. Ratan Singh and Chait Singh were also arrested.[69] During the hearing of the Garden Reach Taxi Dacoity Case at Alipore Court in 1915, Ratan Singh claimed that his taxi had been hired from Howrah Railway Station by some Bengali gentlemen ('babus'), and he had been ordered to drive through Harrison Road, Chitpur Road and Grey Street to a place where 'cinematograph pictures' were exhibited. Some of the occupants got off near the cinema and secured a supply of food from a confectioner's shop. Ratan Singh then drove them through Kidderpore to Sonai Bazar, where three persons sitting by the roadside joined them. He was then ordered to go to the juncture of Garden Reach Road and Circular Garden Reach Road, and instructed to wait there for twenty minutes. A

hackney carriage appeared and was stopped by some of the babus, who took about half an hour to transfer the money bags. When he tried to prevent them from driving away with the loot, he was thrown out of the car. He identified Patit Paban Ghosh, a revolutionary, as one of the babus.[70] Ratan Singh, Babu Singh and Bharat Sao, a Jat jeweller from Kidderpore, succumbed to police pressure and revealed incriminating details about the others. The police first isolated Ratan Singh and Babu Singh from the other prisoners, especially Chait Singh, with whom they shared a close bonding. The interrogators were instructed to grill

Babu Singh (Courtesy West Bengal State Archives)

them with utmost strictness. In Ratan Singh's case third-degree methods may have been applied, since he reportedly displayed signs of insanity; after his revelations the police decided to go easy on him, describing him as a man of little importance who was losing his 'reason' in prison, and who had been waylaid by Dewan Singh and unwittingly inducted into the revolutionary underground.[71]

By becoming a witness for the prosecution, Babu Singh, Chait Singh's 'intimate' friend, provided information and evidence on the link between Chait Singh and the *Jugantar* revolutionaries. As a reward, the charges against him were dropped.[72] Bharat Sao revealed that Bhagwan Das's jewellery shop where he worked, at Watgunge, Kidderpore, was the meeting point for Bengali revolutionaries and the Sikhs, and he was in their confidence along with his employer Bhagwan Das and his fellow employee Nanda Lal Shah, a middle-aged Arya Samajist. According to Bharat Sao, one of the revolutionaries who regularly visited the shop premise was Asutosh Ghosh, a Kidderpore resident from birth. He was a schoolteacher in his late thirties who worked at the Mitra Institution in Bhawanipore. Asutosh read the newspapers to which Bhagwan Das subscribed, and discussed war news with them from 1914. After the *Komagata Maru* passengers landed and were confronted by the authorities at Budge Budge, he and other bhadralok visitors took great interest in the incident, and 'persuaded' Bharat Sao to establish contact between them and Sikh bodies such as Bara Sikh Sangat and Howrah Khalsa Dewan. Asutosh was assisted in his efforts by a circle of young bhadraloks living in Kidderpore. He worked closely with Durga Charan Bose, also in his late thirties and a life-long Kidderpore resident, who taught at South Suburban School and was a partner in the coal business managed from their family home by his two brothers. Bholanath Banerjee, an unemployed youth from Kidderpore in his late twenties with no 'visible anarchist past', previously engaged in odd jobs at the docks and supported by his father, was accused of being involved. Also accused were Nut Behari Haldar or 'Gebu' from Kidderpore, and Narendranath Chatterjee, a comparatively new resident of the area. These neighbourhood bhadralok militants were soon joined by Dewan Singh, Chait Singh and Ratan Singh. Bharat Sao reported hearing 'scraps' of conversation between Ratan Singh and Asutosh on the former being thrown out of a car without coming to any real harm, and of suspicious cash transactions. He described Asutosh and Durga Charan as the 'chief conspirators', implying that they congregated at the shop to melt looted jewellery and exchange ill-gotten notes and money. During the identification proceedings at Alipore Jail, he 'at once' recognized Chait Singh 'and exhibited the signs of the greatest terror at the sight of him'.[73]

Chait Singh first came to the notice of the police during the investigation into the Corporation Street robbery in December 1915. When he was found with his car at Bhawanipore and questioned regarding his movements that very evening, he stated that he had been waiting there for over an hour. The statement was read as 'false' since the Deputy Commissioner who interrogated him 'on examining the car found the engine still quite hot'. The manager of the Indian Motor Taxi Cab company claimed that he saw a Bengali in Chait Singh's car in front of the Grand Hotel in Chowringhee at 6.30 p.m., about half an hour before the robbery in Corporation Street was executed. Chait Singh claimed he had taken the Bengali passenger to the Columbia Rink, and that another taxi driver, Genda Singh, had witnessed this. But Genda Singh denied seeing them. The police thought Chait Singh's claim of picking up a passenger for such a short walking distance was 'extremely improbable because from the Grand Hotel to the rink across the maidan is only 150 to 200 yards whereas by road it would be more than double the distance'.[74] The manager also stated that the Bengali in the car was covered in a green *alwan* (warm shawl) and this matched the police's claim of possessing 'evidence that one of the *dakaits* was wearing a green *alwan*'.[75]

Chait Singh's bail was arranged by the *Jugantar* revolutionaries he worked with. To celebrate his release, they participated in two elaborate 'feasts' at Bhawanipore, where sheep were slaughtered to cook curry and liquor was consumed. These convivial gatherings, where Sikh chauffeurs and Bengali babus rubbed shoulders, indicated the forging of an anti-colonial alliance among young men that temporarily dissolved class, caste, linguistic and regional barriers. The celebration was short-lived. Chait Singh was arrested for a second time alongside his *Jugantar* friends, and sentenced to indefinite imprisonment under wartime repressive measures. He had developed a following among fellow cab drivers who initially tried to cover his tracks.[76] In the end, the police secured sufficient information on his involvement in the revolutionary 'outrages'. They learnt that 'Tiger' Jatin Mukherjee, chief leader of *Jugantar*, who was killed by the authorities at Balasore in 1915, was supplied a motorcycle in Calcutta whenever he needed one with Chait Singh's help, by his friend Bhagat Ram. They also established Chait Singh's connections with Ratan Singh and their joint participation in 'taxi-cab dacoities'. Bharat Sao reported that the two were very close and that they had once visited Bhagwan Das's shop in connection with a quarrel they had with a Brahman over a woman, which resulted in a court case. The police identified Chait Singh as the driver in 'Khaki uniform' of the red 'A' class taxi (number A67) belonging to the Indian Motor Taxi Cab company; the automobile was employed in November–December 1915 during the heists at Cornwallis Street and Corporation Street. A 'reliable' source in Calcutta reported after his arrest:

> . . . one of the leaders of the revolutionary party had mentioned the fact that the police recently arrested two of their most trusted and daring drivers and that no information as to their present whereabouts could be obtained. This remark was evidently made in connection with the arrest and confinement in jail of Chet Singh and Rattan Singh.[77]

Wartime security laws such as the Defence of India Act (1915) or older provisions such as Regulation III of 1818 applied to Dewan Singh and Chait Singh ensured long-term, indefinite incarceration, supplemented with deportation to Punjab and confinement in 'village domiciles'. These measures suppressed the Sikh revolutionary network in and around Calcutta. It was noted that 'although this enquiry has not been productive of much information, it has . . . had a good result in showing the Sikhs in Calcutta that the police have their eye on them. Since the enquiry started, the taxi-cab drivers have been well aware of it.'[78] Once again, by treating the taxi drivers as potential criminals, colonial law and policing demonstrated their entwined roles as instruments of labour control.

Bharpur Singh, Attar Singh and Kartar Singh were recommended for removal and internment in their villages in Punjab by the police. Application of the Defence of India Act was suggested for Pertab Singh due to his reluctance to reveal what he knew. Sardara Singh, who had returned, accompanied by Harkaur, a woman he had met while working as a contractor in Burma for four to six years, was arrested in Punjab during 1915, kept in the lock-up and ultimately ordered to remain confined to his village.[79] As for Dewan Singh and Chait Singh, their convictions were not weakened by imprisonment. In contrast to official accounts where they were criminalized, respectively, as a 'dreg of society' and a ferocious 'fanatic', Bhupendra Kumar Datta, a Bengali revolutionary belonging to *Jugantar* who shared the jail space with them, offered completely different images of the two rebels. Datta described Dewan Singh as a kind and courageous veteran warrior who made new political prisoners feel at home in the prison environment; he treated Datta like a son when they first met. Dewan Singh was apparently 'incensed' when younger revolutionaries contemplated going on hunger strike to protest prisoners' abuse but were in favour of excluding older political inmates. When he and other elderly prisoners insisted on fasting, the strategy of boycotting food was given up by the youth brigade. Unlike the British officials, who saw him as a secretive figure exuding an aura of quiet menace, Datta saw Chait Singh as a 'tall man' with a 'heart-felt, open' smile who sang 'bhajans' (spiritual songs) and combed his long hair while sitting in the prison yard.[80] In early 1918, Chait Singh was transferred to Lahore.[81]

Inter-provincial models of repression proved useful in dealing with Sikh and other revolutionaries in Bengal who had forged bonds of inter-provincial solidarity. A draconian formula of suppressing wartime opposition enforced on a wide scale in Punjab was eventually adopted to curb the rebels in Bengal. A high-ranking colonial policeman later claimed that the sharp reduction of revolutionary activity was made possible by enforcing the special powers of censorship, search and arrests under the Defence of India Act, an emergency legislation pressed for by the Punjab government under the governorship of Michael O'Dwyer. This helped extend police powers to a degree that was not possible under 'ordinary' colonial laws of repression, such as the Criminal Procedure Code and the Indian Evidence Act. After the assassination of Basanta Chatterjee, Deputy Superintendent of Police, by revolutionaries in Calcutta (June 1916), the Bengal authorities turned to the 'special powers' that had proved to be 'effective' in Punjab.[82]

Conclusion

While the local press dissected the character of government action regarding the *Komagata Maru*, a relationship was established between bhadralok revolutionaries and Sikh workers in wartime Calcutta and its surroundings. Unlike the public sphere of print, the microworlds of secret action were not subject to legal and other political constraints placed by the government. The revolutionary underground subordinated the identity of the Sikh activists as workers to that of nationhood, while depending on the labour they performed in the urban milieu. The Sikh activists, in turn, found an organized channel of subverting British authority through the revolutionary network. So far, their relationship with Calcutta and its suburbs had been confined by the entwined conditions of migration and livelihood. The nationalist revolutionary milieu connected them for the first time with planned political action. The colonial authorities undermined their convictions, often portraying them as instruments of bhadralok revolutionary intrigue, as fanatical conspirators with a tendency to 'quarrel' by making troublesome disruptions wherever they went, and as men of 'loose' morals, their political criminality being laced with alcoholic and sexual deviations. The police were satisfied that the arrests and searches undertaken in 1916 would serve as a stern warning to those who had the potential to join revolutionary activities in future, and suitably intimidate the migrant workers from Punjab in Calcutta, Howrah and the suburbs, permanently deterring them from engaging in movements opposing the state. This was not to be. In the upsurge against capitalism and colonialism in the years following the First World War, a section of Punjabi Sikh workers, while turning leftward, echoed the legacy of Ghadar and consciously focused on the memory of the *Komagata Maru*, which had symbolically propelled the migrants towards participation in local politics.

NOTES AND REFERENCES

[1] Sumit Sarkar, *Modern India 1885–1947*, Delhi, 1983, pp. 147–48.
[2] *Report on Native Papers in Bengal 1914.*
[3] Ibid.
[4] Ibid.
[5] Ibid.
[6] Ibid.
[7] *Report on Indian Owned English Newspapers in Bengal 1914.*
[8] *Capital,* 9 July 1914.
[9] Ibid.
[10] *Report on Indian Owned English Newspapers in Bengal 1914.*
[11] *Report on Native Papers in Bengal 1914.*
[12] Ibid.
[13] Ibid.
[14] Ibid.
[15] *Weekly Reports of Intelligence Branch, Bengal Police 1915.*
[16] *Indian Owned English Newspapers in Bengal 1914.*
[17] Ibid.
[18] Ibid.
[19] *Report on Native Papers in Bengal 1914.*
[20] *Report on Indian Owned English Newspapers in English 1914.*
[21] *Report on Native Papers in Bengal 1914.*
[22] Ibid.
[23] Home (Political) WBSA 322/1914 (1–31).

[24] *Weekly Reports of Intelligence Branch, Bengal Police 1914.*
[25] 'The Ditcher's Diary', *Capital*, 4 November 1914.
[26] Nalini Kishore Guha, *Banglay Biplabbad*, Calcutta, reprint, 2012, p. 151.
[27] Home (Political) WBSA 322/1914 (1–31).
[28] Ibid.
[29] *Weekly Reports of Intelligence Branch, Bengal Police 1920.*
[30] Home (Political) WBSA 95/1919.
[31] *Weekly Reports of Intelligence Branch, Bengal Police 1914.*
[32] *Report on Indian Owned English Newspapers in Bengal 1914.*
[33] Ibid.
[34] *Report on Indian Owned English Newspapers in Bengal 1914.*
[35] Ibid.
[36] *Report on Native Papers in Bengal 1914.*
[37] *The Statesman*, October–December 1914.
[38] *Report on Native Papers in Bengal 1914.*
[39] Ibid.
[40] Ibid.
[41] Ibid.
[42] Ibid.
[43] Ibid.
[44] Ibid.
[45] *Report on Native Papers in Bengal 1915.*
[46] *Weekly Reports of Intelligence Branch, Bengal Police 1915.*
[47] *Sandesh*, Boisakh 1322 (April–May 1915), pp. 28–29.
[48] Eva Willis, 'Indians at War', *Modern Review*, July 1916, pp. 736–40. Edited by Ramananda Chattopadhyay, this English periodical was the sister publication of *Prabashi.*
[49] *Weekly Reports of Intelligence Branch, Bengal Police 1915.*
[50] For a historical treatment, see Himadri Banerjee, 'The Other Sikhs: Punjabi-Sikhs of Kolkata', *Studies in History*, 28 (2), 2012.
[51] Intelligence Branch of Bengal Police (IB) 454/1916 (13/16).
[52] Ibid.
[53] IB of Bengal Police 689/1919.
[54] IB of Bengal Police 454/1916 (13/16).
[55] Ibid.
[56] Ibid.
[57] IB 307/1915. IB 398/1916.
[58] IB 454/1916 (13/16).
[59] IB 689/1919.
[60] *Annual Report on the Police Administration of the Town of Calcutta and its Suburbs for the year 1915.* IB 664/1916 (50/16).
[61] IB 664/1916 (50/16).
[62] IB 454/1916 (13/16). IB 664/1916 (50/16). IB 689/19. *Annual Report on the*

Police Administration of the Town of Calcutta and its Suburbs for the year 1915. Weekly Reports of Intelligence Branch, Bengal Police 1915.

[63] *Annual Report on the Police Administration of the Town of Calcutta and its Suburbs for the year 1915.*

[64] *The Statesman*, 4 November 1915.

[65] *The Statesman*, 11 December 1915.

[66] *Report on Native Papers in Bengal 1914. Annual Report on the Police Administration of the Town of Calcutta and its Suburbs for the year 1915. Report of the Committee on Industrial Unrest in Bengal 1921.* According to the report on post-war industrial upsurge, 150 drivers of the Indian Motor Taxi Cab Company were on strike during 12–14 December 1920.

[67] IB 454/1916 (13/16).

[68] IB 664/1916 (50/16). IB 454/1916 (13/16).

[69] IB 454/1916 (13/16).

[70] *The Statesman*, 3 July 1915.

[71] IB 454/1916 (13/16).

[72] IB 664/1916 (50/16).

[73] IB 689/1919.

[74] Ibid.

[75] Ibid.

[76] IB 664/1916 (50/16). *Weekly Reports of Intelligence Branch, Bengal Police 1915.*

[77] IB 689/1919.

[78] IB 454/1916 (13/16).

[79] Ibid.

[80] Bhupendra Kumar Datta, *Biplaber Padachinha* (Footsteps of Revolution), Calcutta, 1999, pp. 35, 42.

[81] IB CID Index 2.

[82] J.C. Curry, *The Indian Police*, London, 1932, pp. 293–94.

CHAPTER FOUR

The Long Memory

The horizon of the post-war political landscape in Calcutta and its surroundings was extended and altered by anti-colonial mass movements, labour activism and the emergence of the left. This was also the period when migrations from Punjab and the size of the Sikh labour force increased. The diasporic identity of the Sikh migrant workers converged with the wider labour movement. To the Sikh migrants who joined post-war strike waves and formed unions in the 1920s and early 1930s, an unofficial commemoration of the *Komagata Maru*'s voyage became inseparable from contemporary resistance to domination by colonial capital. They engaged with, worked upon and simultaneously moved beyond the boundaries of ethnolinguistic and religious identities and the social content of nationalism by focusing on a self-aware position based on organized class action. This understanding was linked with the lived experiences of migration and imperial exploitation, the components of identity that had come to the forefront during the voyage of the *Komagata Maru* and underlined the actions of Sikh revolutionaries in a wartime city. The earlier tendency, evident during 1914–15, to subordinate the identity of migrant workers to that of nationhood was transformed in the post-war context as livelihood issues took on the form of systematic protests in the city and beyond.

Post-War Upsurge

The Sikhs in Calcutta,[1] classified by colonial census makers as practitioners of one of the 'minor' religions, worked mostly as sepoys and traders during the first decade of the twentieth century. A marked growth of the Sikh population was registered during the inter-war period. The majority had migrated to the city since 1901.[2] In 1911, 980 Sikhs lived in Calcutta and its suburbs; they fell within the wider population of 1,/43 Punjabi emigrants and included 171 Sikh women. Most Sikhs were adult men of a working age, between 20 and 35 years.[3] Ten years later, the population of Sikhs rose to 1,485. While they continued to engage in business, the number of soldiers declined; instead, many came to be employed as taxi drivers. The drivers and owners of 'mechanically driven vehicles' and their families lived in Calcutta and Howrah; the Sikh chauffeurs were classified within them.[4] With the introduction of and increase in motor vehicles during the second decade of the century, the pattern of Sikh employment changed. Inside the Calcutta municipal area, the highest concentration of Sikhs was in Bhawanipore, where the ex-soldier turned taxi driver, Chait Singh, had joined a wartime revolutionary network. They were also to be found, probably employed as sepoys, in Fort William and the maidan. The rest were scattered across Jorasanko and Colootola in the north, Ballygunge and Tollygunge in the south and Garden Reach, the industrial suburb of Calcutta associated with shipping. Half of the male population was unable to read and write, illiteracy was very high among women, and the population consisted mostly of working men between the ages of 20 and 40 years.[5] By the early 1930s, 4,713 Sikhs were recorded as Calcutta residents, having replaced Jains as the principal group within 'minor' religious communities. Nearly half of the Sikh population lived in Bhawanipore, and three-quarters were distributed in this area and in the neighbourhoods of Ballygunge and Tollygunge.[6] The migrants adjusted to the city through networks built on common vocations, shared workspaces and living quarters, the congregations of faith. Within the religio-linguistic bond of the community, distinctions were present between the high and the low. This was evident in the police dossiers, where the officials repeatedly referred to the owners of substantial assets as sensible, 'educated', amenable to persuasions of the government and loyal, while the propertyless workers or those without significant capital assets were viewed as volatile, potential troublemakers and criminals.[7]

Labour upsurge of the late 1910s and the early 1920s found resonance among them; labour was incorporated by the ongoing Non-Cooperation and Khilafat Movements, the chief vehicles of popular anti-imperialism. The post-war mass upsurge was guided by the demands for India's self-government and the protection of the Ottoman Caliphate, the headquarters of Sunni Islam, from Anglo-French invasions. In this wider climate of Hindu–Muslim unity and populist militancy,[8] the echoes of Ghadar from the war years resurfaced and the protest mentality of the post-war years showed signs of spreading in the colonial army. In 1921, Santa Singh of Ludhiana, sepoy and driver of the 23rd Indian Mechanical Transport Company, was charged with spreading disaffection in the ranks. He had 'used words in favour of the Khilafat Committee and Non Co-operation, and was found guilty and sentenced to suffer rigorous imprisonment for two years.'[9] He had complained of poor wages, urged other soldiers to resign, promised better-paid work with the Khilafat Committee and advocated wearing of 'swadeshi or Gandhi cloth' in late October 1921. At his court martial held a month later, one *havildar*, two lance naiks and two sepoys of the same company testified against him and he claimed in defence that they were his enemies, having harboured personal hostility towards him. He served time in the Alipore Central Jail, a familiar destination of political prisoners in the city. In 1923, 'an officer reported that he seemed very discontented, and that he was met by several motor car drivers on his release'.[10] During the months that followed, he briefly returned to his village and received a taxi driver's license in Calcutta. He travelled to Rangoon to stay with his brother, a milkman, and his movements were watched. Finally, he again made his way back to Calcutta, finding employment at 4, Russell Street as a driver of a private car.[11] Others had tried to organize risings within the army during the war. Influenced by the post-war anti-imperialist mass movements, Santa Singh had encouraged mass resignation from colonial service, an altered strategy to weaken the empire. The transition from being a recalcitrant sepoy driver to a civilian transport worker, his journey from the army barracks to the Alipore Jail to Rangoon and his return to Calcutta, and the aim of sowing 'sedition' in the ranks of the army at a time of organized anti-colonial upheaval resonated with similar patterns and movements from the immediate and distant past. It was as if Chait Singh's and Dewan Singh's resistance to colonial authority had seeped through his actions in a changed political context in a new way. The accumulated experiences of rebel soldiers of the preceding century, of Pathan and Sikh soldiers who had been court-martialled or who had left the army, had filtered down across the decades; they had directly and indirectly touched the route he had taken.

The Sikh presence in the service sector as drivers explains their participation in the post-war world of strikes and union formation. The taxi-cab and the private cars plying in the streets had come to symbolize speedy transport and urban luxury. Those who drove these vehicles, in contrast, suffered from low pay and police repression. The intrusion of the mechanical vehicle in the 1910s had expanded the field of urban policing in Calcutta and turned drivers into rebels and protestors. During the strike wave of 1920–21, the protest mentality of industrial and service-sector workers found an organized outlet in a climate of material hardship; the taxi and professional motor-car drivers went on short-lived strikes in the city and displayed a militant tendency to step beyond the restraints imposed by the mostly middle-class labour leaders. One hundred and fifty drivers employed by the Indian Motor Taxi Cab Company, the wartime employers of Chait Singh and Ratan Singh, went on strike during 12–14 December 1920. They demanded a rise in their commission from 11 per cent to 15 per cent, smaller deduction for empty miles when cabs ran without passengers, and dismissal of oppressive supervisory staff. They alleged that the firm had not fulfilled its promise to raise their commission to 12.5 per cent; this was the term of settlement reached leading to an end of the strike.

This strike was followed by a longer strike. Held a month later, during 12–26 January 1921, it involved 3,000 taxi drivers and chauffeurs of private cars. As in 1915, this was a direct result of protracted differences with the police over new regulations. The rules interfered with the livelihoods of the workers by prohibiting the practice of carrying attendant-companions and imposing medical checks on drivers, which adversely affected those who were older. During September–October 1920, the association of taxi and private automobile drivers had opposed the new regulations being planned, and sent their objection in writing to the Police Commissioner of Calcutta. The Commissioner replied in detail, dismissing their misgivings. A situation of confrontation emerged whereby the workers tried to cling to the existing working conditions, opposing police interference and waging a war of attrition, while the police tried to change and control them and their work through a series of manoeuvres from above. On 2 January 1921, the association held a meeting at Town Hall. It was decided that a strike would begin on 26 January unless a fresh petition being sent to the Police Commissioner yielded a favourable reply by 25 January. On the night of 11 January, matters suddenly escalated when Issur Singh, a taxi driver, was arrested and hauled to a police station for 'continued disobedience of the traffic police officer' and refusal to show his license. Other drivers on the spot protested against his treatment and immediately went on strike. By 12 January, all taxi drivers of the city had stopped work. Though this was 'a breach of programme', the strike was endorsed by their association. On 16 January, a mass meeting of strikers at Wellesley Square under the auspices of the association spoke on the negative implications of the new regulations, particularly medical tests on existing drivers, making it practically impossible for many of them to earn a living. The strikers also appealed to the drivers of private cars to join the action. Consequently, on the next day, most drivers of private cars also participated in the strike.

In the face of widening protests, the Police Commissioner announced that he had recommended the appointment of a committee of enquiry to look into the rules. He promised that the police would allow attendants to accompany the drivers without attaching any condition, and accept the medical certificate of any doctor depending on the committee's report. He also agreed to receive a deputation of strikers in order to reach a negotiated settlement. On 18 January, the strikers reassembled at Wellesley Square. As the leaders briefed the drivers on the meeting with police authorities, they were frequently interrupted by shouts from the audience that they would not accept medical tests and would carry attendants who did not possess a license. They also demanded a withdrawal of the case against Issur Singh. On 20 January, the Commissioner agreed to drop medical examination of old drivers if the committee of enquiry agreed, and issued a communiqué announcing its formation. This conciliatory strategy was abruptly abandoned the next day when the government suspended all existing driving licenses of motor cars. The president of the association along with the owners of automobiles now began a negotiation with the Commissioner. Clearly on the back foot, the president agreed to drop the demand regarding Issur Singh's case on 22 January. On 24 January, the association and the owners accepted the Commissioners' proposals and the suspension order on driving licenses was lifted. The drivers returned to work on 25 January, having prematurely started and been pressured into ending their strike. The results of industrial actions demonstrated uneven gain for the workers engaged in this sector. While the stoppage of work directed against a specific concern in December 1920 by taxi drivers secured higher earnings, the cease-work by taxi and private car drivers in January 1921 failed to overturn new police regulations.[12]

The life of a taxi driver as a worker, mostly Sikhs from Punjab, was subject to continuous police interference. The police apparatus acted as a managerial force on behalf of the colonial authorities and business enterprises with the aim of replacing older drivers and vehicles as disposable labour and outdated means of service against a backdrop of rapid growth in productive forces, which benefited the owners rather than the workers; the aim was to control the workforce physically and impose curbs on used vehicles, the instruments of service production, which most drivers as workers did not own. Ageing drivers and automobiles became the chief targets of police authorities. The police attempted to legitimize the measures of control in the name of road safety and 'standardization' of taxi services. By 1918, the number of motor vehicles in Calcutta streets was over 5,000, including motorcycles; a 'regrettable rise in fatal accidents' was also noted. In the course of the 1920s, a series of government plans to control the taxi trade were implemented. In 1921, the number of taxi-cabs decreased owing to the imposition of new government rules and 'more frequent inspection', ostensibly aimed at 'a more efficient taxi-cab service'. The police hoped the numbers would decline further for the sake of an 'efficient standard of service' in the future, demonstrating reliance on a policy which would rid the workforce and hired cars of 'old' elements. They were also happy that they enjoyed the 'power delegated . . . to deal with drivers' licenses'. They were quick to note that the establishment of 'a separate traffic court with a stipendiary Magistrate as well as a bench of Honorary Magistrates has proved of great value in dealing with drivers'.[13] This coincided with the government's expectation that heavy motor vehicles would increase on the roads with the inauguration of a bus service by the Tram Company in the city, and the service would soon be extended to the suburbs.

In 1922, a depression hit the motor trade as the impact of the new regulations was felt more acutely, interfering with the service and the livelihood of the workers. The number of taxi-cabs decreased due to 'weeding out old unserviceable cars' and floating of new models, in keeping with revised rules. Fewer drivers were issued licenses as the new rules effectively cut down the number of professional drivers and the vehicles they had driven so far. The number of people injured and killed from collision with taxi-cabs kept rising between 1920 and 1922 despite these restrictions, confirming that the rules were not aimed at saving lives but for increasing control of the rulers over the profitable transport sector and the often recalcitrant drivers. By 1923, the rules had taken full effect. The depression in the motor trade was waning as new taxi models were imported by owners of taxi companies. There was a decrease in the number of people killed as well. By 1928, there was a huge increase in the trade and further regulations were imposed on cabs. Old taxi meters were 'thoroughly examined' and the police followed the same policy in relation to them as was evident in the case of drivers and cars a few years before: those found to be 'old' and 'defective' were replaced. New models, deemed luxurious and comfortable, were introduced in taxi fleets. It was noted that 'a favourable state of the motor market' led to an increase in the number of taxi-cabs. The new cabs registered in 1928 were of 'the latest six-cylinder type giving spacious passenger accommodation and greater riding comfort'.[14] Thirty-six saloon model taxi cars were registered. The police boasted that of the 1,356 cabs plying for hire in Calcutta, 952 or over 70 per cent had been on the road for less than three years. 'Special attention' was given to the garages of taxi-cabs. No cab was registered without garage accommodation. The number of vehicles allowed to 'stand on the street all night and suffer abnormal deterioration' was 'considerably reduced'.[15] This was accompanied by close supervision of training schools through regular inspection at working hours. Severe tests were imposed on driving license applicants and the topography test was imposed on all taxi drivers. These restrictions did not lead to immediate protests. The workers, in the absence of a surge in labour resistance, were forced to adapt to the changes, and may have seen a rise in earnings. The police thought that there had been an increase in the number of licenses of all kinds due to an increase in motor traffic and higher income for drivers as they were needed in a climate of sectoral expansion in their line of work.[16]

The Turn Leftwards

Work as a realm of intensified labour exploitation made way for an affinity towards political radicalism. From the second half of the 1920s, an identifiable left tendency emerged among the Sikh workers living in the city and the suburbs. In November 1927, during the birth anniversary celebration of Guru Nanak, a *diwan* (mass congregation) was held at the Bara Sikh Sangat on 172 Harrison Road. Gurdit Singh, who had shifted to Calcutta that year, delivered a 'fiery speech' before 600 men and women, citing 'indignities' inflicted on the Sikhs by the government. An 'objectionable' Punjabi leaflet in Gurumukhi script, printed at the Kavi Kutia Press of Bhawanipore, was circulated. Signed by Teja Singh Sorabha and Inder Singh Hoshiarpuri, it stood for a theology of self-liberation from below:

> The Guru was born to deliver the labourers from the oppressions of the rulers. The same oppressions are committed now as in those days. . . . Be united.

Listen to the commands of the Guru. Realize the ideal of the Guru. Unite as
the labourers have done all over the world and throw off the yoke of slavery.
Awake and arise. Break the fetters of slavery.

The handbill urged the Sikhs to subscribe to *The Kirti*, a labour journal
published by communists in Punjab. They were also asked to join the Bengal
Kirti Dal, located at 29, Russa Road, North Bhawanipore. It was to be a local
branch of the Kirti Kisan Party of Punjab, a counterpart of the Workers and
Peasants Party of Bengal (WPP); both were open organizations of the illegal
Communist Party of India (CPI). The police sensed a joint influence of
'Ghadar revolutionaries' and 'the Bolshevik flavour' behind this initiative.
A Bengal Kirti Dal Committee was established in December 1927. A 'Sikh
Agent' reported on a private meeting of the 'Kirti Dal Committee' held on
3 December 1927 at 29, Russa Road, at the residence of Mahendra Singh,
a bus owner and a member of the Gurudwara Prabandhak Committee,
Bengal. Among the office bearers elected to the executive committee were
Balwant Singh Granthi of the Ballygunge Gurudwara; Bhag Singh, a bus
driver; Genda Singh, a bus driver of the Tramways Company; Gurdayal
Singh Patiala, of 10, Justice Dwarka Nath Road, a medicine dealer;
Mahendra Singh, a bus driver and owner; and Sawadagar Singh of Kavi
Kutia Press. No programme of work had been planned, but the president
Teja Singh Sorabha (Safri) and secretary Inder Singh Hoshiarpuri, a motor-
car driver from 9, Alipore Road, were working on it.

The overwhelming working-class composition of the Bengal Kirti
Dal attracted government attention from its inception. The police hoped
the group would be ineffective. A letter from 14, Elysium Row by S.S.H.
Mills, Deputy Commissioner, Special Branch of Calcutta Police, to Cleary,
Personal Assistant to Director, Intelligence Bureau, Home Department,
New Delhi, with copies to the Deputy Inspector General, CID, Special
Branch, Lahore, Punjab and F.P. McKinty, Intelligence Branch, Bengal
Police, forwarded the Sikh agent's report. Mills observed:

> My own impression is that this Dal will come to an untimely end, unless it is
> supported with funds from outside. I am, however, endeavouring to keep in
> close touch with its activities. Teja Singh Safri, is, of course, well known, and
> I am endeavouring to ascertain the antecedents of Inder Singh Hoshiarpuri.

As expected, the Sikh agent reported on 18 December that a constitution,
deemed luxurious and comfortable with the following rules:

1. This party will be named the 'Kirti Dal, Bengal'.
2. There is no limit to the membership of this party.
3. Every member will be required to pay a monthly subscription of *annas* four only. Any one of any nationality may be a member of this Dal by paying *annas* four only per month.
4. This party will not take part in any religious quarrel. It will not interfere with any religious movement.
5. In order to unite the workers of Bengal, Bihar and Orissa, and Assam this Party will start branches in different places in those provinces.
6. The Head Office of this Party shall remain in Calcutta.
   . . .
8. This party will shortly carry on its propaganda by publishing a newspaper of its own.
9. This paper should contain well written articles to save the *kirti*s (workers) from the hands of the oppressors.
10. The labour conditions in different countries should be made known to the *kirtis* in Bengal, Bihar and Orissa and Assam.
11. The grievances of the *kirtis* should be brought to the notice of the Bengal and Indian Government. This party should try to ameliorate the conditions of the workers in the Provinces named above.

In April, a worried letter from CID, Lahore, reached Cogwill of IB in Calcutta:

> Information has been received that Calcutta is being made a centre of the Kirti Group, that the Bengal Kirti Dal is in close touch with Bengal revolutionaries on one side and with the Kirti group in the Punjab on the other side, and that messsages are being exchanged between Calcutta and Amritsar through special messengers. It is further reported that the organizers of the Kirti Movement are trying to set up a regular system of communication between Calcutta and the Punjab, as they are afraid of their correspondence being censored by Government if sent by post.
>
> . . . I am desired to pass on the above for your information. . . . The Intelligence Bureau, Simla, is also being informed.[17]

Soon, the CID was accused of trying to crush the nascent Kirti Dal through infiltration, harassment and persecution. Genda Singh, employed by the European-owned Calcutta Tramways Company, was threatened with dismissal unless he refused to resign from his post as the Kirti Dal's president. Consequently, Genda Singh had to give up his employment. *Akali*, a newspaper, reported on 25 August 1928:

> Since the organization of Kirti Dal in Bengal the CID of Calcutta appears to be bent upon and determined to crush it. Sometimes its agents try to get into it, and sometimes useless attempt is made to put pressure on the workers. Ultimately they took rest only after removing S. Gainda Singh, President of the Kirti Dal from Tramway Company's Service. It is stated that the company, on the strength of CID reports, ordered S. Gainda Singh, a patriot, that he should resign from the presidentship of the Kirti Dal, otherwise his service would be dispensed with. Hearing this Sardar Gainda Singh resigned his appointment.

Tight police control and surveillance on Sikh dissenters, practised from 1914 onwards, was never given up. The officials tended to close in on political activists through indirect routes of victimization and removal when legal means of prosecution were not at their disposal.

By early August, the connections between Bengal Kirti Dal and the WPP were being keenly followed. Sohan Singh Josh, a Ghadar revolutionary turned early communist from Amritsar, wrote to Muzaffar Ahmad, one of the early communist leaders from Bengal, requesting him to write for *Kirti*, which Muzaffar received and read regularly. Josh wanted Muzaffar to write an article 'giving your views' on the All India Workers and Peasants Party's constitution in the making, or 'some other article' by 15 August: 'You should do it positively as the articles of all the comrades are being published in the columns of the "Kirti" save and except that of yours.' He acknowledged receiving *Ganabani*, the mouthpiece of the Bengal WPP edited by Muzaffar Ahmad, and asked him to underline important sections in red, possibly for the purpose of translation, exchange and discussion. He promised to do the same when sending *Kirti*. The police instantly surmised: 'It is pretty clear from this that the "Kirti Dal" of Amritsar is getting in closer touch with the Workers' and Peasants' Party in Bengal.'[18] Meanwhile, gathering information on and stereotyping of leftist opponents continued. The Punjab police sent its views on Kirti Dal as a grouping of 'Sikh extremists' from Amritsar. Sohan Singh Josh was described as 'weak and ineffective', while Baba Bhag Singh Canadian, a Ghadar veteran, was projected as 'a drunkard and a womanizer'. The surveillance report from Punjab thought the organization was without prospects and could only become effective in the future if it became actively involved in agrarian issues, particularly the question of landownership.

In 1928, Bengal Kirti Dal's office was shifted to Gurdit Singh's house at 27/2, Ashutosh Mukherjee Road in Bhawanipore, from its previous location at 35/17, Padmapukur Road. Later that year, Sohan Singh Josh visited Gurdit Singh and other members of Kirti Dal. He had arrived in Calcutta and headed for the Bengal WPP office; local communist activists, including prominent figures such as Abdul Halim and Dharani Goswami escorted him. A Special Branch officer, watching the Bengal WPP office at 2/1, European Asylum Lane, reported on 5 September 1928:

> This morning at about 8 a.m. a Punjabi aged about 30/35 years, tall, having moustaches and beard, fair complexion, strong build wearing long coat (achkan), pyjama, nagra shoes and a pagri, came to the above place with a small bedding and a handbag in a 2nd class phaeton. This Punjabi was searching for Muzaffar Ahmed of 2/1, European Asylum Lane, of 'Ganavani' office, and his name was ascertained to be Sohan Singh. He was coming from the Punjab. The watchers were instructed to keep an eye over him.

The next day, Assistant Sub-Inspector Brojendra Kumar Roy Chowdhury of Special Branch reported on 'Suspect Sohan Singh who stopped at 2/1 European Asylum Lane':

> I was on secret watch duty over the above mentioned suspect who was temporarily residing at 2/1 European Asylum Lane. At about 7.30 a.m. the suspect accompanied by suspect Dharani Goswami came out and went on foot up to the junction of Lower Circular Road and Dharmatolla Street. Therefrom they both got into a Motor Bus and landed from it just in front of Jagoo Babu's Bazaar. Soon after he met a Punjabi there and the three were shadowed to the premises No. 23 Harish Mookherji Road. After waiting for about an hour there, they came out of that place and were then shadowed to 32 Asutosh Mookherji Road. Here they waited for about 20 minutes and then were shadowed to 35/17 Paddo Pukur Road. Here they waited for about 45 minutes after which they again got into the premises No. 32 Ashutosh Mookherji Road. I waited there till 1 p.m. but as they did not come out I left them there.
>
> Again was on the same duty. At about 5.45 p.m. two Punjabis came from outside and entered into 2/1 European Asylum Lane. At about 6.30 p.m. the suspect accompanied by the aforesaid Punjabis and suspect Halim came out. The two Punjabis were pointed out to Constable Chandan Singh by me. They all then hired a taxi No. T.655 at Circular Road and drove away. I could not

follow them by a taxi, which was not available at that time. The suspect had a bedding and a suit case with him. So I got into a Motor bus and went to Howrah Station. On my arrival there I found them all talking to one another in an inter class compartment of 1 Up Punjabi Mail. I requested one of the railway employees to have his ticket checked. The employee found him (the suspect) in possession of an inter class ticket No. 000007 from Calcutta to Amritsar. At about 7.45 p.m. suspect Halim bade him good-bye and the two Punjabis waited there till the train started.[19]

The 'suspects' mingling with the 'comrades' were a source of anxiety. Their trans-regional, transcontinental and internationalist connections were apparent when Special Branch noted that 100 copies of *India and the Next War* by Agnes Smedley were in possession of Muzaffar Ahmad: 'they were probably brought here during the last visit of Sohan Singh Josh of the Amritsar Kirti Dal'.[20] By October, 'several visits' had been 'exchanged' between Dharani Goswami of Bengal WPP and Prithi Singh of Bengal Kirti Dal, the focus being the activities of the latter group. Dharani had apparently advised the inclusion of Bengali members into the Dal, with the aim of popularizing it at the local level. The executive committee of the Dal, according to the police, was thereby 're-constructed' with Mohini Mohan Haldar as president, Genda Singh as vice president, Tincori Banerji as secretary, Inder Singh Hoshiarpuri and Prithi Singh as assistant secretaries, and Balwant Singh Granthi as treasurer.[21] Prithi Singh was later identified as a former apprentice in the French Motor Car Company at Bhawanipore, who had arrived in Calcutta at the end of 1926. He had read up to Middle English Standard, studied Civil Engineering, had served in Mesopotamia for three years during the war and returned after the armistice.[22] The Bengali office-bearers were expected to help enlist local members. Mohini Mohan Haldar was reported to be a homeopathic practitioner residing at 275, Kalighat Road, and a member of the South Calcutta Congress Committee. Tincori, a clerk of the Bengal Nagpur Railway's office at Garden Reach, was the assistant secretary of the Bengal Nagpur Railway labour union and lived at 6/1, Kali Lane. Both were acquaintances of Prithi Singh who had encouraged them to join the Dal. Balwant Singh was suspected of making arrangements 'to preach communistic and revolutionary principles among the rank and file of Sikhs' by bringing out a fortnightly newspaper called *Lal Jhanda*, the print organ of the Bengal Kirti Dal in Gurumukhi script, and guided by the principles of the Dal's headquarters in Amritsar.[23]

Combined Actions

The Kirti Dal established connections with communists as well as with those belonging to the Congress-affiliated labour movement. One of the leading activists they closely worked with in the late 1920s was Gurdit Singh. As a political prisoner in 1923, Gurdit Singh had petitioned the government and demanded that his personal property left on the *Komagata Maru* be returned. The Government of India, while admitting that sealed boxes belonging to him had indeed been sent on the special train to Ludhiana, refused to take any responsibility for misplacing them.[24] His relationship with the state remained antagonistic. He had become active in labour and community meetings soon after his arrival in Calcutta, attracting police attention.[25] His memoirs on the voyage of the *Komagata Maru*, sharply indicting the empire and colonial racism, were translated and printed from Calcutta in 1927.[26] In 1928, he also started civil proceedings against the government regarding the ship's journey and treatment of its passengers during 1914.[27]

Gurdit Singh's activities, along with the wider political developments in which Sikh workers and migrants were engaged, came to be watched and reported each week by police agents, once his vocal presence had been noted. He regularly addressed well-attended meetings of Punjabi Sikhs and other men and women. The police observers following his speeches at Sunday *diwans* in gurudwaras and public meetings repeatedly accused him of 'seizing opportunities' to attack the colonial regime. On 8 January 1928, 'intemperate speeches' were made by Pandit Murali Dhar of Kanpur and Gurdit Singh at a Sikh *diwan* held in the Ballygunge Gurudwara. Murali Dhar stated that being a resident of a part of the country where the Revolt of 1857 had broken out, he had 'declared himself free', and said that he 'would make India free at any cost' in 1925. If the Sikh soldiers had not fought against the mutineers, the 'red-faced men' would not have been able to rule India. The speaker appealed to the Sikhs to join in the cause of freedom as 'death was preferable to a life of shame'. He ended his speech with a reference to imperialist incursions into China, appealing to all Indians not to assist the British in any way against the Chinese people. Gurdit Singh endorsed his views. He thought that the Sikhs had committed a great sin by helping the English to suppress the Revolt. By referring to the victims of the uprising of 1857 to western interventions in China during the late 1920s, a trans-regional, transcontinental and internationalist appeal against imperialist powers was being launched in the meetings in which Gurdit participated.

Local issues, linked with everyday coercive practices of colonial administration, were also raised, and this annoyed the police. At a private meeting of twenty Sikh bus and taxi owners held at Gurdit Singh's Bhawanipore residence on 10 February, it was decided that a Sikh motor syndicate would be formed to check 'the alleged *zulum* of the Police'. The Khalsa Motor Syndicate emerged with Gurdit Singh as president of the owners' association. On 11 March, at a meeting in Ballygunge Gurudwara with the aim of popularizing the syndicate,

> Gurdit Singh, as usual, seized the opportunity of hurling invective at the police, whom he criticized as 'demons let loose' and 'parasites sucking the life-blood of the people'. The police, he alleged, went about in Calcutta sending up the poor Sikh drivers on petty charges, and allowing the more wealthy who were able to pay bribes to go scot-free.[28]

He was arrested on 16 March, to answer a charge of delivering a seditious speech at Mirzapur Park on 3 March. He was granted bail and ultimately acquitted by the Chief Presidency Magistrate.[29] He issued a Punjabi pamphlet in Gurumukhi script drawing attention to his continued persecution by the state 'to hamper him in the civil suit, in connection with the "Komagata Maru" case, which he has first instituted in the High Court'. The response in his support was immediate:

> As was expected, the arrest of Baba Gurdit Singh was the main subject of discussion at the Diwan held at Ballygunge on the 25th instant, and the speeches were noticeably more violent and bitter than usual. Bhag Singh, Assistant Secretary of the Kirti Dal, read a pamphlet, the theme of which was that it was now time for the Sikhs to draw the sword, as non-violence had been of no avail. All the speakers paid high tribute to the character and work of Gurdit Singh. Dharam Singh, concluding a speech eulogizing the virtues of Gurdit Singh, said that in the event of another war the Sikhs would 'beat the Government with shoes and make them clear out, bag and baggage'. Balwant Singh requested the Sikhs to muster strong at Bankshall Court on the 28th when the Baba would appear to stand his trial. . . . Gurdit Singh announced his intention of exposing the vagaries of the Government in the Court.[30]

At an Akali meeting on 1 April, in the presence of 400 Sikhs at 9 Bagmari Road, Gurdit Singh was honoured for standing up to the government:

The latter seized the opportunity of making an impassioned speech, wherein he alleged that he had been arrested because he was organizing and giving life to the Calcutta Sikh Community. He was charged, he said, with bringing into hatred and contempt Government established by law in India, the law being similar to the law of dacoits who would order their victims to open their safes on the point of the revolver. To him the whole of India was a jail.

Gurdit Singh allegedly proclaimed that he wished to inform 'the "fiend" Government that his bones would be too hard for them to crack'.[31] The time to limit tyranny was 'fast approaching' when people would resist with the sword. The police were annoyed to find that even the normally obedient Punjabi Sikh segments were sympathizing with him.

> As exemplifying the mentality of the educated Sikh community in Calcutta, it is interesting to note that although they have frequently expressed their displeasure at Gurdit Singh's extravagant political speeches in the Gurudwaras, yet no sooner is he arrested on a charge of sedition than he is the object of sympathy.

On 22 April, a *diwan*, with Balwant Singh presiding, was held at Ballygunge Gurudwara, at 105, Bakulbagan Road; it was attended by 350 men and 200 women. Thamman Singh proposed that if a war broke out in the future, Sikhs should refrain from helping the government; they would remain passive having been subjected to many indignities after having helped in the last war. Gurdit Singh agreed, and

> regretted that Sikhs, whose heads were dedicated to the service of the Gurus, should serve in the army for a pittance of Rs 15 a month and should slaughter human beings. What was worse still, they joined the C.I.D. and carried to the ears of the authorities stories against their own countrymen.[32]

He declared that British soldiers deserved no rewards for they served their king, but Indian soldiers deserved awards for killing their compatriots in the interest of the British Raj. He concluded that he could be 'sent to jail for saying these things, but he was not afraid as they were already confined in a bigger jail'.

These views matched some of the radical analyses on empire, colonial governance and repressive state apparatus stemming from the left, and worried the authorities. The police encouraged Raghubir Singh, projected as a moderate and a loyalist, to successfully expel Gurdit Singh from a position of influence in the owners' association. In June, it was observed with satisfaction that a split in the Bengal Khalsa Bus Syndicate was imminent, as moderates were refusing to accept the leadership of Gurdit Singh for his 'extreme political views'. Raghubir Singh, secretary of the association, had asked Gurdit to step down as president 'as early as possible'. After tendering his resignation, Gurdit sarcastically told the loyalist brigade that they will have to approach him again to guide them since the Police Commissioner would never help them. This was followed by a private conference of prominent Sikh leaders on 9 June, where it was decided that if the authorities failed to redress their grievances, they would take recourse to *satyagraha* (passive resistance) and ask Gurdit Singh to lead them. However, Gurdit could not regain his foothold within the syndicate, which opted for close collaboration with the police; this meant accepting government control and patronage at a time when the transport sector was expanding and yielding profits. Since the association was composed of owners, the police could easily outmanoeuvre Gurdit Singh. This was evident from a report on a Bus Syndicate meeting held on 20 July on the roof of its Bhawanipore office at 79, Padmapukur Road. Raghubir Singh expressed satisfaction over the Calcutta Police Commissioner's sympathetic attitude to their deputation. The meeting requested owners to make the drivers obey the orders of the traffic police. The police happily noted that the syndicate had 'cooperated with the police in dealing with taxi and bus traffic in the neighbourhood of Chowringhee, and the results so far have been very satisfactory'.[33]

Other speakers in Gurdit Singh's milieu, representing the Sikh community from below, joined and championed the communist-led left movement in Punjab, locally represented by the Bengal Kirti Dal. Gurdit Singh endorsed and participated in these efforts. At a *diwan* held at the Ballygunge Gurudwara on 15 January 1928, in the presence of about 500 Sikhs, Mahtab Singh and Mangal Singh exhorted the Sikhs to be ready to sacrifice their lives in the cause of their religion and country. The latter's appeal also held up Soviet Russia as an example to follow. The mélange of ethno-religious identity with nationalism and communist internationalism displayed the many influences shaping the activists and their audience. Explicit left appeals were also made. On 1 July, at a *diwan* held in Bakulbagan Gurudwara and presided over by Balwant Singh Granthi, around 260 persons, 60 of whom were women, gathered. 'The object of the *diwan* was to advocate the necessity for joining the Kirti Dal. Speeches were made by Bhag Singh, Assistant Secretary of the Dal, and Prithi Singh, a member. The speeches were anti-Government in tone, but there was nothing unusual or alarming about them.' Prithi Singh also printed and circulated a membership application form in Gurumukhi from Kavi Press, Bhawanipore:

> I beg to submit to the Jathadar Saheb of the Kirti Dal, that I am very much distressed owing to serfdom under the rich and the Government. So I am ready to make all sorts of sacrifices, under orders of the Kirti Dal, Bengal, to found a Labour Government. Please oblige me by enrolling me as a member of the Kirti Dal, Bengal. I have read and heard the rules and bye-laws of the Dal, and am sending the annual subscription of 4 Annas herewith.[34]

Soon, plans were afoot to bring about an 'amalgamation' of the Bengal Kirti Dal with its regional counterpart, the Workers and Peasants Party of Bengal. This was evident on the eve of a proposed all-India conference of the different regional groups led by Communist Party members. By late 1928, the police were well aware that the Bengal communists, with the help of Kirti activists, were planning to host an all-India WPP meeting alongside the annual Congress session to be held in December at Calcutta.[35] On 5 November 1928, Muzaffar Ahmad, who had been away in Bombay and so had been unable to meet Sohan Singh Josh when the latter visited Calcutta in early September, wrote to him:

> I draw your attention to the fact that Sikhs in Calcutta form a Bengal Branch of the Punjab Party. This is really ludicrous. I held a Conference with some of them and what I understand is that the workers themselves are not unwilling. . . . I will make the Bengal Kirti Dal at least a branch of the Bengal Party. . . . Also print a notice . . . addressing the Punjabi workers, Sikhs, Hindus and Mussalmans in Calcutta and near about.

He wanted the Kirti members to deal with two specific points in the notice – what the Kirti Dal stood for, and the relationship between different regional parties organized by the left. Muzaffar Ahmad suggested that the notice should put forward the position that all the regional parties led by communists were working with the same principles and programmes, and would unite as one in the coming conference.

Planning of the event led to joint activities. On 11 November, a public meeting of the Sikhs was held in Calcutta under the aegis of the Bengal WPP. The aim was to publicize the party's programme among the workers, particularly among the Sikh migrants, and obtain their assistance during the forthcoming All-India Workers and Peasants Party Conference. Philip

Spratt, sent to assist communists in India by the Communist Party of Great Britain (CPGB), spoke first and explained the programme of the party, advising labour organizations to join ranks. Other speeches focused on the oppressions of the colonial state, as well as of the Indian moneylenders, zamindars and capitalists. At the end of the month, Spratt, Muzaffar Ahmad and executive committee members of the Bengal WPP made further practical plans to work closely with Kirti members in view of the coming merger in December, and chose Sohan Singh Josh as the conference president. The police thought Josh had been instrumental in convincing Bengal Kirti Dal members to work with Gurdit Singh when he visited the city. He

believed that this cooperation would strengthen the group.[36] A meeting of the reception committee of the All-India WPP Conference was held on 28 November at European Asylum Lane, where P. Dinda presided in the presence of Muzaffar Ahmad, Abdul Halim, Philip Spratt, Dharani Goswami, Nirod Chakraborty, Balwant Singh and Genda Singh. The discussion touched on the number of delegates who would be coming, the method of voting and other details.

Genda Singh (Courtesy West Bengal State Archives)

A month later, this was followed by the hosting of what was described by the police as 'the first conference of its kind in India'. Among prominent representatives from Bengal, the United Provinces and Bombay were noted representatives from Punjab, including Ferozuddin Mansoor, Sohan Singh Josh, Mangal Singh and Gurdit Singh. B.F. Bradley and Philip Spratt of the CPGB, active respectively in Bengal and Bombay, and Jack Ryan, a communist from Australia representing the Pan-Pacific Trade Union Congress, attended the conference, emphasizing its internationalist orientation. Sohan Singh Josh allegedly delivered an 'objectionable' presidential address at Albert Hall, College Street, a hub of the anti-colonial public sphere in the city, where 300 leftist delegates had congregated. He 'began by referring to the "Komagata Maru" incident at Budge Budge, on which occasion, he said, Punjabis had been brutally murdered. He then attacked the Congress policy and said that they must demand complete independence.'[37] He stressed on close affiliation with the League Against Imperialism, Communist Third International and the Pan-Pacific Trade Union Secretariat. In reference to strikes, he spoke of internationalist solidarity in the form of monetary assistance from Soviet Russia. He envisaged a 'coming war' between the communists and the British empire; once direct combat against British capitalism began, mass strikes and sabotage were to be adopted as methods and all means of communication destroyed so that the British government faced a combined attack from two sides – the Soviet Union and the communists from India. In anticipation of such a day, he advocated launching a campaign to discourage potential recruits from joining the colonial army; turning to the imperial practice of enlistment drives in Punjab, he upheld similar views long circulated by anti-colonial Punjabi circles. The militant mood at the conference was observed along with a march across the city at the conclusion of the event to publicize left activism; the procession responded to anti-capitalist, anti-imperialist slogans, demanded a workers' government, and carried forty red flags.[38] The conference, held alongside the annual session of the Indian National Congress (INC), also had another purpose. Left activists, trade unionists and workers 'invaded' the Congress conference tent, and demanded the adoption of 'complete independence' as the declared goal of Indian nationalism; under gathering pressure from below, the Congress leaders agreed to consider this and adopted it as policy in the following annual session at Lahore.[39]

The colonial state was already prepared to strike at the militant labour and communist movement. Speeches were being recorded in detail, and perhaps embellished to suit the imperial strategy of uprooting the left opposition from the political landscape. Hansen, Deputy Commissioner of Calcutta Police, felt that a 'distinct advance' in proceeding against the communists and leftists could be made on the basis of views expressed at the All India WPP conference. After communist and militant labour leaders were arrested in March 1929 and stood trial at Meerut, a 'legal defence fund' was established in Calcutta to raise money for those on trial and campaign against the arrests; the initiative involved activists from a Sikh background. In his letter to the Central Defence Committee of Meerut prisoners in Delhi, Abdur Rezzaq Khan, secretary of the Meerut Trial Defence Committee in Bengal, wrote that the fund-raising body formed in May included Balwant Singh of the Bengal Kirti Dal. The correspondence between Punjabi and

Bengali communists continued, indicating a relationship of shared concern and personal warmth in the face of repression. In April 1929, Halim wrote to Ferozuddin Mansoor enquiring about the state of the Communist Party in Punjab, stressed the need for renewed campaign among workers and peasants following the Meerut arrests, reported his ill-health and conveyed his 'heartfelt' love to Baba Bhag Singh Canadian. Ferozuddin replied that the fight had to go on and that Bhag Singh Canadian was keeping well. Though Gurdit Singh briefly turned left before moving to a position of permanent affiliation with the Congress, the handful of activists who had joined the Bengal Kirti Dal remained within the communist fold. Inder Singh Hoshiarpur, Genda Singh, Balwant Singh, Ajit Singh and Prithi Singh were regarded by the colonial authorities as 'Sikh members' of the Communist Party of India, active among the diaspora living in Calcutta and Budge Budge, especially transport workers from Punjab.[40]

In late April 1930, an enquiry was made by the Special Branch, Calcutta Police regarding a letter written by Prithi Singh from 118, Manoharpukur Road, Bhawanipore, to Hari Singh, a carpenter engaged at the Lilooah railway workshop in Howrah. Prithi Singh wanted Hari to print 'ABC of Communism' in Gurumukhi, promised to send Rs 100 for this purpose and declared that the translated manuscript covered four exercise books. Confidential enquiries at the Lilooah workshops yielded nothing. Hari Singh could not be traced.[41] During the early 1930s, Abdul Halim was in 'close touch' with local communists from a Sikh background. In 1933, the government thought he was making plans with his Sikh comrades to import Russian oil cheaply via Budge Budge and utilize the profit for spreading communist propaganda in India. Since oil products imported into Calcutta passed through the oil depot at Budge Budge, surveillance was mounted on the possible arrival of Soviet ships carrying petroleum and propaganda, and on Sikhs with communist convictions connected with the transport of oil in South Bengal. However, the British official requested to keep watch revealed the paradox of capitalism-in-crisis and the submerged yet ever-present inter-imperialist competition; he felt such a development was to be welcomed as Russian oil could only drive the depression-era high prices of petroleum downwards. He labelled 'current' prices as 'scandalously high', as the market was controlled by American corporate monopolies such as Standard Oil.[42]

Halim was also suspected of deploying Harnam Singh, a communist from a Sikh background, as a courier of confidential communist correspondence; in a letter to Muzaffar, Halim mentioned sending some letters through him.[43] In the early 1930s, Mangal Singh, who had been dismissed from Tata Steel Works at Jamshedpur, was in touch with several communist activists in Calcutta, including Abdul Halim, Somnath Lahiri and Santa Singh. He also maintained contact with Munsha Singh Dukhi, a revolutionary poet with a Ghadar past who had established the radical Kavi Kutia Press at Bhawanipore. Viewed as 'an experienced and influential labour agitator' in the language of the state, Mangal Singh worked with Manik Homi, a Parsi worker, and Phanindra Nath Dutta, an unemployed youth from a bhadralok background who had studied engineering at the nationalist technical school at Jadavpur in Calcutta. The latter corresponded with Halim on action. His brother, Nagendra Chandra Dutta, a political prisoner, had died in jail during the late 1910s. Phani wrote to Halim in 1934 that he and 'Comrade' Mangal Singh were organizing unemployed workers, and that about 1,000 of them had gathered at a meeting in Jamshedpur where the causes and remedy of unemployment had been explained in leftist terms.[44]

Though Muzaffar Ahmad spent the first half of the 1930s in prison, the police thought he had been keen to organize Sikh janitors and recruit them to the communist party.[45] In the course of 1932–33, the Calcutta Committee of the CPI gained acceptance among the left in Bengal as the successor of the communists who had been active in the WPP. According to a Special Branch report (20 August 1934), the party included and was supported by 'Sikh revolutionaries' such as Balwant Singh Pardesi and others. Genda Singh was also an active member. The party had 'control' over the City and Motor Transport Workers Union. It was connected with communists in New York through the Sikh representatives of the Ghadar Party in Calcutta. Members of the party were noted for their militancy, and the Sikh members played a prominent role during public gatherings. At a meeting at Hazra Park on 28 April 1934, the Kirti Dal organized a meeting where a red flag with the hammer and sickle emblem was hoisted. Abdul Halim, Genda Singh and Balwant Singh Pardesi spoke against imperialist occupation, exploitation by capital and advocated a future government based on the rule of workers. Genda Singh led the rallying slogan, 'Communist Party Ki Jai!' (Victory to the Communist Party!). Balwant Singh Pardesi hoped for a day of freedom for all under the red flag.[46]

The cordial relationship between communist organizers and Sikh labour activists survived into the 1940s. Sardar Kehr Singh, a Ghadar veteran from Canada, executive committee member of Bus Drivers' Union and volunteer at a Congress mass meeting in 1945, defended the communists against the accusation that the former had cut microphone wires to sabotage the meeting. He stressed on the unity of all anti-colonial forces as the 'need of the hour', and regarded 'baseless accusations against individuals and parties' as undesirable.[47] When the Communist daily *Swadhinata* (Liberation) was started in 1946, Pritam Singh of the Bus Workers' Union and Bachan Singh, representing Giribala Motor Transport, sent goodwill messages in Urdu, projecting the paper as a mouthpiece of workers and one that will focus on their suffering. Bachan Singh hoped it would unite the workers with the rest of the masses and 'unmask' imperialism.[48]

The communist activists from a Punjabi Sikh background in the inter-war period continued to represent a militancy inherited from their struggles as migrant workers, first politicized by the Ghadar tendency to confront imperialism from below and then moving towards Leninist internationalism. Saroj Mukherjee, a communist leader from Bengal, recalled Genda Singh as an active organizer of the CPI-led Transport Workers Union in the early 1930s. In 1934, Genda Singh had delivered a 'seditious' speech against the state at a communist rally to celebrate 'May Day' in the maidan (open ground). He was speaking at a time-honoured protest spot in Calcutta, the space in front of the Ochterlony Monument, a colonial landmark later renamed Shahid Minar (Martyr's Column). During the same period, other prominent figures of the Calcutta Committee, such as Abdul Halim, Somnath Lahiri, Ranen Sen, Saroj Mukherjee and Balwant Singh Pardesi, were also tried for disrupting a Congress meeting, circulating leaflets abusing Gandhi and the colonial government, and threatening police officers. In prison, Genda Singh and other communists were stripped of their status as political prisoners and treated like ordinary convicts. Genda Singh had appealed to the crowd to uproot the British Raj and throw the regime into the sea. Consequently, he was sentenced to rigorous imprisonment for one year. To this jail term was added another three months. On 10 May, undeterred by the presence of police watchers, he had shouted 'British Raj Barbad' ('Destroy the British Government') at another communist public meeting in a park.[49] By speaking out in the open, Genda Singh and other activists from the late 1920s and early 1930s marked a shift from the forms of resistance adopted at wartime, an era of short-lived resistance, transient gestures and words of subversion. Fully articulated political programmes were being uncovered through public speech. The organized and self-aware militancy of post-war labour movements had made this transition possible. The times of silent action and secret propaganda were over.

Conclusion: The Long Memory

In Genda Singh's speech at the foot of the Ochterlony Monument, the motif of the ocean, associated with the *Komagata Maru* and other ships of 'sedition' carrying migrant workers across long stretches of water, had surged forth to haunt and offend the colonizers. He had inverted the water-bound experience of Sikh migrant workers and consigned the empire to the sea. His speech indicated that in the inter-war period, the expatriate militancy of the wartime Ghadar Movement and the symbolically defiant references to the *Komagata Maru* were a latent shadow of the past that surfaced in labour rallies and speeches of left and militant labour activists. They appeared as sources of inspiration in the present and as traumatic memory incorporated within the repeated drives for fresh mobilization against colonial capital and resistance to imperialist state authority. They also merged with and conveyed an explicit vision of an alternative society after decolonization, one that was no longer bound by the rule of private property and profit.

A direct reference to the experiences aboard the *Komagata Maru* could be found in the lectures of Gurdit Singh. Though leaving behind his early communist association in the city, he had joined a socialist labour current present within and subordinate to the Congress nationalist platform. Gurdit Singh continued to recall the ship's journey in public meetings. In Budge Budge, which he revisited as the president-elect of a district labour conference in June 1932, he was welcomed on behalf of the local population. A chorus of little girls started the proceedings with a song dedicated to workers. Ideological differences surfaced when the sole communist speaker, Abdul Momin, criticized Gandhi and the Congress leadership for compromising with capitalists. His speech was regarded as unfair by Subhas Bose, Jalaludin Hashmi and other Congress labour leaders who dominated the conference. Some tried to object while he was speaking but Gurdit Singh allowed him to continue. Others echoed the wider contours of the left and communist positions. Sudhin Pramanik, who addressed the meeting in Bengali as chairman of the conference reception committee, spoke of the hardships endured by Gurdit Singh and his struggles on behalf of labour, and welcomed him on behalf of the people of Budge Budge. Focusing on the oppressive labour relations practised by different oil and petrol concerns located in the town, he referred especially to the misbehaviour and exploitative strategies of the management of the

Burma Shell Company. He requested the conference to adopt a policy to confront the company for its treatment of workers in the factories at Budge Budge and Golmuri. Pointing at the rotten society (*galito samaj*) and the tyrannical administration (*shecchachari shashantantra*), he pronounced that the '[t]ime had . . . come for the capitalists to be careful as to how they behave with their labourers'.[50] Condemning capitalism and imperialism, he declared that these systems will be overthrown, that capital was not the master of the working class, and that the Meerut trial showed how the workers had frightened the capitalists.

Gurdit Singh was overwhelmed by a sense of *déjà-vu* while addressing the assembled crowd of 4,000 men and women: 'He was glad to address the Budge Budge people in their own place, he loved Budge Budge as he was intimately connected with the place . . . described how he and the rest of the crew of the Komagata Maru were treated by the Canadian as well as the English Government.'[51] He recalled his direct experience of contesting, within legal bounds, colonial racism and the navigation and immigration laws applied against people of dark skin, and being persecuted by the state. He also consciously linked and situated this past within a personal and wider frame of social resistance from below; he stated he was born a peasant who had spent his life among workers, and planned to spend what remained of it in the same way. While opposing capitalism and empire-building, he praised the Soviet Union as a workers' state, envisaged India as a country ruled by workers in the future, and advocated unity of labour free of factional differences, so that workers could become 'invincible'. The speech, delivered in Urdu, was translated into Bengali by Jalaluddin Hashmi, a Congress trade unionist, for the benefit of those who could not scale the language barrier. The latter went on to add that the task of the workers' movement was to defy those in power.[52] Not merely as an individual, unique 'episodic' memory, Gurdit Singh was sharing his experience on the ship with others as 'memory-knowledge', rooted in a rejection of the colonial condition from below. Labour activists and workers from different ethno-linguistic-religious and political backgrounds absorbed this as listeners, as transmitted experience of imperial violence and victimization to be claimed and shared by all.[53] For them, the past was unfolding in the present urging action, and individual memory was taking on the form of class memory. In these gatherings, the *Komagata Maru* returned to lead other voyages of opposition, mobilization and resistance.

NOTES AND REFERENCES

[1] For a historical survey of the Sikh diaspora in Calcutta, see Himadri Banerjee, 'The Other Sikhs: Punjabi-Sikhs of Kolkata', *Studies in History*, 28 (2), 2012. A sketch of Sikh residents of the city is also to be found in Pijush Kanti Roy, 'Sikh' (Sikhs), *Kolkatar Pratibeshi* (Calcutta Neighbours), Calcutta, 2002, pp. 132–64.

[2] L.S.S. O'Malley, *Census of India 1911, Volume VI, City of Calcutta, Part I: Report*, Calcutta, 1913, pp. 20–26.

[3] L.S.S. O'Malley, *Census of India 1911, Volume VI, City of Calcutta, Part II: Table*, Calcutta, 1913, pp. 14, 28.

[4] W.H. Thompson, *Census of India, 1921, Volume VI, City of Calcutta, Part I: Report*, Calcutta, 1922, pp. 38–39. The maidan was an open space at the centre of the city, adjoining the Europeanized Chowringhee and Dalhousie areas of imperial control.

[5] W.H. Thompson, *Census of India, 1921, Volume VI, City of Calcutta, Part II: Table*, Calcutta, 1922, pp. 10, 17, 28.

[6] A.E. Porter, *Census of India, 1931, Volume VI, Calcutta, Parts I and 11*, Calcutta, 1933, p. 102.

[7] *Weekly Reports of Intelligence Branch, Bengal Police 1914*. IB file number suppressed at the time of consultation. Contains 'Reports on the Political Situation and Labour Unrest in Bengal' from 1928 to 1932. Also, KPM/SB/00445/05 (PS 503/42).

[8] For details on the context and trajectory of the twin mass movements launched in India after the First World War under Gandhi's leadership, see Sumit Sarkar, *Modern India 1885–1947*, Delhi, 1983, pp. 165–227.

[9] IB 454/1916 (13/16).

[10] Ibid.

[11] Ibid.

[12] *Report of the Committee on Industrial Unrest in Bengal 1921*.

[13] *Annual Reports on the Police Administration of the Town of Calcutta and its Suburbs for the years 1918–1928*.

[14] Ibid.

[15] Ibid.

[16] Ibid.

[17] IB 185/1928 (87/28).

[18] Ibid.

[19] Ibid.

[20] Ibid.

[21] Ibid.

[22] IB 111/1928 (191/28).

[23] IB 185/1928 (87/28).

[24] Home (Political) WBSA 180/1923.

[25] IB 111/1928 (191/28).

[26] Darshan S. Tatla, 'Introduction', *Report of the Komagata Maru Committee of Inquiry and Some Further Documents*, edited by Darshan S. Tatla, Chandigarh, 2007, pp. 1–28.

[27] IB file number suppressed at the time of consultation. Contains 'Reports on the Political Situation and Labour Unrest in Bengal' from 1928 to 1932.

[28] Ibid.

[29] Ibid. Also, *Annual Report on the Police Administration of the Town of Calcutta and its Suburbs for the year 1928*.

[30] IB file number suppressed at the time of consultation. Contains 'Reports on the Political Situation and Labour Unrest in Bengal' from 1928 to 1932.

[31] Ibid.

[32] Ibid.

[33] Ibid.

[34] IB File number suppressed at the time of consultation. Contains 'Reports on the Political Situation and Labour Unrest in Bengal' from 1928 to 1932.

[35] IB 185/1928 (87/28).

[36] Subodh Roy, ed., *Communism in India: Unpublished Documents 1925–1934*, Calcutta, 1998, pp. 51–53.

[37] IB 210/1927 (23/27).

[38] Ibid.

[39] Suchetana Chattopadhyay, *An Early Communist: Muzaffar Ahmad in Calcutta*, Delhi, 2011, p. 180.

[40] IB 210/1927 (23/27). IB 210/27 (41/27).

[41] IB 185/28 (87/28).

[42] IB 111/1928 (191/28).

[43] IB 210/1927 (23/27).

[44] IB 210/1927 (41/27).

[45] IB 168/1922 (1935–51).

[46] Manju Kumar Majumdar and Bhandudeb Datta, eds, *Banglar Communist Andolaner Itihas Anusandhan* Calcutta, 2010, pp. 71–76.

[47] *What happened at the Deshapriya Park meeting and thereafter?* Calcutta, 1945.

[48] Samir Dasgupta, ed., *Gana Andolane Chapakhana: Communist Party o Samadarshi Sangbadpatrer Kramaparjay*, Calcutta, 1996, p. 163.

[49] Saroj Mukhopadhyay, *Bharater Communist Party o Amra* (*Communist Party of India and Ourselves*), Vol. I (1930–41), Calcutta, 1993, pp. 61, 78. Majumdar and Datta, eds, *Banglar Communist Andolaner Itihas Anusandhan*, pp. 75–76. Also, IB CID Index 4 (I), p. 139. The IB Index contains a short sketch of Genda Singh, born in 1892 at Ferozepur, and his association with the Kirti Dal and the Communist Party of India.

[50] IB file number suppressed at the time of consultation. Contains 'Reports on the Political Situation and Labour Unrest in Bengal' from 1928 to 1932.

[51] IB 497/1927 (168/27).

[52] Ibid.

[53] IB 185/28 (87/28). IB 497/27(168/27). Memory formation of individuals is

explored by E. Tulving, 'Episodic and semantic memory', in E. Tulving and W. Donaldson, eds, *Organization of Memory*, New York, 1972, pp. 382–402. An analysis of workers' memory of past struggles in the North Indian context can be found in Chitra Joshi, *Lost Worlds: Indian labour and its forgotten histories*, Delhi, 2003, pp. 11, 236. For an understanding of social dimensions of memory, see James Fentress and Chris Wickham, *Social Memory*, Oxford, 1992. For discussions on memory and action, see Aleida Assmann and Linda Shortt, 'Introduction', in Aleida Assmann and Linda Shortt, eds, *Memory and Political Change*, New York, 2012, pp. 3, 4.

Dismantling the Cage

A compulsion to dismantle the cage built by the empire of capital marked the protests and campaigns of workers from Punjab in Bengal. When the *Komagata Maru* was forcibly guided to the Budge Budge docks in 1914, the Punjabi Sikh workers, a minute part of the population in Bengal, were not visible either as a community or as political actors. As mentioned, uprooted from the soil by colonial land revenue policies and expelled from any position of ownership, the majority of Sikh travellers belonged to a migratory workforce. Making a precarious living in the formal and semi-formal Anglo-American and other empires across Asia and the Americas, the commodity they were selling was their labour power. As insecure subjects of market fluctuations in labour demand, they were frequent victims of racial exclusion as a form of labour control; this was explicitly evident during the voyage of the *Komagata Maru*. Exposed to radical socialist, anarchist and diasporic nationalist movements, many were interested in self-organization as workers through the 'Ghadar' tendency. The activists among them drew widespread sympathetic response; they encouraged and led struggles against racist impediments in seeking work, movements for labour dignity and bred protest mentality against imperialism.

The question of class was complicated by the context of anti-colonial protests. The *Komagata Maru*'s arrival, the attendant state repression and related controversy turned the focus in the direction of this migrant labour diaspora and enabled the entry of Punjabi Sikh workers into local politics. Motivated by the Ghadar Movement and interconnections between revolutionary nationalist groups, a short episode of resistance emerged where Sikh taxi drivers and janitors, the lesser folk who could be ignored so far, became a source of disquiet to the colonial authorities. Surveillance, an essential part of policing, already alert to the anti-colonial challenge posed by migrants returning from overseas, began concentrating on those turning towards radical action at a local level. While they were suppressed during the First World War, the activities of people of their 'social sort' continued to be watched in the post-war period as self-aware labour militancy became manifest in their ranks. In this study, an attempt has been made to trace the threads of radical responses among Punjabi Sikh workers, and their interactions with colonial state apparatus, especially imperial surveillance, and local political currents with trans-regional dimensions. The aim has been to show the ways in which migrant workers and activists from a Punjabi Sikh background, though small in number, adapted themselves to local processes of resistance to colonial authority and capitalism, even if contexts, strategies, forms of protest and politics changed over the decades between the 1910s and the 1930s. Imperial surveillance, however, never lost track of these dissenters and rebels, and the intelligence gathered on them frequently led to prosecution.

They could be jailed or temporarily deported to Punjab. The Punjabi Sikh engagement with the left was a route plagued by repeated official persecution.[1] The milieu of labour and politics during the 1930s and 40s was further complicated by the emergence of various left fractions, the wider climate of another impending world war, and the interplay of nationalist and communal mobilizations. Left-leaning Sikh activists were active within a spectrum of inter-war labour politics which involved the Communists, the Congress Left and smaller left groups that emerged in the course of the 1930s. Multiple individual and changing affiliations marked their positions. Fragmented and splintered actions of the activists demonstrated that some remained consistent while others participated in various anti-colonial groupings without developing any permanent attachment. Guided by anti-colonial perspectives from below, they were mostly willing to coordinate their actions with the parties and leadership dominating the regional movements in and around Calcutta, while maintaining connections with Punjab.

Munsha Singh 'Dukhi' (the mournful one), for instance, was linked with Kirti Dal and other radical streams which emerged among Punjabi migrants in Bengal. Originally from Jalandhar, he resided at 66, Padmapukur Road, where he owned a shop selling cloth and motor accessories. He had been to America and the Far East, was convicted in the Second Supplementary Conspiracy Case at Lahore on 5 January 1917, and sentenced to life imprisonment. He was released on 23 April 1920, due to a Royal Amnesty for political prisoners.[2] Munsha Singh was also listed among twenty-eight passengers of the *Komagata Maru* who were 'still at large' during late 1914, in the *Report of the Komagata Maru Committee of Inquiry*.[3] This connection was recalled by the police when he resurfaced in the late 1920s in Calcutta as one of the figures behind Kavi Kutia Press, 'rendezvous of Sikh seditionists, particularly those who had been abroad'. Dukhi was noticed in 1927 as the anti-colonial poet who ran *Kavi* magazine, a short-lived diasporic literary initiative of '*Komagata Maru* fame'. Balwant Singh Pardesi, his close associate, was the magazine's publisher. 'Dukhi' and 'Pardesi' (the outsider), as chosen names, may have indicated their sense of alienation from existing society.

Pardesi, born in 1892, had come to Calcutta at the age of 8 with his father. He participated in the Non-Cooperation and Civil Disobedience Movements, and was interned in Alipore Central Jail during 1920–21. In 1930, he was again imprisoned there alongside Subhas Bose, Kiran Sankar Roy and other Congress leaders. Pardesi moved between Communist, militant left, Congress Left and labour circles in the city, and utilized his connections with various gurudwaras to advocate anti-colonial programmes. He became Head Granthi of the Bakulbagan Gurudwara in February 1929. He was known for distributing proscribed copies of *Kirti* and Ghadar literature for Punjab in Calcutta. He arranged an 'Akhand Path', a continuous reading of the *Guru Granth Sahib*, in memory of the revolutionaries Bhagat Singh, Raj Guru, Sukh Dev and Jatin Das. In touch with absconding revolutionaries from Punjab and in correspondence with Ghadar activists of California, he had allegedly visited Punjab and formed a communist group in Lahore during September 1931. Expelled from Bengal in 1932, he lived in Nankana Sahib and attended the activities of the communist-led Kirti Kisan Party. Participating in the Kirti Kisan conference at Nankana Sahib, he condemned the masses for not exerting themselves to secure the release of the Ghadar conspiracy case prisoners indicted during 1914–15. Kept under constant police surveillance when forced to stay in Punjab, he was accompanied by Sajjan Singh, who had also lived in Bengal briefly. Sajjan was regarded as the self-proclaimed murderer of Mrs Curtis, wife of a British military officer in Punjab, in January 1931; the police thought Sajjan, having vowed to assassinate Europeans, had stayed at the Howrah Gurudwara and visited Calcutta to procure arms while claiming that he was seeking employment as a security guard. Balwant Singh Pardesi returned to Calcutta in the early 1930s and was active in the communist fold; he came back again with his family on 28 June 1935, and put up at 105, Bakulbagan Road, his familiar space in Calcutta. He remained in close touch with Genda Singh, who was the same age as him and belonged to the Communist Party of India (CPI). They had often worked together. Pardesi also retained links with Gurdit Singh who belonged to the Congress Left. He continued to maintain communist and nationalist anti-colonial connections. In July 1939, he was organizing a combined contingent of Bengalis and Punjabis in order to take them from Calcutta to Lahore and court arrest in a *kisan morcha* (peasant rally). He visited Lahore to meet Sohan Singh Josh and other communists, discussing ways of linking Punjab with Bengal. He had reportedly declared that Bengal communists and terrorists were in favour of combined action. In September 1939, he allegedly claimed that the Bengali revolutionary terrorists were willing to start a campaign if Britain declared war on Russia. Pardesi was active as a Congress activist in the Quit India Movement of 1942; he went underground, and was arrested and released that year. In 1943, he was employed as a librarian in the Guru Nanak Khalsa library at Nankana Sahib, and he remained quiet during the rest of the war. In June 1945, he proclaimed support for the social interests of peasants and workers. His whereabouts were not known from then till August 1956, when he returned to Bengal. In December that year, he joined Texmaco, a corporation owned by the Birla business house, at Belghoria near Calcutta. Though the dossiers lost track of him after this, it was evident that he played an active role in the political life of Calcutta and its surrounding areas during every major mass anti-colonial movement from the late 1910s to the early 1940s.[4]

The Sikh Sunday *diwan*s (mass congregations) remained crucial public spaces for mobilizing workers and other class segments along nationalist, sectional and left lines within the diasporic community. This was evident from the late 1920s when Gurdit Singh and others addressed co-religionists on a range of issues. Political activists from other linguistic and religious backgrounds were also invited to speak on special occasions. Though there were noticeable exceptions, women attended but seldom spoke in these gatherings. The police reports on these meetings contained details on the number of participants and the composition of the crowd; locales and themes were also discussed. These revealed the spectrum of Sikh political activism in the city. An annual meeting of the Khalsa *diwan* was held during 13–15 April 1928 at Kansaripara Road, Bhawanipore, at which 400 Sikhs from Calcutta and its neighbourhood were present. What was evident was social demography and mood of organized opposition from below: 'They were representatives of the lower class of Sikhs in Calcutta including the taxi drivers and the durwans, but the educated Sikhs on the whole kept away from the meeting.' References were made to political repression and arrests in Punjab. Leaders of the labouring class, including non-Sikh activists, were present: 'Though supposed to be religious, politics were indulged in freely.'⁵ At Bakulbagan Gurudwara, on 19 February 1928, Gurdit Singh asked 500 Sikhs including 150 women to boycott the Simon Commission, in keeping with the positions of the Congress and the Left. On 20 May, at a *diwan* at Bakulbagan where 300 men and 150 women were in the audience, Balwant and Gurdit spoke about the oppression of the Motor Vehicles Department directed against Sikhs engaged in the motor trade, and requested drivers and owners to join the Bus Syndicate; Gurdit Singh asked the Sikhs to vote for the Congress candidate of Bhawanipore constituency in the Calcutta Corporation by-election. Although linked with the Congress, Gurdit Singh was also connected with the communists during this period.

A visibly weakened communist influence remained after the Meerut arrests in March 1929. The Naujawan Bharat Sabha, a youth group founded in Punjab by Bhagat Singh among others and influenced by the Ghadar current in Punjab, gained popularity among left-inclined radical Sikh activists. A branch was visible in Calcutta during the second half of 1929. Like Kirti Dal, it established connections with the Kavi Kutia Press. On 11 June 1929, a *kavidarbar* in Ballygunge Gurudwara was organized by the Naujawan Bharat Sabha; 250 Sikhs, including women, attended the meeting, which was presided over by Ratan Singh Sevak. Chait Singh referred to the Nankana Sahib massacre of 1921 in Punjab. Hazara Singh of Kirti Dal asked Munsha Singh to read out the first issue of *Sanjwal*, a Punjabi labour organ printed in Gurumukhi. Inder Singh recited Punjabi poems on the life of Guru Arjun Singh and Muslim oppression. Communal, communist and religio-regional identities emerged, but no common ground could be arrived at. That various groups of the Left in Punjab were seeking entry into Bengal was apparent on 10 July, when Munsha Singh Dukhi published the rules and regulations of the Bengal branch of the Naujawan Bharat Sabha from the Kavi Kutia. A youth league that denounced caste and religion, describing itself as being dedicated to the complete independence of India and to driving out 'slavery', the group aimed to organize in the form of a committee composed of general members and an executive consisting of seven elected members. A week later, a printed membership application form in Punjabi of the Naujawan Bharat Sabha was made available in Gurumukhi script. On 31 July, the Sabha held a public meeting of 100 Sikhs at Dwarkanath Mitra Square supporting Bhagat Singh and Batukeswar Dutta as heroes for having thrown bombs in the Imperial Legislative Assembly. While they made some inroads, the Kirti Dal almost vanished. On 4 December 1929, the Commissioner of Calcutta Police reported:

> An informal meeting of the Bengal Kirti Dal was held at the house of Balwant Singh Pardeshi at No. 35/17, Poddopukur Road, on the 27th November, at which Balwant Singh, Pirthi Singh, Inder Singh and a few others were present. It was decided that as the Dal was practically moribund something should be done to improve it, and it was proposed that they should hold another conference in the near future and ask a suitable Bengali to act as President.
>
> Note: The Bengal Kirti Dal as an association is a complete failure. Meetings of this nature have been held for months but have not been productive of results of any practical value.[6]

The radical youth enjoyed little success. At a meeting held by the Naujawan Bharat Sabha on 31 December, New Year's eve, at 96, Asutosh Mukherjee Road, only twelve members were present. The meeting was presided over by Surain Singh. Balwant Singh proposed that they must change their creed as the Congress had done and hoist a flag with the inscription 'Independence or Death'; subsequently, 'by common consent a red flag with yellow inscriptions was hoisted after midnight'.[7]

The group's adherents were persecuted. On 15 February 1933, five Punjabi Sikh workers were arrested as 'terrorists' linked with the Naujawan Bharat Sabha and Kirti Dal. They had occupied a room on the third floor of 6, Ganga Prasad Mukherjee Road, Bhawanipore, and four of them worked as drivers. At the time of the police raid at 5 a.m. in the morning, they had been asleep. Two aluminum bombs and a phial containing strong sulphuric acid were found among their effects. Although they claimed that the incriminating objects had been planted by the police and that they were being framed, the state dismissed their plea. On 20 May, they were convicted under the Arms and Explosives Substances Act (Act VI of 1908) and sentenced to six years' rigorous imprisonment. Bhagat Singh, the alleged ringleader, and the others were suspected of having imbibed a toxic mix of militant left-wing convictions and terrorist violence while living and working

6, Ganga Prasad Mukherjee Road (Photo by Ritaj Gupta)

in Calcutta. The Kirti Dal and Naujawan Bharat Sabha were instrumental, according to the police, in instilling a revolutionary tendency among them. All were from Hoshiarpur district in Punjab, and had migrated to Calcutta as young workers in search of livelihood.

Bhagat Singh, born in 1908/1909 in Mahilpur, had passed middle school in 1923 and arrived in Calcutta in 1924. He had learnt driving at the Gopal Motor Training School in the city and worked as a bus driver 'under private masters' till 1933, when he was jailed. His co-accused were Banta Singh, born in 1912, also from Mahilpur, a bus driver; Pakkar Singh, born in 1908, a bus driver; Dhanna Singh, born in 1912, a taxi driver who had read up to fifth class in his village school; and Amar Singh, born in 1908. They were literate; diaries, leaflets and handbills in Gurumukhi were found in their possession. Others had also been arrested in the preceding years for advocating militant socialist views. Anak Singh, born in 1905 at Ferozepur and supposedly a member of the Hindustan Socialist Republican Army (HSRA), had been picked up in October 1930, committed to Presidency Jail and detained at Hijli Camp for political prisoners in March 1931. In June that year, he had been expelled from Bengal. In the case of the Bhawanipore five in 1933,[8] their shared district of origin, Punjabi neighbourhood network, livelihood, social location in the big city, and association with leftists active among transport workers were probably enough to criminalize them. The very factors that had brought them together could be utilized to project them as 'conspirators' by the state. Amar Singh died in a Multan prison. Bhagat Singh, Pakkar Singh and Dhanna Singh were released from the Bengal jails in 1938, having

Banta Singh
(Courtesy West Bengal State Archives)

Dhanna Singh
(Courtesy West Bengal State Archives)

Pakkar Singh
(Courtesy West Bengal State Archives)

been granted remission after five years. Pakkar Singh's friendship with a Punjabi Sikh warder in Rajshahi Jail led to the latter's dismissal on the ground of being associated with a 'terrorist', generating a minor bureaucratic controversy.

The police followed Dhanna Singh from the jail gate to Gurudwara Jagat Sudhar at 31, Rash Behari Avenue. This gurudwara's location in the Kalighat area, adjacent to Bhawanipore, represented the local extensions of the Punjabi Sikh diaspora in south Calcutta. The Singh Sabha, which managed the gurudwara, had also vouched to receive Bhagat Singh and send him to Punjab. Before his release from Dum Dum Central Jail, Bhagat Singh had written a secret letter in Punjabi. Intercepted by the police, the letter was interpreted as an instance of his enduring interest in left-wing political positions. He had wanted to know about the ongoing hunger strike in Punjab jails; he had also been eager to know about the opinion of the communist and socialist leaders regarding this move and

Bhagat Singh (Courtesy West Bengal State Archives)

whether they had been consulted on this matter. Bhagat Singh is physically described in the jail records as being a Hindu/Sikh of average height (5 feet 8 inches), fair, of having reasonably good health, with a scar just below his left eye and another scar at the root of the outer side of his left index finger.[9] There is an image of Bhagat Singh, developed from a glass negative, in the Calcutta Police records. It is unlikely that the man in this picture is the famous revolutionary who was hanged in 1931, for the image is of an older person. Apparently, neither the photographer nor the officials saw any irony or symbolism in the photo, filed away with thousands of others as a routine procedure, a mundane exercise in identification, a matter of records. Set against the background of an endless corridor inside a house of incarceration, the prisoner stands with his left hand still in handcuffs, holding the chains. The right hand is free. He wears a defiant and slightly sarcastic expression. The image seems to suggest that he might have given up on religious customs. Yet the Singh Sabha of 31, Rash

Behari Avenue, in its letter to the colonial authorities, had offered to look after Bhagat Singh prior to his release. This act of solidarity, which consisted of claiming an absent individual as a member of the congregation, seemed to indicate empathy for rebels and victims. It is also to be remembered that Balwant Singh, Genda Singh and others attended and spoke at the *diwan*s in this particular gurudwara. Once again, communitarian anti-colonial radicalism seemed to have struck a chord within the diasporic community despite different political persuasions.

Gurdit Singh continued to represent the left wing within the Congress. At a public meeting in the Ballygunge Gurudwara on 14 March 1930, in the presence of 500 Sikhs, he praised Gandhi and prayed for the success of Civil Disobedience. At a second *diwan* held two days later, Sikhs were urged to support the Congress in the Calcutta Corporation elections. In January 1931, . Gurdit Singh and Balwant Singh Pardesi were among leading community leaders responsible for carrying out Congress propaganda among the Sikhs of Calcutta. Gandhi, Subhas Bose and J.M. Sengupta were praised during nationalist mobilization of city Sikhs.[10] The police also observed that at the 'so-called' religious *diwan*s, Balwant Singh Pardesi, Gurdit Singh and others delivered inciting speeches, sang songs seeking 'annihilation' of the British Raj and tended to support the Subhas Bose faction of the Bengal Congress.[11] In the backdrop of Civil Disobedience, the spectrum of Sikh activism was manifested through pulls in different political directions. The gulf between the Congress supporters and those of the Communist Left, at a time when the CPI had parted ways with the INC, was sharply visible. On 3 January 1931, a *diwan* was held at the Sikh Gurudwara on Main Sewar Road, presided over by Balwant Singh Pardesi. Around 450 Sikhs, including 150 women, were present. Sajjan Singh made an 'inciting speech' asking the audience to plunge 'headlong' into the national movement, resist oppression and follow Gandhi. He urged boycotting of British cloth and appealed to young men to take the places of the leaders who had been arrested. Mahendra Singh endorsed Gandhi's programme, but also praised Bhagat Singh for having embraced the gallows and shown the path to liberty. Genda Singh of Bengal Kirti Dal, 'the Sikh communist organization in Calcutta', labelled Gandhi as a capitalist and argued that they must not identify with his programme.

Five *diwan*s were held during early 1932, on 31 January, 7 February, 14 February, 21 February and 28 February; all were presided over by Balwant Singh Pardesi and held at the 'New Gurudwara' at Rash Behari Avenue, Kalighat. At the first *diwan*, Sajjan Singh delivered 'a most objectionable speech', claiming that the government was suppressing the Sikh religion and instigating Muslims to attack Sikhs in Kashmir. He asked the Sikhs to follow Gandhi and Nehru. In contrast, 'Genda Singh read out a very inciting and seditious poem urging labourers to shout revolution, to hoist the red flag and to destroy the present Government and establish labour rule.'[12] He asked the assembled crowd to follow the Soviet model for attaining labour dignity. Around 500 persons were present, including 150 women. The tone turned more aggressively communal in the following meetings where Sikh speakers, including those associated with the Congress Left, projected Sikhs as Hindus. At the second *diwan*, attended by about 650 Sikhs including 150 women, and the third *diwan* attended by 600 Sikhs including 200 women, money was collected by Balwant and Sajjan for 'distressed' Sikhs suffering from Muslim attacks. Balwant claimed that if the government failed to check 'lawlessness' and communal violence against Sikhs, it was 'unfit to rule over Hindus'. While Genda Singh upheld the Soviet Union, the nationalists promoted other examples. The communal agenda would return. On 31 July, at Jagat Sudhar, communal, anti-Muslim positions were stridently expressed and communists clearly did not have much of a voice at the meeting. Allotment of 55 per cent seats in the Punjab council to Muslims by the government through the scheme of Communal Award was discussed. Akali and Shiromani Prabandhak opinions were held up to condemn 'the Moslem attitude in Punjab' by pro-government speakers such as Raghubir Singh, who wanted Sikhs to stay away from Congress-led anti-colonial movements.

Anti-colonial considerations dominated most of the gatherings; however, gender and caste, the sources of inequality and impediment to united efforts, were occasionally discussed as fissures dividing the community. On 26 June, at Jagat Sudhar, Mahendra Singh asked those present to study the histories of Ireland, China and America to learn lessons in 'patriotic self-sacrifice'. A Sikh committee of eighteen members, including Gurdit Singh, Bibi Sukhowant Kaur (whose husband had been transported), Balwant Singh and Sajjan Singh (who had been expelled from Bengal), and Genda Singh were elected. On 17 June, Sukhowant Kaur read a poem on self-sacrifice, martyrdom and killing the enemy: 'This is yet another inciting oration the lady has made in the course of the last month of Sikh diwans.'[13] Genda Singh 'read a speech exhorting workers to establish a raj similar to that which existed in Russia and destroy capitalists'.[14] Upon enquiry, the police learnt that Sukhowant Kaur was the wife of Lachaman Singh, of 20, Justice Dwarakanath Road, a supporter of the Bengal Congress leader C.R. Das during 1919–20. She had worked with C.R. Das's wife, Basanti Debi, and others during the post-war mass upheavals. In 1930, she had picketed with the women activists Bimal Pratibha Debi, Santi Das and Indumati Debi. On 7 August, at Jagat Sudhar, in the presence of 600 people, while Genda Singh 'made usual communistic speech against capitalism' and Udam Singh read a 'poem on communist lines about destruction of capitalists', Sukhowant Kaur spoke of the necessity to start a women's organization and their political representation in the law-making bodies. On 24 July, at Jagat Sudhar, a Sunday *diwan* was held under the auspices of Ballygunge Singh Sabha, presided over by Balwant Singh Granthi. Bir Singh, a communist, 'read out his weekly poem containing the usual slogans about the Raj of the Proletariat'.[15] He emphasized the Soviet model and reminded the gathering of 300 Sikh men and 100 women of Bhagat Singh, Batukeswar Datta and Rajguru, who had given their lives for the country, and of 'how Lenin in Russia had given up everything'. He repeated the plea that 'they must raise the Red flag and destroy the capitalists'.[16]

In the Sunday *diwan*s, untouchability was condemned within the community. On one occasion, Gurdit Singh formally accepted bread from the hands of an 'untouchable' or an outcaste, to break the barriers of caste; others followed his example. Discussions on communal lines continued, and the idea of a joint electorate was put forward as desirable for a multireligious nation, affirming the nationalist position. At the same time, it was felt that if the principle of communal division was retained, Sikhs should receive their share; reservation of seats for Sikhs was demanded in the Calcutta Corporation and the Bengal Legislative Council. Guru Nanak was projected as a figure of unity admired by followers of all three major religions in Punjab. On 23 August, 600 people including 200 women attended the *diwan* at Jagat Sudhar. Narain Singh Panchkhal condemned the Communal Award for causing divisions among Hindus, Muslims and Sikhs, and demanded a joint electorate and two seats for Sikhs in the Calcutta Corporation. A resolution was passed along these lines. It seems that an attempt was being made to diffuse the communal tensions that had been evident in the previous months.

On 11 September, a *diwan* was held to welcome Gurdit Singh upon his release from the prison. Pratap Singh of 31, Asutosh Mukherjee Road read the welcome address, containing the 'usual reference to his connexion with Komagata Maru incident'.[17] Communists, Akalis and transport union activists were present along with Bachan Das Sharma, a Punjabi activist from a Hindu background. Seven hundred people attended the meeting. Class issues as labour demands surfaced repeatedly in late 1932. On 23 October, at the 'usual Sunday diwan' at Jagat Sudhar, Ratan Singh Sevak presided over a meeting of 500 Sikhs, including 100 women. Referring to the strike at the Titagarh jute mills, Genda Singh said that the strikers had been dispersed by the police with sticks while on their way to Calcutta to represent their grievances. As drivers and conductors of the Sikh community were also workers, assistance should be given to the striking jute workers. He requested the audience to attend a solidarity meeting which was to be held at Albert Hall on the same day to express their support. On 20 November, a Sunday *diwan* was held at the Jagat Sudhar Gurudwara with Chattar Singh presiding. Addressing a congregation of 600 Sikhs including 200 women, Genda Singh exhorted Sikh drivers, conductors and labourers to be united and to maintain their dignity as workers. He predicted, probably in a millenarian vein, that the time was soon approaching when the capitalists would be destroyed.

The leftist emphasis on class solidarity continued to be expressed alongside parochial grievances and communal positions. Occasional speakers, such as Mangal Singh, who was a bus owner, commented on the unreliability of Bengali leaders and on being singled out for persecution in Bengal by the police for being Sikh rather than Bengali. Gurdit Singh, Balwant Singh and others referred to 'Muslim despotism' over Sikhs under the Mughals, especially Aurangzeb. However, they always argued that British rule was worse. These forays into restricted visions of Sikh identity politics were accompanied by combined work with activists from Muslim and other backgrounds in wider fronts. So, the consciousness of Congress Left leaders from a Sikh background was paradoxical. Their political identity revealed an unresolved social juxtaposition of experiences as workers and an inability to go beyond received belief systems, including mythical versions of the past. The interplay of sectional and wider considerations was shaped by the orientations of leadership, organizations, programmes, objectives and movements at critical conjunctures. The primacy of positions taken depended on the nature of mobilization. Communists and nationalists attended Sikh *diwan*s to put forward competing political positions, ideologies and actions. For instance, Genda Singh tried to appeal to drivers and conductors along class lines, while others stressed on 'patriotic' or communal unity. Some gurudwaras were preferred by certain speakers. There was a marked tendency to appear in the same space again and again since the audience, coming from the local neighbourhoods, was 'captive' and familiar.[18]

The fractions and factions continued to make their presence felt without any major shift in the diverse and overlapping political positions present within the diaspora. By the early 1940s, the police were of the opinion that '[t]he local Sikhs have no strong organization which follows any definite political programme.'[19] The politically moderate and socially conservative leaders of the Singh Sabha, the largest Sikh organization in Bengal which managed the gurudwaras and community life around it, were unpopular with the 'extremist sections' of the community. The Akali Dal and the Punjab Naujawan Sabha openly broke with them. The Akali Dal fell out with the Singh Sabha leaders owing to differences over financial matters, namely checking the accounts of their religious council, the Bara Sikh Sangat. The Naujawans, as left militants, opposed British imperialism and capitalism; they were against the Singh Sabha, which refused to directly accommodate anti-British words or actions, and saw it as the conduit of institutionalized loyalism within the community. In 1941, speakers of the Naujawan Sabha advocated an armed movement for freedom, rejecting Gandhian non-violence as 'sterile and ineffective'. In June 1941, Sarbans Singh, 'a starter of route No. 3' and a Naujawan member, advocated a combined effort of youth, workers and peasants to remove British imperialism and capitalism. On 26 January 1942, the Sabha observed independence day at D.N. Mitra   Square, when Gernail Singh Arshi recited a poem condemning the exploitation of India by 'foreign dacoits', urging people to end it along with capitalism. Shibnath Singh and Bachan Das Sharma shouted objectionable slogans: *'British government dhangsa houk!'*, *'British hukumat murdabad!'* (May destruction overtake the British government!). Both were arrested and served with orders preventing them from attending meetings, assemblies and processions for a year. Gernail Singh Arshi was expelled from Bengal and confined within the limits of the revenue estate of Rashin in Dehlon, Ludhiana. Apart from left radicalism, a tendency was present to work with the Hindu Mahasabha as a platform of the radical communal right. The police also observed the influence of the local left and the Subhas Bose-led initiatives which had connected the Sikhs with Bengal politics from the 1920s: 'The more politically advanced section being dissatisfied with other groups joined the Progressive People's Front and Forward Bloc.'[20]

The prominent Punjabi Sikh activists involved in radical politics in Calcutta continued to be men of humble background. A police note on

Kishen Singh, son of Hardit Singh of Ludhiana, and a resident of 11, Harish Mukherjee Road, recorded that he was born in 1898 and was a tailor by profession. He was noticed when he participated in a procession from Hazra Park to Ochterlony Monument in 1931, in connection with the observance of 'Dinesh Gupta Day' to honour the Bengal revolutionary who had survived an aborted attack on Writers' Building and had been hanged that year. In 1933, he was active as a member of Kirti Dal and Akali Dal, and in 1942, he was a member of the leftist Progressive People's Front (PPF), being present when its action wing, the National Volunteer Corps, was formed. He urged all aid to Britain and Russia by organizing guerrilla squads at a meeting of the PPF at his residence, and was accepted as a member of its sub-committee to fight the Japanese invasion.

Pratap Singh of Ludhiana, a resident of 57/2, Bondel Road, was also kept under watch. He was a member of the Bengal Labour Party (BLP), a public organization in which several communists were active as the CPI was officially banned. He was first spotted by police agents at a meeting of the newly formed Bengal Bus Drivers and Conductors Association on 25 August 1939, where two Bengal communist organizers, Paresh Chakraborty and Sailen Mukherjee, urged the union members to come under the red flag. In 1940, he was active in BLP meetings in Calcutta. He took a keen interest in raising funds for the miners of Jharia Coalfields, and was arrested, convicted and sentenced to one month's rigorous imprisonment; he was also fined for holding an unauthorized meeting at a city park. In 1941, he was again active in trade union work alongside Bengali leaders. In 1942, he organized a study circle in south Calcutta on behalf of the PPF.

Bir Singh Sanjhwal, also from Ludhiana, Punjab and a resident of 6/1, Rup Narain Nandan Lane, was similarly active in the PPF. Born in 1897, he was noticed upon his arrival in Calcutta for the first time in 1928, when he was introduced to Dharani Goswami by Balwant Singh Pardesi on 30 November, at the Sikh Gurudwara at Bhawanipore. His links with the CPI continued as the communists kept changing the public name of their organization under repressive conditions. In 1931, he visited the office of the open organization of the CPI, Samya Raj Party, at 9, Bhabanath Sen Street, and had a discussion with Aghor Sen, a communist leader, about the party manifesto and other matters. He entertained Muzaffar Ahmad at a garden party on 15 November 1931, when the latter was granted a short break from prison life to visit Calcutta on medical grounds. In 1932, Bir Singh was elected a member of the executive committee of the Samya Raj

Party. He was convicted under Section 124A and 153A of the Indian Penal
Code and sentenced to 'Rigorous Imprisonment' for two years on both
counts (sentences to run concurrently) by the Assistant District Magistrate,
Alipore on 31 October 1932, for delivering seditious speeches at Jagat
Sudhar. Towards the middle of 1934, he was released from jail and he left for
his native village in Punjab. In 1935, he returned from Punjab and resumed
labour activism in Calcutta. This involved engaging in internationalist
movements organized by the Left. He became a member of the executive
committee of the PPF against war and fascism. In 1936, he was active in the
CPI-led Workers' League, including its various internationalist campaigns
– solidarity with Republican Spain and opposition to British policies in
Palestine. He was again active in the felicitation of Muzaffar Ahmad upon the
latter's release that year after having served an eight-year sentence following
his conviction as chief accused in the Meerut Communist Conspiracy Case
(1929).

The CPI's decision to work in cooperation with Congress Socialists from
the mid-1930s meant that Bir Singh too was active in joint movements.
Condemnation of firing on strikers at Pondicherry by French authorities,
solidarity towards Port Trust workers and Bengal Nagpur Railway strikers
were some of the actions he participated in. As a trade unionist, he worked
in the Motor Workers' Union, which came under the influence of the
Workers' League. Later, he left the CPI fold, serially joining several smaller
leftist groups. In 1937, he joined the Radical Socialist Party (RSP) along
with former CPI member Aghor Sen and worked among textile workers
and peasants. In 1938, he was one of the founders of the Motor Transport
Workers' Union and became the secretary of the Majdoor Dal (Workers'
Party). At a street hawkers' meeting held at the foot of the Ochterlony
Monument (30 November 1938), he narrated the sufferings of hawkers at
the hands of the police. In 1939, he joined the Communist League and was a
member of the Provincial Committee of Bengal Bus Drivers and Conductors
Association. He worked with Saumyendra Nath Tagore, formerly of CPI,
who had turned to Trotskyism. He also maintained contact with the Radical
Revolutionary Party led by Bepin Ganguly, who wanted him to enlist ex-
soldiers from the Sikh community to train revolutionary nationalists in
the use of firearms. According to the police, Bir Singh recruited ex-sepoys,
Arjun Singh and Bhagwan Singh, for this purpose. He was with the RSP
again in 1940, attended Naujawan Sabha meetings in 1941 and worked
with the PPF in 1942. Though his 'ostensible means of living' was hawking,

he was suspected to be an 'important member of a terrorist party in Bengal', and a link between Sikhs and Bengali nationalist revolutionaries.[21] Though he was primarily a leftist political activist on the labour front, the state detected in his actions an echo of Ghadar, encompassing militant trade unionism and revolutionary nationalism.

For his political past, Bachan Das Sharma from Ludhiana, of 49 A, Chakraberia Road (South), Bhawanipore, Calcutta, was interrogated at length by the police in 1943. He claimed he was addicted to *ganja* (cannabis) and opium, could hardly move and no longer had anything to do with politics. However, he offered insight into the life of Punjabi immigrants in Calcutta and political organizations of Sikhs in the city. Brahmin by caste and Hindu by religion, he was 35/36 years of age at the time of the interview. His father was a grocer in Ludhiana, and Bachan depended on an eating house which he ran from his address in Calcutta, with assistance from his younger brother. He had previously worked in the hotel of Basant Singh from Amritsar at 45, Asutosh Mukherjee Road for five years, gaining some experience in the business of eateries. In 1932, he was the editor of *Sanjwal,* started by Maha Singh (who had died by the time of the interview), Munsha Singh Dukhi (who had left the city and whose whereabouts were no longer known) and Sundar Singh (who had also died). Although he enjoyed the post 'in name only', he claimed to be the editor and was paid Rs 15 or Rs 20, while Maha Singh ran 'the whole show'. Though he never wrote anything, Bachan was sentenced to six months of rigorous imprisonment in 1932/1933 for publishing 'seditious matter'. Subsequently, he was sentenced to one year on the ground of rioting; later, his sentence was reduced to six months. Others convicted with him were Gurdit Singh (who had become a security prisoner in 1941), Maha Singh, Sundar Singh (who died in jail), Mangal Singh (bus owner) and Prithi Singh. Bachan also worked as a hawker of the Punjabi journal *Desh Darpan,* edited by Niranjan Singh Talib. Balwant Singh Pardesi was also associated with it. Bachan Das drew Rs 2 per day as salary for this work. Niranjan Talib, whom the police regarded as a 'de facto owner of the Kavi Press', had been imprisoned as a wartime security prisoner. He was a Congressman and campaigned for the release of political prisoners. Bachan attended these meetings. On 26 January 1941 (observed as independence day by the nationalists), he was arrested for shouting 'congress' slogans and served a notice preventing him from joining meetings and protest movements: 'Since then I keep aloof from all such meetings. Even I do not go to the Gurudwara.'[22]

Bachan was familiar with the political divergences among Punjabi groups. While working for *Desh Darpan*, he had come across the Naujawan Sabha located on the second floor of 48, Chakraberia Road (South). Niranjan Talib was connected with the group. Bachan did not join the Sabha; its members derisively called him a 'Gandhite', the 'follower' of a 'bania', taunted him as 'old', and flaunted themselves as the 'youth' (*naujawan*). They played carrom and organized meetings, poetry contests and study circle lectures. He never took part in any of these activities. He denied being connected with the Akali Dal since he was not a Sikh and could not join. He was aware that Niranjan had written against the Akalis having fallen out with them, and that this had led to 'a quarrel at the Gurudwara'. Since he was addicted to opium, despite being a 'staunch Congress supporter' in the past, he did not participate in the Quit India Movement of August 1942 or the nationalist protests of 1943. To ward off police attention, he emphasized that he was no longer connected with any political activism or activists: 'I still maintain that I am innocent. I am addicted to opium and Ganja and as such I am incapable of doing anything.'[23]

Another former activist interviewed by the police was Harnam Singh Kanka of Ludhiana and 31, Rash Behari Avenue (Singh Sabha office). He knew Bachan Das Sharma as a seller of newspapers on the streets of

48 Chakraberia Road (South), where the Naujawan Sabha was located

Calcutta. Harnam Singh was an ex-sepoy turned schoolteacher of Sikh boys and girls in Calcutta at Jagat Sudhar. The school closed down during the Japanese bombing of Calcutta. When he was questioned, he was 57 years old and working as a clerk for Singh Sabha, the controlling committee of Jagat Sudhar. He had joined the army in 1910 and retired in 1921. He had served in Afghanistan and China: 'I fought in the last Great War.' He came to Calcutta in 1931. He knew Niranjan Talib as a prominent organizer of the community and paper editor, but refused to say anything against him and his friends, whom the police suspected of attempting to bring about 'disaffection' among Sikh soldiers in Calcutta. He claimed ignorance of any such activity in the city. He admitted that he had been arrested in 1924 in his village for joining the Akali or Gurudwara movement, but denied having formed an Akali Regiment in Calcutta. He had lived in 6/1, Rup Narayan Nandan Lane up to May 1940, having rented the whole house from Jagat Seth, a Marwari trader of Harrison Road, and paying a monthly rent of Rs 75. Living in one room, he had let out the other rooms to subtenants: Punjabi, Sikh and Bengali motor drivers. In May 1940, he shifted to 30, Beni Nandan Street, which he rented for Rs 70. His subtenants there were even more impoverished, 'Madrasi beggars and menials'. He was living in the world of immigrant labourers as a semi-permanent slum landlord, when

Gurudwara Jagat Sudhar, 1940 (Photo by Richard Bear)

he shifted to Jagat Sudhar in June 1942. His work involved being in charge of the accommodation of *musafirs* (travellers) staying in the three rooms allotted to them for seven days or less at the gurudwara. He claimed that there was no question of charging rent, but the money donated by them was collected and entered in the register entrusted to him. He had no connection with the Naujawan Sabha. Among Sikh activists in Calcutta, he admitted knowing Giani Meher Singh, who had no fixed place of residence and was expelled from the city in 1941. He also knew Mula Singh, who worked as watchman (*durwan*) at Alipore; Mula Singh's son attended the school run at the gurudwara before they left Calcutta. He also knew the poet Arshi, a member of the Naujawan Sabha, who also left Calcutta in 1941. The police learnt that Mula Singh, an Akali and religious preacher, worked as a doorkeeper for a Nepali general at 3, Judges Court Road, in the upper-crust neighbourhood of Alipore. Connected with Subhas Bose but not the Congress, he was suspected of spreading disaffection against the British Raj among Sikh soldiers who attended gurudwara meetings at Jagat Sudhar.[24]

Radical Sikhs in Calcutta were watched, expelled from the city and its suburbs and prevented from speaking in public meetings or taking part in processions. As the Second World War began, social tensions generated further protests with radical dimensions. The murder of a Calcutta taxi driver, Chaman Singh, by two Afro-American soldiers provoked a wildcat taxi strike for two days by Sikh drivers. At the funeral cortege, which took on the form of a quiet protest march, the police spotted a bus driver carrying two flags inscribed with the communist symbol of hammer and sickle. The man, who clearly refused to remain quiet, was shouting that the Americans, who were guests in India, had abused the hospitality of the country and committed homicide. At a protest meeting held in the premises of the Taxi Association in Bhawanipore, Milki Singh requested the drivers and owners to send a deputation to the Police Commissioner of Calcutta to find ways and means of preventing such incidents in future. The police recorded the comments made by a Sikh taxi driver: 'It is impossible to have any confidence in American justice. . . . Tyranny has exceeded all limits. An innocent man has been killed. The Americans are oppressing us in our own country. American goondas [hooligans] have slaughtered our brother.'[25] These angry outbursts prompted the Police Commissioner and the Bengal government to request American authorities in Delhi to prohibit soldiers from carrying knives in the streets of the city.[26] In the compartments of racialized subjecthood, it is interesting to note that racist remarks were not directed at black soldiers. Instead, North American (and white) justice was again called into question.

Drivers continued to be suspected as potential rebels. 'Information supplied by a source' was recorded in the dossiers:

> In Calcutta no Sikh organization, based on terrorist lines, has so far been formed, but as the bulk of the Sikh population there is made of motor-drivers, who left their home province after committing some acts of moral turpitude or after absconding in criminal cases, they are apt to participate in cases of loot and plunder if the situation in Calcutta deteriorated.
>
> Those Sikhs, who run a lucrative business, will return to the Punjab as soon as Bengal is invaded from the East, but the Darwans and motor-drivers who do not possess taxis of their own are likely to remain behind and take part in the commission of dacoities. Their targets would especially be banks and houses and godowns of rich Marwaris and businessmen where they had been employed and which places they know intimately.[27]

Sikh taxi-driver and co-pilot with American GIs in Calcutta, 1945
(Source: www.library.upenn.edu/collections/sasia/calcutta1947/)

Also, rumours were rife that they might engage in 'Fifth Column' activities to paralyse the Indian administration if Subhas Chandra Bose marched into India with Japanese forces.[28] The colonial stereotype of Sikh workers as propertyless, 'disloyal' troublemakers in the city and the region had persisted in the immediate aftermath of the *Komagata Maru*'s voyage, and enjoyed a long life in the inter-war and Second World War years, whenever the need to control them arose from above. At the end of the war, as partition loomed over Bengal and Punjab, communalization of regional politics quickly overpowered radical currents from below. As left organizational drives and unity along 'class' rather than 'religious community' lines were sidelined in Calcutta, the image of the Sikhs as 'troublemakers' came to be associated with Hindu rioters.

During a crisis in which those above them in the rungs of the social hierarchy played a leading role and emerged as principal beneficiaries, the 'slow persistence' towards class unity pursued by Sikhs and other workers broke down. The complex 'contradictions of hierarchies' within labour, based, on 'ascriptive affiliation' to and social support drawn from religious community in an insecure and uncertain world, the compartmentalized work regimes they were subject to, and the competitions that enabled the capital to manage workers by setting one group against another, were a part of their everyday lives.[29] These elements paved the way for their participation in mass murder. During the Great Calcutta Killings of 1946–47, which took on the grisly form of a civil war between Hindus and Muslims, a considerable section of the Sikh diaspora, including cab drivers and other working-class segments, were mobilized and reorganized under Hindu communal leaders who were upholding local proprietorial concerns. Sikhs as assassins and musclemen on the Hindu side in Calcutta generated fear and panic amongst residents of Park Circus, a predominantly Muslim neighbourhood. Though an attack was anticipated, the Sikhs never arrived. In the fever-driven nightmares of a middle-class Bengali Muslim youngster, for two consecutive years following the riot of 1946, their menacing images could not be wiped away. They found a place, decades later, in his autobiographical recollections.[30]

Hindu middle-class segments also shared this sense of terror-ridden antipathy. A bhadralok youth from Bhawanipore, who later attained superstardom on Bengal's silver-screen, felt Punjabi Sikh taxi drivers were an unpleasant burden on the Hindu neighbourhoods during the communal conflagration. According to him, the police did not stop their petty criminal transgressions. Their anti-social, thuggish behaviour was tolerated by

Hindus who deployed them against Muslims. Consequently, they turned into alcoholic extortionists and demanded protection money from passers-by at night. They also became predators in the dark, harassing and insulting women.[31] It has been argued, however, that despite the role of Sikhs as active participants in the carnage, there were 'instances of intercommunal help' with Sikhs and Muslims saving lives by ignoring the barbed-wire fences of religious divisions in certain neighbourhoods.[32]

The riots accompanying India's independence from colonial rule demonstrated the restricted reach of 'class-oriented' social identity, mass mobilization and political programmes within different segments of the urban working class at a time when the left forces, which formed a 'third bloc' within the political spectrum, were on the retreat. As the late colonial state and dominant political parties enforced communal polarization and violence, the militancy of Sikh workers in Calcutta was channelled to fight with and murder ordinary Muslims, including workers. This sanguinary history has effectively erased the other histories of self-awareness as working people among segments of Punjabi Sikhs from the 1910s to the 1940s in Bengal, and their contributions to collective efforts where 'class' surfaced in consciously organized and latent forms. This study has attempted to record those actions since they made their way into police dossiers as challenges to imperial authority and colonial capital. Though noticed by the rulers, they have remained largely unaddressed in historiography. As they joined labour unions and political organizations, the Punjabi Sikh workers attempted to transcend diasporic boundaries and attendant constraints imposed on them as a minority within a small minority. They tried to assert themselves by confronting the existing social relationships which placed them at the lower end of class divisions. Collectives in the form of small left groups emerged, dissolved and surfaced again. They reflected a persistent need to constitute, not just community-orientated congregations centred around shared religious consciousness, belief and practice, but other agencies of intervention to change socio-material conditions.

The attention of colonial surveillance was devoted to Punjabi Sikh worker-dissenters. The police dossiers noted the diverse cycles of protest and acted as sources offering regular doses of information on their activities. A critical reading of the police records reveals the intersectionality of diasporic relationships and labour conditions which informed radical political action of workers from Punjab in Bengal. The conjunction of political protests and social ties produced political groups and unions to lead them. These efforts were underlined by the repeated search for an agency linked with overlapping class-oriented and community-based actions. The dossiers unveil social resistance and political mobilization in response to coercive strategies from above. They offer glimpses of structures of feeling borne of desperation and destitution. The sources also indicate the extent to which the state engaged with those deemed as opponents or belonging to an oppressed category with a potential for waging a war of opposition. Between stereotypical representations and demonization as subversives, between prosaic surveillance and imaginary exaggerations with literary touches, the records are an invaluable guide to a conflict which was never concluded.

The voyage of the *Komagata Maru* as an 'event' within the flow of historical time had found multiple echoes in the experiential, political and social spheres, acting as a motivating force, a conduit of militant consolidations, a field of not just fleeting combinations but organized bonding, capable of merging with various streams of activism.[33] While the activists were anxiously observed by the colonial state, the inconclusive nature of the official records also meant that the migrants, who appeared in the pages as labourers in search of employment, as drivers and janitors, as tailors and hawkers, could easily disappear. Sometimes, they left without a trace. Occasionally, they resurfaced or those bearing the same names echoed their already distant actions. Sometimes, the actions themselves were an echo of certain words, gestures or patterns registered during earlier periods of protest. The name of Chait Singh (alternatively spelt as Chet Singh), for instance, remained inseparable from a persistent shadow of enduring opposition. Repeatedly inscribed in changed contexts across the passing years, Chait Singh was listed among the arrested passengers of the *Komagata Maru* in 1914.[34] The most significant figure bearing the same name was that of the rebel taxi driver who committed revolutionary robberies in 1915 to assist a coming uprising at wartime, and ended up as a detainee in 1916. The third Chait Singh, who could have been the second, appeared as an anti-colonial speaker at a Naujawan Bharat Sabha meeting in 1929. One way or another, he cut a figure of defiance challenging imperial authority. His exact identity could never be mapped through reports. The sense of resistance he conveyed could never be fully contained or comprehended by those sent to watch him.

NOTES AND REFERENCES

[1] Himadri Banerjee, 'The Other Sikhs: Punjabi-Sikhs of Kolkata', *Studies in History*, 28 (2), 2012, p. 277.

[2] IB 185/1928 (87/28). 'IB' stands for dossiers of Intelligence Branch of Bengal Police.

[3] Darshan S. Tatla, ed., *Report of the Komagata Maru Committee of Inquiry and Some Further Documents*, Chandigarh, 2007, p. 138.

[4] IB 185/1928 (87/28). Manju Kumar Majumdar and Bhandudeb Datta, eds, *Banglar Communist Andolaner Itihas Anusandhan,* Calcutta, 2010, pp. 71–76.

[5] IB file number suppressed at the time of consultation. Contains 'Reports on the Political Situation and Labour Unrest in Bengal', 1928–32.

[6] Ibid.

[7] Ibid.

[8] 'Bhawanipore [Bhahbanipur] five' were the drivers described in the passage earlier – the men arrested from 6, Ganga Prasad Mukherjee Road, Bhawanipore, and tried and sentenced on the charge of possessing explosives.

[9] IB 267/33. IB CID Index 4 (I).

[10] IB file number suppressed at the time of consultation. Contains 'Reports on the Political Situation and Labour Unrest in Bengal'1928–32.

[11] IB 185/1928 (87/28).

[12] IB file number suppressed at the time of consultation. Contains 'Reports on the Political Situation and Labour Unrest in Bengal',1928–32.

[13] Ibid.

[14] Ibid.

[15] Ibid.

[16] Ibid.

[17] Ibid.

[18] Ibid.

[19] Kolkata Police Museum (KPM)/SB00446/05. The museum contains an archive of the dossiers of Special Branch, Calcutta Police.

[20] Ibid.

[21] Ibid.

[22] IB 313/1941.

[23] Ibid.

[24] Ibid.

[25] Rajsekhar Basu and Sanjukta Dasgupta, 'History of Kolkata Police: A Research Study by Calcutta University', unpublished manuscript, pp. 111–13.

[26] Ibid.

[27] KPM/SB/00445/05 (PS 503/42).

[28] Ibid.

[29] This conceptual understanding is drawn from a theoretical framework of how the 'biography of labour' can be written. See Amiya Kumar Bagchi, 'Workers and the

Historians' Burden', in K.N. Panikkar, Terence J. Byres and Utsa Patnaik, eds, *The Making of History: Essays Presented to Irfan Habib*, Delhi, 2000, pp. 276–77.

[30] See Anisuzzaman, 'Introduction to the Fourth Edition', *Muslim Manas o Bangla Sahitya* (The Muslim Mind and Bengali Literature), Calcutta, 1999, p. 12. For historical references, see Banerjee, 'The Other Sikhs: Punjabi-Sikhs of Kolkata', pp. 286–87. Suranjan Das, *Communal Riots in Bengal 1905–1947*, Delhi, 1991, pp. 181–83.

[31] See Uttam Kumar Chattopadhyay, *Hariye Jaowa Dinguli Mor* (My Lost Days), Calcutta, 2013, p. 97.

[32] Das, *Communal Riots in Bengal*, p. 181.

[33] For a sociological discussion on the materiality of 'events', see Tomas Pernecky and Omar Moufakkir, 'Events as Social Phenomena', in Omar Moufakkir and Tomas Pernecky, eds, *Ideological, Social and Cultural Aspects of Events*, Boston, 2015, pp. 1–11.

[34] Tatla, ed., *Report of the Komagata Maru Committee of Inquiry*, p. 112.

Bibliography

PRIMARY SOURCES

Official Records

Annual Report on the Police Administration of the Town of Calcutta and its Suburbs, selected years.

Bengal Home (Political) Records, selected years.

Bengal Intelligence Branch Records, selected years.

Census of India, selected years.

KPM/SB: dossiers of Special Branch, Calcutta Police, Kolkata Police Museum archive.

Report of the Committee on Industrial Unrest in Bengal 1921.

Report on Native Papers/Indian owned English Newspapers in Bengal, selected years.

Report of Special Branch of Calcutta Police, selected years.

Weekly Reports of Intelligence Branch, Bengal Police, selected years.

Non-official Records

Capital

Curry, J.C., *The Indian Police*, London: Faber & Faber, 1932.

Modern Review

Sandesh

The Statesman

What happened at the Deshapriya Park meeting and thereafter?, Communist Party of India pamphlet, Calcutta, 1945.

Printed Primary Sources

Bhattacharyya, Ananda, *Remembering Komagata Maru: Official Reports and Contem-porary Accounts*, Delhi, 2016.

Dasgupta, Samir, ed., *Gana Andolane Chapakhana: Communist Party o Samadarshi Sangbadpatrer Kramaparjay*, Vol.1, Calcutta, 1996.

Majumdar, Manju Kumar and Bhandudeb Datta, eds, *Banglar Communist Andolaner Itihas Anusandhan*, Calcutta, 2010.

Tatla, Darshan S., ed., *Report of the Komagata Maru Committee of Inquiry and Some Further Documents*, Chandigarh, 2007.

Roy, Subodh, ed., *Communism in India: Unpublished Documents 1925–1934*, Calcutta, 1998.

Waraich, Malwinder Jit Singh and Gurdev Singh Sidhu, eds, *Komagata Maru, A Challenge to Colonialism: Key Documents*, Chandigarh, 2005.

Memoirs/Reminiscences

Anisuzzaman, 'Introduction to the Fourth Edition', *Muslim Manas o Bangla Sahitya*, Calcutta, 1999.

Chattopadhyay, Uttamkumar, *Hariye Jaowa Dinguli Mor*, Calcutta, 2013.

Datta, Bhupendra Kumar, *Biplaber Padachinha*, Calcutta, 1999.

Dey, Mukul Chandra, *Japan theke Jorasanko: Chithi o Dinalipi, 1916–1917*, edited by Satyasree Ukil, Calcutta, 2005.

Guha, Nalini Kishor, *Banglay Biplabbad*, Calcutta, reprint, 2012.

Mukhopadhyay, Saroj, *Bharater Communist Party o Amra*, Vol. 1 (1930–41), Calcutta, 1993.

O'Malley, L.S.S., *Census of India 1911, Vol. VI, City of Calcutta, Part I: Report*, Calcutta, 1913.

O'Malley, L.S.S., *Census of India 1911, Vol. VI, City of Calcutta, Part II: Table*, Calcutta, 1913.

Singh, Baba Gurdit, *Voyage of Komagata Maru or India's Slavery Abroad*, edited by Darshan S. Tatla, Chandigarh, 2007.

SECONDARY SOURCES

Books and Articles

Assmann, Aleida and Linda Shortt, eds, *Memory and Political Change*, New York, 2012.

Bagchi, Amiya Kumar, *Private Investment in India 1900–1939*, Cambridge, 1972.

Bagchi, Amiya Kumar, 'Workers and the Historians' Burden', in K.N. Panikkar, Terence J. Byres and Utsa Patnaik, eds, *The Making of History: Essays Presented to Irfan Habib*, Delhi, 2000.

Bagchi, Amiya Kumar, *Perilous Passage: Mankind and the Global Ascendancy of Capital*, Delhi, 2006.

Bald, Vivek, *Bengali Harlem and the Lost Histories of South Asian America*, Cambridge, Mass., 2013.

Banerjee, Himadri, 'The Other Sikhs: Punjabi-Sikhs of Kolkata', *Studies in History*, 28 (2), 2012.

Banerjee, Himadri, 'Remembering Komagata Maru: Its Many Journeys, 1914–2014', *South Asian Diaspora*, 8 (2), September 2016.

Basu, Subho, *Does Class Matter? Colonial Capital and Workers' Resistance in Bengal, 1890–1937*, Delhi, 2004.

Chakraborty, Subhas Ranjan, 'The Journey of Komagata Maru: Conjuncture, Memory and History', *South Asian Diaspora*, 8 (2), September 2016.

Chakravorty, Upendra Narayan, *Indian Nationalism and the First World War (1914–1918)*, Calcutta, 1997.

Chattopadhyay, Suchetana, *An Early Communist: Muzaffar Ahmad in Calcutta*, Delhi, 2011.

Chattopadhyay, Suchetana, 'Closely Observed Ships', *South Asian Diaspora*, 8 (2), September 2016.

Chattopadhyay, Suchetana, 'War-time in an Imperial City: The Apocalyptic Mood in Culcutta (1914–1918)', in Roger D. Long and Ian Talbot, eds, *India and World War I: A Centennial Assessment*, London and New York, 2018.

Cheng, Lucie and Edna Bonacich, 'Introduction', in Cheng, Lucie and Edna Bonacich, eds, *Labor Immigration under Capitalism: Asian Workers in the United States Before World War II*, Berkeley, 1984, pp. 1–56.

Cheng, Lucie and Edna Bonacich, eds, *Labor Immigration under Capitalism: Asian Workers in the United States Before World War II*, Berkeley, 1984.

Das, Suranjan, *Communal Riots in Bengal 1905–1947*, Delhi, 1991.

Deepak, B.R., *India China Relations: In the first half of the 20th Century*, Delhi, 2001.

Deshpande, Anirudh, *British Military Policy in India, 1900–1945: Colonial Constraints and Declining Power*, Delhi, 2005.

Dijk, Cornelis, *The Netherlands Indies and the Great War 1914–1918*, Leiden, 2007.

Ellinwood, D.C. and S.D. Pradhan, *India and World War I*, Delhi, 1978.

Fentress, James and Chris Wickham, *Social Memory*, Oxford, 1992.

Gera Roy, Anjali, 'Making and Unmaking of Strangers: The Komagata Maru Episode and the Alienation of Sikhs as Undesirable Persons', *Sikh Formations*, 12 (1), 2016.

Gera Roy, Anjali, 'Immobile Mobilities and Free-flowing Sikh Movements from Punjab', *South Asian Diaspora*, 8 (2), September 2016.

Gera Roy, Anjali, *Imperialism and Sikh Migration: The Komagata Maru Incident*, New York, 2017.

Gera Roy, Anjali and Ajaya K. Sahoo, 'Introduction to the Special Issue: The Journey of the Komagata Maru: National, Transnational, Diasporic', *South Asian Diaspora*, 8 (2), September 2016.

Gera Roy, Anjali and Ajaya K. Sahoo, *Diasporas and Transnationalisms: The Journey of the Komagata Maru*, New York, 2017.

Gould, Harold A., *Sikhs, Swamis, Students, and Spies: The India Lobby in the United States, 1900–1946*, Delhi, 2006.

Gupta, Partha Sarathi and Anirudh Deshpande, eds, *The British Raj and Its Indian Armed Forces, 1857–1939*, Delhi, 2002.

Hobsbawm, Eric, *On History*, London, 1999.

Hussain, Nasser, *The Jurisprudence of Emergency: Colonialism and the Rule of Law*, Ann Arbor, 2003.

Johnston, Hugh, 'The Surveillance of Indian Nationalists in North America, 1908–1981', *B.C. Studies*, Vol. 78, Summer 1988.

Johnston, Hugh, *The Voyage of the Komagata Maru: The Sikh Challenge to Canada's Colour Bar*, Vancouver, 1995; first edition, Delhi, 1979.

Joshi, Chitra, *Lost Worlds: Indian Labour and its Forgotten Histories*, Delhi, 2003.

Kawashima, Ken, *The Proletarian Gamble: Korean Workers in Interwar Japan*, Durham and London, 2009.

Kuwajima, Sho, *Indian Mutiny in Singapore (1915)*, Calcutta, 1991.

Maienborn, Claudia, Klaus von Heusinger and Paul Portner, *Semantics*, Vol. 3, Berlin, 2013.

Mawani, Renisa, 'Law and Migration Across the Pacific: Narrating the *Komagata Maru* Outside and Beyond the Nation', in Karen Dubinsky, Adele Perry and Henry Yu, eds, *Within and Without the Nation: Canadian History as Transnational History*, Toronto, 2015.

Mazumdar, Sucheta, 'Colonial Impact and Punjabi Emigration to the United States', in Lucie Cheng and Edna Bonacich, eds, *Labor Immigration under Capitalism: Asian Workers in the United States Before World War II*, Berkeley, 1984, pp. 316–36.

Metscher, Randall J., '"Emden" in Spencer', in C. Tucker, ed., *The European Powers in the First World War: An Encyclopedia*, New York, 2013.

Mizukami, Kaori, 'Staying in Japan, Working beyond Japan: Perspectives from Japanese Sources on the Ghadar Movement', *The Panjab Past and Present*, Vol. XXXXV, Part II, No. 90, October 2014.

Moufakkir, Omar and Tomas Pernecky, eds, *Ideological, Social and Cultural Aspects of Events*, Boston, 2015.

Mukherjee, Mridula, *Colonizing Agriculture: The Myth of Punjab Exceptionalism*, Delhi, 2005.

Pernecky, Tomas and Omar Moufakkir, 'Events as Social Phenomena', in Omar Moufakkir and Tomas Pernecky, eds, *Ideological, Social and Cultural Aspects of Events*, Boston, 2015, pp. 1–11.

Prashad, Vijay, *Everybody was Kung Fu Fighting: Afro-Asian Connections and the Myth of Cultural Purity*, Boston, 2002.

Puri, Harish K., *Ghadar Movement: Ideology, Organization and Strategy*, Amritsar, 1983.

Ramnath, Maia, *Haj to Utopia: How the Ghadar Movement Charted Global Radicalism and Attempted to Overthrow the British Empire*, Berkeley, 2011.

Roy, Pijush Kanti, *Kolkatar Pratibeshi* (Calcutta Neighbours), Calcutta, 2002.

Sarkar, Sumit, *Modern India 1885–1947*, Delhi, 1983.

Sohi, Seema, *Echoes of Mutiny: Race, Surveillance, and Indian Anticolonialism in North America*, New York, 2014.

Sood, Malini, *Expatriate Nationalism and Ethnic Radicalism: The Ghadar Party in North America*, Hamden, 2000.

Strachnan, Hew, *The Oxford Illustrated History of the First World War*, Oxford, 2014.

Sundaram, Chandar S., 'Arriving in the Nick of Time: The Indian Corps in France, 1914–15', *Journal of Defence Studies*, 9 (4), October–December 2015.

Talbot, Ian, *Punjab and the Raj, 1849–1947*, Delhi, 1988.

Torpey, John, *The Invention of the Passport: Surveillance, Citizenship and the State*, Cambridge and New York, 2000.

Tulving, E. and W. Donaldson, eds, *Organization of Memory*, New York, 1972.

Yong, Tan Tai, *The Garrison State: Military, Government and Society in Colonial Punjab, 1849–1947*, Delhi, 2005.

Unpublished Manuscripts/Papers

Bains, Satwinder Kaur, 'Resistance Struggle: Facing Lies, Deception and Racism', paper read at workshop on 'Charting Imperial Itineraries 1914-2014: Unmooring the Komagata Maru', University of Victoria, 15–16 May 2014.

Basu, Rajsekhar and Sanjukta Dasgupta, 'History of Kolkata Police: A Research Study by Calcutta University', unpublished manuscript.

Bhandar, Davina, 'Memories, Placement and the Return of the Forever Forgotten: Memorialization of the Komagata Maru', paper read at workshop on 'Charting Imperial Itineraries 1914–2014: Unmooring the Komagata Maru', University of Victoria, 15–16 May 2014.

Dhamoon, Rita Kaur, 'Unmooring the Komagata Maru: Denaturalizing Settler Colonialism and Cacophonies of Difference', paper read at workshop on 'Charting Imperial Itineraries 1914–2014: Unmooring the Komagata Maru', University of Victoria, 15–16 May 2014.

Dua, Ena, '"Race", National Historiographies and Transnationality: The Ghadars and the Writing of Canadian and Indian History', paper read at workshop on 'Charting Imperial Itineraries 1914–2014: Unmooring the Komagata Maru', University of Victoria, 15–16 May 2014.

Fletcher, Ian, 'In Exercise of Their Rights of British Citizenship: The Komagata Maru and the Paradox of Imperial Citizenship before the First World War', paper read at workshop on 'Charting Imperial Itineraries 1914–2014: Unmooring the Komagata Maru', University of Victoria, 15–16 May 2014.

Mongia, Radhika, 'Terms of Analysis: Methodological Lessons from the Komagata Maru', paper read at workshop on 'Charting Imperial Itineraries 1914–2014:

Unmooring the Komagata Maru', University of Victoria, 15–16 May 2014.

Singh, Milan, 'Re-Writing the Context Around the Komagata Maru: A Case for South Asian Women's Migration to Canada', paper read at workshop on 'Charting Imperial Itineraries 1914–2014: Unmooring the Komagata Maru', University of Victoria, 15–16 May 2014.

Somani, Alia, 'Past Wrongs and New National Imaginary: Remembering the Komagata Maru incident', paper read at workshop on 'Charting Imperial Itineraries 1914–2014: Unmooring the Komagata Maru', University of Victoria, 15–16 May 2014.

Index

Ahmad, Muzaffar, 122, 124, 129, 130, 133, 154, 155
Akali (newspaper), 122
Akali, 159
  meeting, 126
  movement, 158
  opinion, 150
  Regiment, 158
Akali Dal, 153, 154, 157
Akhand Path, 142
American
  authorities, 37, 159
  -controlled Philippines, 2
  corporate monopolies, 132
  -cut clothes, 69
  goods, 80
  goondas, 159
  justice, 159
Americans, 159
  in Asia, 80
Amrita Bazar Patrika, 81, 83, 91
Amritsar, 11, 35, 37, 41, 71, 121–22, 124, 156
Amritsar massacre, 90
Associated Press, 86

babu (Bengali gentleman), 36
Ballygunge, 114

Gurudwara, 120, 125, 126–28, 144, 149
  Singh Sabha, 151
Bara Sikh Sangat, 88, 89, 90, 106, 119, 153
Barabazar, 87
Barishal Hitaishi, 82
Basu, Babu Bhupendra Nath, 85
Basumati, 15
Bengal Intelligence Branch (IB), 20, 50–52, 54, 56–58, 61–63
Bengal Kirti Dal, 120–24, 128–32, 145, 148
Bengalee, 22, 44, 81, 82, 84, 87, 88, 93
Bhabanipur, 96, 98; *see also* Bhawanipore
bhadralok
  background, 86, 133
  militants, 106
  revolutionaries, 3, 100, 104, 109, 110
  youth, 100, 161
Bhawanipore, 43, 96, 97, 99, 100, 104, 106, 107, 114, 119, 120, 123, 124, 126, 128, 129, 132, 133, 143–47, 154, 156, 159, 161; *see also* Bhabanipur
Biswas, Kapil, 34
Bolshevik Revolution, 3
boycott, 79, 80, 85, 144

British
  empire, 3,4 5, 7, 9, 14, 28, 39, 49,
    71, 78, 79, 83, 84, 86, 95, 100,
    131
  government, 28, 32, 36, 38, 39, 55,
    131, 153
British Columbia (BC), 4, 21, 39, 54–
    56, 66, 81, 95
British India, 61, 63
Budge Budge, xi, 1, 4, 6, 7, 16, 20, 21,
    24–26, 29, 33–35, 38, 43, 49, 55,
    60, 86, 90–93, 97, 106, 130, 132,
    135, 136, 140
  Railway Station, 1, 25, 33, 35, 43
  riot / riot case, 24–26, 34, 43, 57, 70,
    86, 88, 90–93, 95
Burma, 2, 18, 56, 57, 97, 99, 104, 108,
    136
Burma Shell Company, 136

Calcutta, xi, 1, 4–6, 9, 13–15, 16–21,
    30–31, 34, 50–51, 68–69, 78–79,
    86–88, 104, 109, 121, 125–26,
    129, 133–34, 142–44, 146–47,
    153, 154, 155, 156, 158, 159,
    160, 162
  anti-colonial network in, 71, 74
  communist activists in, 133
  docks, 22, 52, 55, 61
  European soldiers in, 16
  headquarters of imperial authority in,
    50,
  imperial surveillance in, 95
  intelligentsia in, 79,
  journalists, 86
  metropolitan, 8
  Punjabi diaspora in, 9, 132, 156
  revolutionary underground in, 7, 78,
    97, 108–09
  Sikh soldiers in, 158
  Sikh taxi-cab drivers in, 104–05, 115,
    159, 160
  Sikhs in, 96, 97, 100, 104, 113–14,
    127, 129, 144, 149, 156, 159, 162

Calcutta Budget, 91
Calcutta Committee of the CPI, 133,
    134
Calcutta Corporation, 144, 149, 151
Calcutta Police, 32, 51, 57, 58, 60, 61,
    120, 128, 131, 132, 145, 148
Calcutta Tramways Company, 121
Canada, 1–4, 20, 21, 23, 28, 35, 41,
    53–55, 57, 66, 68, 70, 72
Canadian, Baba Bhag Singh, 122, 132
Canadian government, 2, 56, 81, 96
Capital (periodical of colonial capitalists),
    86, 110 n8, 111 n25
Carmichael (Lord), 15
Central Intelligence Department / CID
  Bengal, 61, 88, 122
  headquartered in Delhi and Simla, 50
  Lahore, 121
  Punjab, 28, 51, 55, 90, 105
Chait Singh, 97
China, 2, 16, 31, 60, 97, 99, 125, 150,
    158
Chittagong, 55, 57, 62
Cleveland, (Sir) Charles, 20–22, 34, 52,
    53–58, 60, 63
College Square, 16, 83
Collin Street, 92
colonial capital, 5, 7, 8, 9, 14, 17, 19, 49,
    53, 61, 63, 65, 76 n31, 86, 113,
    135, 162
Colootola, 114
Commissioner of Police / Police
  Commis-sioner
  Bombay, 73
  Calcutta, 51, 58, 63, 68, 116, 117,
    128, 159
Communist Party of India / CPI, 120,
    132–34, 143, 149, 154, 155
Corporation Street, 103
Cumming, 22, 27, 32, 34, 40, 41, 50,
    54–56, 59, 60, 63, 71, 90

Dainik Basumati, 94
Dainik Bharat Mitra, 15, 91

Dallas-Smith, (Captain) E.D., 67
Das, Narain, 29, 40
Deputy Commissioner of Police
    Calcutta, 51, 120, 131
    Punjab, 73
Deputy Inspector General, CID (Lahore,
    Punjab), 120
Deputy Inspector General, IB (Bengal),
    50, 51, 57–58, 62, 120
Deputy Superintendent of Police
    Calcutta, 109
    Punjab, 28, 88
Dey, Mukul Chandra, 77 n72, 77 n73
Dhaka Military Police Battalion, 67
Dhanushkodi, 70, 71
District Association in Bengal, 85
Dixon, G.W., 62
Duke, (Sir) William, 21, 34, 50, 91
'Dukhi', Munsha Singh, 133, 144, 156
Durga Das Lane, 100

East/Eastern Asia, 2, 18, 19, 48, 55, 61,
    63, 64, 67, 69, 74, 99
Emden, 6, 17, 18, 19
Englishman (The), 82, 83

First World War, 3, 14, 13, 101, 110,
    141
Foo Sang, 62, 66

Gandhi, 83, 84, 86, 115, 134, 135, 149,
    150
German
    airships (Zeppelin), 17
    cruiser(s), 18, 19
    invasion, 16, 19
    navy, 17, 19
    'spies'/agents, 68, 70
    Vice-Consul's house, 73
    warship, 6
    vessels, 17
Ghadar, 20, 39, 65, 66
Ghadar, 3–5, 8, 9, 19, 20, 21, 29, 38,
    39, 49, 53, 62, 64–66, 68–70, 72,
    73, 75, 78, 94, 96–100, 104, 110,
    115, 120, 122, 133–35, 140, 142,
    144, 156
    activist, 3, 78, 142
    doctrine, 54
    literature, 29, 97, 100, 142
    revolutionary, 120, 122
    tendency, 8, 20, 21, 38, 64, 75, 78,
        94, 134, 140
Ghadar Movement, 3, 8, 9, 39, 54, 70,
    72, 96, 100, 135, 140, 156
Ghadar Party, 3, 53, 54, 68–70, 72, 99,
    104
Ghadar-di-Gunj, 3, 38
Goswami, Dharani, 123, 124, 130, 154
Government Press, 66
Governor of Bengal, 15, 42, 90, 91
Guha, Nalini Kishore, 86
Guru Granth Sahib, 27, 142
Gurudwara Jagat Sudhar, xi, 147
gurudwara(s), xi, 30, 39, 42, 90, 97–99,
    104, 105, 120, 125–28, 144, 147
Gurumukhi, 10, 35, 39, 62, 119, 124,
    126, 129, 132, 144, 146

Hablul Matin, 85
Halim, Abdul, 123, 130, 132–34
Harrison Road, 90, 105, 119, 158
Hindustan Ghadar, 3
Hindustani (The), 38, 64
Hitavadi, 80, 90
Hong Kong, 4, 26, 31, 37, 39, 43, 54–
    57, 60, 61, 65, 69, 72, 85, 99
Hooghly
    district, 71, 72
    river, 6, 7, 8, 18, 25, 49, 58
Hongkong and Shanghai Banking
    Corporation (The) / HSBC, 43
Hopkinson, W.C., 21, 54, 92
Howrah, 21, 30, 34, 35, 42, 65, 69, 90,
    96, 97–99, 104–06, 110, 114,
    124, 132, 142
Howrah Gurudwara, 30, 42, 90, 97–99,
    104, 105, 142

Hughes-Buller, R.B., 50, 54, 57, 58, 60, 64, 71, 73
hunger strike, 109, 147
Hussain, Liaqat, 16
Hutchinson, R.H.S., 50, 51, 53, 57, 59, 61, 65

imperialism, 9, 19, 82, 114, 131, 134, 136, 140, 153
Ingress into India Ordinance (V of 1914), 21, 40, 43, 49, 52, 57, 59, 64, 71
Indian Mirror, 91
Indian Motor Taxi-cab Company, 101, 103, 107, 108, 116
Indian National Congress / INC, 3, 131, 149
Indian Telegraph Gazette, 59
Indo-China Steamship Company, 66
Inspector General of Police
  Bengal, 34, 50, 58, 62
  Central Provinces, 52
  CID, Punjab, 55, 67

Josh, Sohan Singh, 122, 123, 124, 129, 130, 143
Jugantar, 72, 97, 100, 101, 106–08

Kanka, Harnam Singh, 157
Karachi, 50, 60
Khan, Amir Mohammad, 23, 28, 29, 41, 42
Khidirpur, 18, 67; *see also* Kidderpore
Khilafat Committee, 115
Kidderpore, 18, 67, 96, 97, 99, 100, 101, 104–06; *see also* Khidirpur
Kirti Kisan Party, Punjab, 5, 120, 142
Kobe, 23, 29, 31, 32, 35, 55, 64

Lahiri, Somnath, 133, 134
Lahore, 35, 37, 41, 68, 69, 78, 90, 109, 120, 121, 131, 142, 143
Lahore Conspiracy Case, 94, 99, 142
Lahore Reserve Force, 67

Lieutenant Governor, Punjab, 22, 43, 60

Mackinnon-Mackenzie, 17, 61
Madras docks, 18
Maharajah of Burdwan, 42
Mal, Jawahar, 23, 29, 30–32, 40
Managing Agency House(s), 61, 101
Mansoor, Ferozuddin, 130, 132
Marwari, 87, 158, 160
Mazumdar, Rukmini Kanta, 24
Meerut
  arrests, 132, 144
  prisoners, 131
  trials, 131, 136
Meerut Communist Conspiracy Case (1929), 155
Meerut Trial Defence Committee, 131
Modern Review, 95, 111 n48
Mohammadi, 16
Moslem Hitaishi, 14, 16, 79
Mukerji, Hari Das, 36
Mukherjee, Saroj, 134
Mulvany, J., 40

Naujawan Bharat Sabha, 144, 145, 146, 153, 155, 157, 159, 163
Nayak, 90, 92
non-cooperation, 25
Non-Cooperation Movement, 114, 115, 142
Newman (Lieutenant Colonel), 25

Ochterlony Monument (Shahid Minar), 134, 135, 154, 155
Omar, Haroon, 73
Outram Ghat, 18, 52

pan-Islam/Islamists, 39, 49, 71, 78, 100, 104
Panchkhal, Narain Singh, 151
'Pardesi', Balwant Singh, 134, 142, 145, 149, 154, 156
Petrie, David, 20, 26, 56
Postal Censor, 1, 72, 95

Prabashi, 79, 84, 93–95, 111 n48
Punjab CID, 28, 51, 55, 73, 90, 105, 120, 121
Punjab Kirti Dal, 122, 124
Punjabi Sikh
  activists, 7, 8, 96, 134, 153
  diaspora, 2, 78, 147
  drivers, 101, 158, 161
  labourers/workers, 1, 7, 8, 10, 48, 110, 140, 141, 145, 162
  migrants, 3, 5, 9
  passengers, 74
  warder, 147

Quit India Movement, 143, 157

Raniganj, 86
Ray, Gnan Chandra, 83
Ray, Sasanka Jiban, 83
Report of the Komagata Maru Committee of Inquiry, 24, 25, 32, 142
Ross, Anna, 1, 95

Samay, 80, 82, 85, 94
San Francisco, 2, 20, 53, 72
Sandesh, 95, 111 n47
Sen, Ranen, 134
Shahid Minar, 134
Sharma, Bachan Das, 152, 153, 156, 157
Sharma, Amar Nath, 90
Sikh drivers, 101–04, 126, 152, 159; *see also* Punjabi Sikh drivers
Sikh troops, 86
Sindhi brothers, 23, 29, 31, 32, 38, 40
Singh, Babu, 100–01, 105, 106
Singh, Bhagat (driver, leader of the 'Bhawanipore five' in Calcutta), 146, 148, 149
Singh, Bhagat (revolutionary martyr from Punjab), 142, 144, 145, 147, 149, 151
Singh, Bhagwan, 37, 39, 155
Singh, Bir, 64, 151, 154, 155

Singh, Dewan, 97–100, 104–06, 108, 115
Singh, Genda, 107, 120, 121, 124, 130, 132
Singh, Gurdit, 4, 6, 7, 20–23, 25–34, 36–41, 54, 64, 82–86, 91, 93, 97, 119, 123, 125–28, 130, 132, 135, 136, 143, 144, 149–52, 156
Singh, Jhawan, 65
Singh, Kahal, 40
Singh, Kehar, 23, 39
Singh, Labh, 39, 101
Singh, Ladha, 56
Singh, Lal, 39
Singh, Mangal, 37, 128, 130, 133, 152
Singh, Mangal (bus owner), 156
Singh, Mastan, 29
Singh, Mohan, 39
Singh, Narain, 36, 38
Singh, Prithi, 124, 128, 129, 132, 156
Singh, Puran, 66
Singh, Ratan, 43, 100, 101, 104–07, 116, 144, 152
Singh, Santa, 40, 115, 133
Singh, Sher, 42, 98, 100, 105
Singh, Sucha 41, 42
Singh, Sukha, 28, 29, 33, 39, 90
Singh, Surain, 36, 37, 41, 60, 145
Singh, Suram, 68
Singh, Tara, 35, 36, 105
Skinner, Jardine, 61, 62
Slocock, F.S.A., 30, 52, 53, 55, 60, 64
Sorabha, Teja Singh, 119, 120
South Africa, 79 83, 84, 86
SS Egypt, 18
SS Japan, 56, 73
Statesman (The), 43, 65, 82, 83, 92
Straits, 56, 70
strike, 80, 112 n66, 113, 116, 117, 152, 159
Superintendent of Police, Bengal, 51
Superintendent of Police, Chittagong, 62
Superintendent of Police, Punjab, 28, 88

Tagore, Rabindranath, 77 n73
Talib, Niranjan Singh, 156
Tatla, Darshan S., 25
Tosha Maru, 62, 66, 72–74, 76 n47

Uriya, Dinabondhu, 24

West Bengal State Archives (WBSA), 9

Workers and Peasants Party (WPP), 129
   of Bengal, 120, 122, 123, 129, 130,
   133
Writers' Building, 50, 60, 61, 154

Yamamoto (Captain), 31
Yat Sang, 54
Yule, Andrew, 61, 62, 99